WAR and WELFARE

Recent Titles in
Contributions in American History
Series Editor: JON L. WAKELYN

WAR and WELFARE

SOCIAL ENGINEERING
in AMERICA, 1890-1925

JOHN F. McCLYMER

CONTRIBUTIONS in AMERICAN HISTORY, NUMBER 84

GREENWOOD PRESS
WESTPORT, CONNECTICUT · LONDON, ENGLAND

Excerpts from John F. McClymer, "The Pittsburgh Survey, 1907-1914: Forging an Ideology in the Steel District," *Pennsylvania History* 41 (April 1974):169-86. Reprinted by permission of *Pennsylvania History*.

Excerpts from John Dos Passos, *1919*, vol. 2, *U.S.A.* (Boston: Houghton Mifflin, 1930). Reprinted by permission of Elizabeth Dos Passos.

Library of Congress Cataloging in Publication Data

McClymer, John F
  War and welfare.

  (Contributions in American history ; no. 84
ISSN 0084-9219)
  Bibliography: p.
  Includes index.
  1. Social service—United States—History.
2. Public welfare—United States—History.
3. European War, 1914-1918—United States.
4. Reconstruction (1914-1939)—United States.
5. United States—History—1898-   I. Title.
HV91.M22   361'.973   79-54060
ISBN 0-313-21129-9

Library of Congress Catalog Card Number: 79-54060
ISBN: 0-313-21129-9
ISSN: 0084-9219

First published in 1980

Greenwood Press
A division of Congressional Information Service, Inc.
88 Post Road West, Westport, Connecticut 06881

Printed in the United States of America

10 9 8 7 6 5 4 3 2 1

For
Joan
and
Peter

Contents

Tables

Preface

America is preeminently the country where there is practical substance in Nietzsche's advice that we should live not for our fatherland but for our children's land.

To do this men have to substitute purpose for tradition; and that is, I believe, the profoundest change that has ever taken place in human history. We can no longer treat life as something that has trickled down to us. We have to deal with it deliberately, devise its social organization, alter its tools, formulate its method, educate and control it. In endless ways we put intention where custom has reigned. We break up routines, make decisions, choose our ends, select means.

—Walter Lippmann, *Drift and Mastery* (1914)

These are a young man's words (Lippmann was twenty-five when *Drift and Mastery* was published), and hyperbole is one of the proverbial excesses of youth. Yet, someone writing in 1914 that his generation stood at the crossroads of the modern age, however enthusiastic his rhetoric,[1] was expressing a greater truth than even he could realize. What Lippmann did understand thoroughly was that a new, modern America had emerged in the half-century or so following the Civil War. What he could not foresee was that the world war would abruptly intrude upon all of his—and everyone else's—calculations. The intrusion of the war upon this vision of scientifically directed social change is the subject of this book.

Postwar disillusionment with prewar ideals is a more than twice-told tale, and I have no desire to rehearse it here. Although historians have vigorously debated the postwar mood, relatively little has been written about the wartime experiences of those who shared Lippmann's vision. And so, this book examines the historical juxtaposition of the developing professions, which collectively we label social engineering, and the war. It will begin with the emergence of a "new" middle class in the quarter century before the war; examine the recruitment of social and settlement workers, public health officials, industrial relations and housing experts, and a host of other new professionals; trace the articulation of their expertise; and analyze the kinds of institutional support they could command in prewar America.

The bulk of the study attempts to tell the story of the war and the experts through the mid-1920s. The war itself of course ended on November 11, 1918, but the "war years"—the patterns of social and political life generated by the war—lasted well into the twenties. War, to employ a distinction of Herbert Marcuse's, is never reasonable, but it can be rational. What Lippmann said of life could be—and was—said by the experts of war: "We have to deal with it deliberately, devise its social organization, alter its tools, formulate its method, educate and control it." The new social experts, we shall see, approached the war in just this spirit. That it was destructive they fully appreciated. But, it was also an opportunity for them to employ their techniques of "social accounting" on an unprecedented scale. Consequently, they did not tend to view war and welfare as antitheses. First the war and then the prospect of postwar reconstruction, a reconstruction that, to their dismay, never occurred, sustained their hopes that America was indeed about to "substitute purpose for tradition."

Chimerical though these hopes ultimately proved, they were grounded in the actual wartime experiences of the experts as well as in their prewar enthusiasm. Experts were swept up in a wide range of war-related activities that, if they did not accomplish their prewar program of social change, did—at least in their own estimation—prove the worth of expertise in solving the problems of war. Surely, they persuaded themselves, the Wilson administration would turn to them to help meet the problems of peace.

When repression and not reconstruction proved to be the order of postwar American life, experts began to appreciate how tragically they had misread the meaning of the war. Errors of this magnitude exact a high price, and this study will attempt to calculate what the war cost the experts. This cost included, amid much else, a full measure of disillusionment; but it was a disillusionment occasioned not by the brute fact that there had been a war but by their growing realization that the war had not meant what they had supposed it would. Experts had flirted with power during the war; they had thought indeed that they had captured it. The Red Scare and what passed for "normalcy" in the early twenties, however, soon disabused them, and experts were once again face to face with their inability to exert the kind of influence to which they felt entitled.

NOTES

1. Lippmann's youthful contemporaries, in fact, found him singularly lacking in enthusiasm. John Reed, who knew Lippmann as a fellow student at Harvard and later as a fellow member of Mabel Dodge's Greenwich Village coterie, wrote of him:

And with him LIPPMANN,—calm, inscrutable,
Thinking and writing clearly, soundly, well;
All snares of falseness swiftly piercing through,
His keen mind leaps like lightning to the True;
His face is almost placid,—but his eye,—
There is a vision born to prophecy!
He sits in silence, as one who has said:
"I waste not living words among the dead!"
Our unchallenged Chief! But were there one
Who builds a world, and leaves out all the fun—
Who dreams a pageant, gorgeous, infinite,
And then leaves all the color out of it,—
Who wants to make the human race, and me,
March to a geometric Q.E.D.—
Who but must laugh, if such a man there be?
Who would not weep, if Walter L. were he?

John Reed, *The Day in Bohemia* (Riverside, Conn.: printed for the author, 1913), p. 42, as quoted in William E. Leuchtenberg, "Walter Lippmann's 'Drift And Mastery,' " in *Drift and Mastery: An Attempt to Diagnose the Current Unrest* (1914, rpt., Englewood Cliffs, N.J.: Prentice-Hall, 1961), p. 14.

About the Author

JOHN F. McCLYMER is Associate Professor of History at Assumption College in Worcester, Massachusetts. He has held a number of post-doctoral fellowships, including a 1979-80 National Endowment for the Humanities Research Fellowship. His articles have appeared in *Prologue*, *The History Teacher*, *Pennsylvania History*, and other publications.

Acknowledgments

This is not a long book, but a long list of people helped make its writing easier and more pleasant. It began as an essay on the Pittsburgh Survey in a research seminar directed by Hugh Cleland. William R. Taylor, also of the History Department at the State University of New York at Stony Brook, patiently supervised the work as it progressed and grew into a coherent whole. The advice of David Burner and Robert Marcus, both of the History Department, and Lewis A. Coser, of the Sociology Department, proved valuable, as did the enthusiastic and numerous late-night discussions with fellow graduate students at Stony Brook. Joseph Garonzik, Isobel Notturno, Patrick Palermo, Russell Snow, and Ronald Story deserve particular thanks.

Milton Cantor, of the University of Massachusetts at Amherst, read many versions of the manuscript and somehow always found the time to offer suggestions and encouragement. Dewey Grantham, of Vanderbilt University, has been another constant friend. His seminar on "Society and Politics in Modern America" (held in the summer of 1975 at Vanderbilt University) was a stimulating intellectual experience. It gave me an opportunity to work with an outstanding scholar and a fine gentleman. A grant from the Immigration History Research Center at the University of Minnesota, Twin Cities, made it possible for me to complete the research for this book and to exchange ideas with the center's director, Rudolph Vecoli. Raymond Cunningham, of Fordham University,

a long-time friend and teacher, not only read sections of this book, he
also helped me to appreciate the historian's craft.

A number of other scholars have read and criticized portions of this
manuscript. They include Charles Estus and Roberta Keane of the
Assumption College Sociology Department; Paul Kleppner of Northern
Illinois University and David Thelen of the University of Missouri, Columbia, both of whom have commented on an early version of the Americanization chapter at the 1976 meeting of the Organization of American
Historians; Richard Juliani, of the Villanova University Sociology Department; and Howard Segal, of the University of Michigan at Ann Arbor.

Librarians and archivists at a variety of institutions cooperated fully
in granting my requests for materials, especially the staffs at the Stony
Brook Library, the Clark University Library, the Vanderbilt University
Library, the University of Minnesota, Twin Cities, Library and, particularly, the Assumption College Library. Early in my research, I had occasion to use the manuscript collections of the Social Welfare History
Archives at the University of Minnesota, Twin Cities, where Clarke
Chambers, its director, was most helpful. Also valuable to me were the
collections of Minnesota's Immigration History Research Center and
several collections at the National Archives in Washington, D.C.

I wish to thank my parents, who sacrificed much to have an intellectual
in the family. My son Peter, who is ten years old, had no part in the
writing of this book; he is nonetheless one of the major reasons I had for
writing it. And, finally, I wish to thank my wife, Joan, who typed most
of the versions of this manuscript and gave me constant encouragement.
She also gave me whatever sense of proportion I possess, for she never
let me pretend that our lives could be organized around *War and Welfare*.

PART I:
The Emergence of Social Engineering

Introduction

On January 2, 1909 the magazine *Charities and the Commons* published the first of three special issues devoted to the findings of the Pittsburgh Survey.* It was a banner day in the history of social engineering in America. Americans had experienced the combined impact of industrialization, urbanization, and immigration in their daily lives for decades, but the Survey was the first systematic and scientific study of the fruits of modernization. Pittsburgh, the self-proclaimed "Workshop of the World," seemed to epitomize both the promises and the perils of the new America that had emerged in the years after the Civil War. "We felt," wrote Survey director Paul U. Kellogg, "that Pittsburgh bore somewhat the same relation industrially to the country at large that Washington did politically."[1] Where Pittsburgh led, the rest of the United States would follow. One went to Pittsburgh to see the future. The people who did so and their colleagues in social and settlement work, public health, industrial relations, housing, and a host of other new professions are the subjects of this book.

The rationale for these new careers was the experts' claim that they could scientifically predict and control the direction, pace, and effects of social change. They thus presented themselves as an answer to what

*This book will discuss the Pittsburgh survey in its three forms: the actual, physical survey (the Pittsburgh Survey), the initial magazine reports published in *Charities and the Commons* and the multivolume final report edited by Paul Kellogg (*The Pittsburgh Survey*).

Robert Wiebe has called the central question of their day: How could order be imposed upon the chaos of change?[2] Change was the dominant fact about America. Its pace seemed relentless; the forms it took, unpredictable. Even those who seemed to march most confidently into the future were often bewildered by what they encountered. John D. Rockefeller I, for example, recalled:

> how often I had not an unbroken night's sleep, worrying about how it was all coming out. All the fortune I have made has not served to compensate for the anxiety. . . . Work by day and worry by night, week in and week out, month after month. If I had foreseen the future I doubt whether I would have had the courage to go on.[3]

Many businessmen, argued Edward Chase Kirkland, sought consolation amid the ups and downs of a business cycle they could not understand by embracing the dogmas of classical economics. Laissez faire may also have given them an effective rallying cry against state regulation of their affairs, but business opposition to regulation has been seriously overstated. Recent research indicates that businessmen were often the strongest proponents of regulation.[4] They cleaved to laissez faire less as a program than as a faith. Faced with the uncertainties of the market, they prayed to an Invisible Hand and besought the providential intercession of Supply and Demand.[5]

Farmers too, according to Richard Hofstadter, sought in myth psychic protection from plunging grain prices. Businessmen though they were, they portrayed themselves not as entrepreneurs but as noble yeomen and identified their cause with the sanctity of the soil.[6] City dwellers, for their part, sought to stave off anonymity by flocking together in countless fraternal orders replete with mystifying names and mystical rituals.[7] Or they sought to make the nuclear family into an emotional bulwark against the pressures of urban life.[8]

Amid this general "search for order," as Wiebe so aptly characterizes the era, were developments that went beyond the defensive or nostalgic. Business consolidation, especially after the Supreme Court had ruled that the Sherman Anti-trust Act applied only to distribution, brought some order to production. Trade unions offered, at least to some segments of the skilled labor force, a measure of job security. And farmers, even though Populism had burned itself out in the 1896 presidential election, successfully lobbied for price supports and parity. The lineaments of a new social order were, by the early 1900s, beginning to become visible.

What would this new order be like? Walter Lippmann spoke for a whole generation of educated youth when he asserted in 1914 that the United States needed to decide, and decide soon, whether it would continue to drift into the future or bring the processes of change under scientific control. This latter alternative he called, with a true believer's zeal, "mastery." "Mastery" expressed in a single word the hopes and ambitions of the first generation of social engineers. To a society buffeted by the winds of change they offered both a vision of stable, predictable development and a series of techniques—social investigation, scientific planning, efficient administration—with which to realize their vision.

Social and settlement workers, public health and recreation experts— these and other social engineers claimed they possessed scientific means of managing social change. On what were these claims to mastery based? How, and how rapidly, did the new expertise develop? What kinds of institutional support, both private and public, did experts seek? To what extent could they challenge existing institutional arrangements and still obtain support? These are some of the questions that prompted this book. They are important because we cannot assess the significance of the expert in modern America until we attempt to answer them.

As the descendants of, and the successors to, this first generation of experts, present-day scholars have accorded them a major role in the making of modern America. So historians have generally followed Lippmann in assuming that the growing complexity of industrial and social arrangements made the expert an indispensable figure. Rowland Berthoff, for example, credited experts with being a key element in "The new political elite . . . which first appeared in the progressive years. . . . " "Scientific and technical experts," he wrote, "commanded a thoroughly modern sort of respect from the common man."[9] A number of other historians have offered the parallel argument that while many of the "reforms" of the early twentieth century were designed to increase the political power of the average voter—the direct election of senators, the short ballot, initiative, referendum and recall measures, and the primary election system are examples—and while the political rhetoric of the day emphasized

the primacy of the popular will, another set of "reforms" was designed
to take some issues out of politics altogether and to entrust them to expert regulation. The city-manager system, factory inspection laws, the
strengthening of the Interstate Commerce Commission and the conservation movement are all examples of this "structural reform" tradition.[10]

Wiebe has provided the most forceful and persuasive version of this
new interpretation of the era. "The heart of progressivism," he wrote,
"was the ambition of the new middle class to fulfill its destiny through
bureaucratic means." Bureaucratic thought, for Wiebe, was "a revolutionary approach to government" that "eventually dominated the politics
of the early twentieth century."[11] Whatever the "heart of progressivism"
may have been, the new social experts were more often dominated than
dominant. Knowledge *could* be power, but only under certain circumstances. Problems had to be perceived generally as both pressing and complex (simple questions do not require expert answers; questions easily
put off do not require answers of any kind). Also, a consensus of expert
opinion had to exist (when experts disagree, nonexperts usually choose,
and their choices are not limited to the options favored by one or another
school of expert opinion). Finally, experts had to occupy at least some
of what noted sociologist C. Wright Mills called the "command posts of
power," or else they had to be able to influence those who did (as we
shall see, decision-makers do not automatically heed, or even seek, expert
advice).

To understand why these conditions were, and are, prerequisites if experts were to exercise actual power, we must briefly survey the place of
the "new" middle class in American society. Mills was the first to call
attention to this new class. What made the class new, he thought, was the
fact that its place in society was based upon its acquisition of some specialized knowledge instead of, as had been the case with the "old" middle
class, a decent capital. The old middle class, in brief, owned something;
the new one knew something.[12]

The meaning of *class,* new or old, middle or other, is one of the oldest
points of contention in American sociology.[13] Although historians are
sensibly reluctant to embroil themselves in this controversy, they are not
reluctant to use the term *class.* It seems to me that historians who use the
term should clearly state what meaning they attach to it. The obligation
is all the greater because, despite the vigor of the controversy, there is
enough agreement among contemporary sociologists about the dynamics

of social stratification for historians to frame meaningful questions about the new middle class.[14]

Virtually all American sociologists, including so-called conflict theorists, have abandoned Marx's view that relations to the means of production determine the social structure. Instead they call attention to additional sources of power. Of these, two are frequently singled out as being of prime importance. One is the rise of various technologies that we can define as sets of rational procedures that are repetitive, obey the law of cause and effect, and utilize efficiency as the criterion of effectiveness.[15] It is this development that makes a "new" middle class possible.

The other major point of agreement is on the significance of the complex organizations that institutionalize these technologies. When the two are brought together, the result—for the historian—is the "new organizational synthesis," of which Wiebe's *Search for Order* is the most influential statement. For the individual seeking to make his or her way in the new America, the result, according to sociologist Talcott Parsons, is "the achievement complex, where achievement may involve either attaining a position of power [in an institutional setting] or utilizing a special or superior competence, or both."[16] Parsons treats "attaining a position of power" and "utilizing a special or superior competence" as equivalents. Whether they are or not, however, is an empirical question, and one that goes to the heart of the position of the new middle class in society. It is also a question requiring historical analysis. That there was, and is, a relationship between knowledge and power is clear. But, as Charles E. Rosenberg has pointed out, "the bare statement that such relationships exist is no longer a meaningful one; it is the task of historians to explore specific instances and define the texture of specific relationships."[17]

For our purposes we can define class in terms of the type of access people have to institutionalized technologies. The "new" middle class, in this usage, are those whose access is through their knowledge of technological procedures. The "old" middle class had, or continued to have, access to older technologies (agriculture, say, or merchandising) through ownership of older and smaller types of institutions (farms or stores). Modern society could not exist without these new technologies, but the technologies require elaborate institutional support. Consider social work. It certainly involved new techniques—casework, for example. But it also involved a new institution, the organized charity society.[18] From the fact that new technologies and new or enlarged institutions develop together comes the conditions specified earlier as to when experts can exercise power. To assess the significance of social engineering we need to determine the extent to which these conditions were fulfilled. How, and how rapidly, did expertise develop? What kinds of institutional support did it require? To what extent did the new social experts control the policies of those institutions? Were there individuals or groups holding positions of power in those institutions who were not experts? What were the relationships between them and the social engineers? The chapters that follow address these questions.

The first deals with the recruitment of the social experts. It focuses on the social settlement as a gateway to a variety of professional careers. The settlements began as cultural missions, bringing the gospel of middle-class respectability to the immigrant poor, and they never altogether lost that character. Even so, the emphasis quickly shifted to the development of social expertise. Chapter 1 examines this impulse toward professionalism and the particular attraction it held for middle-class women.

Chapter 2 uses the Pittsburgh Survey as a case study of the development of expertise. Because the Survey was the experts' first opportunity to analyze systematically the new America, it is an invaluable source for how they viewed the processes of social change. It also serves as an early instance of their developing professional ideology, that is, of their view of their own special qualifications to manage change.

Enterprises like the Survey were expensive. Chapter 3 examines the early history of the institution that financed it, the Russell Sage Foundation. Prior to World War I, the Sage Foundation was the experts' main source of national support; and their attempts to influence its grant decisions provide an excellent opportunity to assess the relationship between those in positions of power, the foundation's trustees, and those possessing special competence. My analysis of foundation politics suggests that the experts were strikingly dependent upon the goodwill of the trustees and that the trustees, for their part, were not dependent upon experts for ideas about how to meet social issues. The alternatives of Parsons's "achievement complex," were not, in this case, at all equivalent. Experts needed the foundation, but they had little or no say in determining what kinds of projects it would support.

This is a contentious book, though I hope in a positive way. The case studies that comprise it cast doubt upon much of what other scholars have said about the role of the expert in modern America. This alone would suffice to make the book argumentative. But it is less directed to testing the "new organizational synthesis" than to suggesting an alternative way of thinking about expertise. The meaning of expertise was finally determined politically. And, as Christopher Lasch has pointed out:

> Anyone who insists on the historical importance of human actions, and who sees history not as an abstract social "process" but as the product of concrete struggles for power, finds himself at odds with the main tradition of the social sciences, which affirms the contrary principle that society runs according to laws of its own. The claim to have discovered these laws is the overriding mystification of social science, which bears the same relation to the later stages of the industrial revolution that the science of political economy bore to the earlier stages.[19]

This book specifically rejects the law formulated by Daniel Bell and others that modern society's increasing reliance upon varying kinds of expertise will make the experts a ruling class.[20] The history of social engineering suggests otherwise. Because experts lacked the institutional means either to develop or implement their ideas, they had to deal with those who possessed those means. Because the necessary resources were scarce, they had to compete for them with nonexperts and with one another. The need to compete, in turn, meant that expert proposals for shaping the future were themselves shaped—and not simply by the inner logic of the proposals themselves. They were also shaped by the logic of the political situation.

Expertise did not spring full blown from the minds of the experts. It was, to borrow Lasch's phrase, "the product of concrete struggles for power." It is to those struggles we now turn.

NOTES

1. Paul U. Kellogg, "Field Work of the Pittsburgh Survey," Appendix E in *The Pittsburgh District: Civic Frontage* (*The Pittsburgh Survey*, findings in six volumes, edited by Paul U. Kellogg, New York: Survey Associates, Inc., 1914), pp. 496-97.

2. Robert Wiebe, *The Search for Order, 1877-1920* (New York: Hill and Wang, 1967). See also Samuel P. Hays, *The Response to Industrialism, 1885-1914* (Chicago: University of Chicago Press, 1957); Rowland Berthoff, *An Unsettled People: Social Order and Disorder in American History* (New York, Harper & Row, 1971); and William E. O'Neill, *The Progressive Years: America Comes of Age* (New York: Dodd, Mead, 1975).

3. Quoted in Edward Chase Kirkland, *Dream & Thought in the Business Community, 1860-1900* (Chicago: Quadrangle Books, 1964), p. 9. Chapter 1, "Panic and Pain," gives numerous examples of anxious tycoons.

4. See Robert H. Wiebe, *Businessmen and Reform: A Study of the Progressive Movement* (Chicago: Quadrangle Books, 1968). For New Left statements of this thesis, see Gabriel Kolko, *The Triumph of Conservatism: A Reinterpretation of American History, 1900-1916* (New York, Free Press, 1967), and James Weinstein, *The Corporate Ideal in the Liberal State, 1900-1918* (Boston: Beacon Press, 1968). For the more traditional view of business hostility to regulation, see Sidney Fine, *Laissez-Faire and the General Welfare State: A Study of Conflict in American Thought, 1865-1901* (Ann Arbor: Mich., University of Michigan Press, 1964).

5. Kirkland, *Dream & Thought in the Business Community.*

6. Richard Hofstadter, *The Age of Reform: From Bryan to F.D.R.* (New York: Vintage Books, 1955), pp. 23-36.

7. See Daniel Boorstin, *The Americans: The Democratic Experience* (New York: Vintage Books, 1973).

8. See Richard Sennett, *Families Against the City: Middle Class Home of Industrial Chicago, 1872-1890* (New York: Vintage Books, 1974).

9. Berthoff, *An Unsettled People,* p. 347.

10. See Thomas K. McGraw, "The Progressive Legacy" and Melvin Holli, "Urban Reform," both in David M. Kennedy, ed., *Progressivism: The Critical Issues* (Boston: Little, Brown & Co., 1971). Two works of Samuel Hays provide influential early statements of this view. See his *Conservation and the Gospel of Efficiency* (Cambridge, Mass.: Harvard University Press, 1959) and "The Politics of Reform in Municipal Government," *Pacific Northwest Quarterly* 55 (October 1964): 157-69.

11. Wiebe, *The Search for Order,* pp. 166, 163. The most spirited critique of Wiebe's view to date is David P. Thelen, *The New Citizenship: Origins of Progressivism in Wisconsin, 1885-1900* (Columbia, Mo.: University of Missouri Press, 1972). Thelen emphasizes the impact of the depression of the 1890s in creating a new political constituency most responsive to consumer issues. See also his *Robert M. LaFollette and the Insurgent Spirit* (Boston: Little, Brown & Co., 1976).

12. C. Wright Mills did not think of this new class as commanding

much in the way of real power. Rather, he argued, it formed an extension of the working class. See his *White Collar: The American Middle Classes* (New York: Oxford University Press, 1951). For an opposing view see Reinhard Bendix, *Work and Authority in Industry: Ideologies of Management in the Course of Industrialization* (New York: Wiley, 1956), Chapter 4.

13. See Charles H. Page's study of the "fathers" of American sociology, *Class and American Sociology* (New York, 1940). Milton M. Gordon's more recent survey, *Social Class in American Sociology* (Durham, N.C.: Duke University Press, 1958), found the controversy equally lively. A reading of Edward O. Laumann, ed., *Social Stratification: Research and Theory for the 1970's* (Indianapolis: Bobbs-Merrill, 1970) produces the same impression.

14. For a fuller discussion of the sociological literature, see Bibliography: Stratification Theories.

15. This definition is taken from James D. Thompson, *Organizations in Action: Social Science Bases of Administrative Theory* (New York: McGraw-Hill Co., 1967), pp. 14-24.

16. Talcott Parsons, "Equality and Inequality in Modern Society, or Social Stratification Revisited," in Laumann, *Social Stratification,* p. 18.

17. Charles E. Rosenberg, *No Other Gods: On Science and American Social Thought* (Baltimore: Johns Hopkins University Press, 1976), p. xii.

18. See Nathan Irwin Huggins, *Protestants Against Poverty: Boston's Charities, 1870-1900* (Westport, Conn.: Greenwood Press, 1971), and Roy Lubove, *The Professional Altruist: The Emergence of Social Work as a Career, 1880-1930* (Cambridge, Mass.: Harvard University Press, 1965).

19. Christopher Lasch, *Haven in a Heartless World: The Family Besieged* (New York: Basic Books, 1977), p. xv.

20. Daniel Bell, *The Coming of Post-industrial Society: A Venture in Social Forecasting* (New York: Basic Books, 1973). This possibility, and the obstacles to it, were analyzed as long ago as Thorstin Veblen, *The Engineers and the Price System* (New York, 1921). John Kenneth Galbraith, *Economics and the Public Purpose* (Boston: Houghton Mifflin, 1973), argues that a "technostructure" has already achieved dominance. Talcott Parsons (see note 16) takes a milder view. Experts, in his view, are the partners in power of those occupying the seats of power.

chapter 1

Recruiting Experts: The Transition of the Social Settlement from Mission to Laboratory

Of all the late nineteenth-century "responses to industrialism" the most innovative and protean was probably the settlement house. The sheer audacity of the idea was astonishing. Young men and women from culti-vated and affluent homes proposed to live among the urban poor, share their lot, and help them improve their lives. Settlement pioneers sought to create a new, extended family that would unite people across class lines; and this new "family" quickly became the home of the new social experts. Not only did the settlements pioneer a wide array of social pro-grams, but they also supplied the trained personnel needed to staff those programs once they were taken over by public agencies. Although we lack the biographical data necessary to determine the exact percentage of ex-perts who began their careers as settlement workers, it is nonetheless clear that the settlement, in the years prior to World War I, was the crucial gate-way to careers in social engineering.

Settlements represented an anomalous mixture of professionalism and familialism. However unlikely such a combination may seem, it becomes less surprising once we realize that settlement workers found their model of professional activity most often in the Protestant ministry. The first generation of experts were, in other words, secular missionaries who sought to make what they considered to be the blessings of middle-class life available to the new urban proletariat. Principal among these bless-ings were the genteel conventions of the Victorian family. In this way settlement work fused family and religious values with professional aspirations. And it attracted, as a result, a particular kind of person, one we may call the "settlement type."

The lack of information about the lives of most settlement workers makes it impossible to describe this "type" with complete confidence, but one historian has compiled "fairly complete biographical information" about 274 "relatively prominent settlement workers."[1] Prominence, of course, is no guarantee of typicality; it is, in fact, almost a guarantee of its opposite. On the other hand, these 274 were the people who set the tone of settlement life. So if we cannot be sure that the "typical" settlement worker fit the settlement "type," we can say that this type was largely responsible for making the settlement what it was.[2] In social history, as in life, prominence is frequently a more reliable guide than typicality.

The settlements attracted the educated and the young. The average age of those studied was twenty-five. Nearly 90 percent had attended college, with more than 80 percent earning a degree. In addition, more than half had done some graduate work. The average term of settlement residency was three years. Often marriage marked the end of that term. One pattern emerges clearly from these few facts. The settlement served as a staging area for highly educated young people on their way from college to some other, more permanent, career and/or marriage. Allen F. Davis, who compiled this profile, suggests an analogy to present-day Peace Corps volunteers that seems quite apt.[3]

Residents were actively religious. Virtually all of them were Protestants, and more than half were Congregationalists or Presbyterians. Of 120 workers whose fathers' occupations could be determined, more than 25 percent (33) were the children of ministers. Most, in fact, came from professional families. Twenty-one were the children of educators, 15 of lawyers, and 7 of doctors. In contrast, only 14 had fathers who were small businessmen.

In addition, settlement workers came from English or Scotch-Irish homes and grew up in cities (60 percent from cities over 25,000 population in 1880; nearly 40 percent from cities over 100,000 population in 1900). Almost all had grown up in the Northeast or the Midwest. And, perhaps most importantly, more than half were women.

The overall profile provides us with several clues about the sort of person who became the new social expert. One is that in terms of economic standing, ethnic origin, and educational attainment, the settlement pioneers were among the most favored segments of the population. They were "haves." Another is that in coming from professional families, settlement workers were familiar with, and likely to be receptive to, the idea of professionalism. Furthermore, coming from cities, it was to be expected they would seek careers in an urban setting.

The commitment to professionalism was virtually contemporaneous with the founding of the settlements.[4] Almost from the outset, the settlement pioneers claimed they utilized empirically proven techniques of social investigation. *Hull House Maps and Papers* had been published as early as 1895.[5] And the preceding year, Julia Lathrop had lectured the National Conference of Charities and Corrections on "Hull House as a Sociological Laboratory."[6] Allied with this emphasis upon research and experimentation was the settlements' attraction as *ad hoc* graduate schools for those seeking entry into the new fields of social expertise. By 1900 a number of settlements were even offering fellowships to those wishing to study the city.[7] Jane Addams commented that in the early 1890s volunteers came to Hull House saying, "We must do something about the social disorder." After 1900, they were saying, "We want to investigate something."[8] In other words, as early as 1900 settlements claimed the training of experts as one of their functions. And even though university-sponsored graduate programs quickly emerged,[9] settlements continued to play this role.

In addition to scientific training and techniques, settlements early displayed a third mark of professionalization: associations. The National Federation of Settlements was organized in 1911. Even before then, however, settlement workers had begun to claim a rightful place at the annual National Conference of Charities and Corrections. The conference held a special session on settlements in 1896; in 1904 it established a new department of "Neighborhood Improvement"; and, in the same year, Jane Addams was elected its president.[10] All in all, it seems fair to say that by 1900,[11] at the latest, settlement workers comported themselves as bona fide professionals.

Aside from these somewhat general considerations, two more specific hints emerge from the profile. One is the major role of women, and the second is the strong religious element. There is an important connection between the two. From the heyday of the benevolent societies in the 1820s, religious service had been a major avenue to social influence for American women.[12] Indeed, one historian has described the "feminization" of American Protestantism.[13]

Addams addressed herself to this in her classic essay, "The Subjective Necessity for Social Settlements." Describing the life of the educated young woman as a sort of prison, "restricted and unhappy," she noted the one exception was when the woman's desires to be productive "are called missionary and the religious zeal of the family carry them over their sense of abuse."[14] Her own school days featured "a concerted pressure" to push her into missionary work, and she noted "the actual activities of a missionary school are not unlike many that are carried on in a Settlement situated in a foreign quarter."[15] Also similar was the work of the "friendly visitor" of the organized charity societies, almost invariably a woman.[16]

In short, young women seeking a "recognized outlet for their active faculties,"[17] found in the settlement house a major source of new possibilities that was at the same time familiar enough to be reassuring. For young men, as well, the ideal of service, derived from religious sources, seems to have been an important motivating force. American Protestantism had viewed the new industrial city with acute misgivings,[18] and few of its attempts to deal with these new conditions had met with much success. Symptomatic of this was the successive moves "uptown" of the established Protestant congregations leaving behind only ineffectual missions for the working classes.[19]

For some young ministers and theology students the settlement seemed a way of redeeming this failure. Graham Taylor, for example, accepted an appointment at the Chicago Theological Seminary on the condition that he be allowed to open a settlement, the Chicago Commons.[20] Similarly, Robert A. Woods was introduced to the settlement movement as a vehicle for the Social Gospel by William Jewitt Tucker, a professor at Andover Theological Seminary and founder of Andover House (later called South End House) in Boston. Woods's association with the settlement movement was lifelong.[21] Allen T. Davis appears to be quite correct in concluding that "many" settlement workers "were directly influenced by the diverse but important effort to create a meaningful faith for an urban, industrial society."[22]

The "meaningful faith" they did create was a least-common-denominator Christianity. Arthur Holden called it "the truly worthwhile Christianity, the Christianity of practice divested of dogmatic considerations." Because it consisted entirely of the injunction to love they neighbor, Holden could find "even in the Jewish houses, a dominating Christian spirit."[23] Although scores of settlements held to far more elaborate denominational creeds,[24] Paul U. Kellogg was right in claiming that Canon "Barnett and his associates [at Toynbee Hall, London] set the type in consistently rejecting sectarian bias and evangelical intent."[25] Andover House was typical. Tucker noted that "the whole aim and motive is religious, but the method is educational rather than evangelistic."[26]

One reason for this divorce of religious motive from ordinary religious practice was the observable failure of the traditional ministry in the new cities. Woods bluntly argued that "the diversity of religious connection among our city population makes it wholly impossible to organize neighborhood life about the church."[27] Divested, then, of its doctrines and its evangelical techniques, this new version of Christianity was little more than a commitment to convert the working class to middle-class values. The first annual report of East Side House in New York City perfectly expressed this faith:

> When men and women who have the power and the knowl-
> edge are ready to live simply and sanely among the people
> for months or years, until they shall have had time to live
> themselves into touch with all the subtle forces that are act-
> ing upon the whole community, then we shall find that in
> that living, new ideas of the needs of the body, unknown
> possibilities for even small incomes, fresh conceptions of
> duty, and hitherto strange ideas of pleasure and recrea-
> tion, will have taken root and made the waste places to
> blossom and bear good fruit.[28]

The second annual report phrased the mission in similar terms: ". . . knowledge and possession of the beautiful, the true, and the good" was a "heritage" of "all of God's children." "We," its resident manager said, "desire to do our part in helping our friends become better men, better citizens, and truer Christians."[29] East Side House was founded by the Episcopal Church Club of New York City and did not formally sever its denominational ties until 1907. Nonetheless, its activities were thoroughly secular from the beginning.[30]

It is clear enough in retrospect that settlement work and other forms of social expertise secularized the religious impulse. To contemporaries, however, just the opposite seemed true. Edward T. Devine, one of its pioneers, claimed social work had "given to thousands an opportunity for a social ministry which they have felt to be religious in every sense."[31]

While previous generations would scarcely have found social work "religious in every sense," Devine's phrase "social ministry" is quite accurate. It recognized that the Protestant clergy provided the first social experts with a professional model, and it also noted the social purpose of their mission.

Mary Kingsbury Simkhovitch's charming pamphlet, *A Settlement Catechism,* assumed the same identity of religion and middle-class values:

> What is a Settlement?
> It is a family living in a neighborhood.
>
> What kind of family?
> A group of people who have had educational and social advantages.
>
> What kind of neighborhood?
> A neglected neighborhood.[32]

Indeed the settlement movement's faith in middle-class culture was virtually boundless. The manifold problems of Pittsburgh, revealed by the Pittsburgh Survey,[33] were due, said Charles C. Cooper, resident director of Kingsley House, of that city, to the fact that the community "lacked . . . in sufficient numbers . . . that solvent of society, a great middle class of cultured, refined, educated and purposeful men and women." This class was "in touch on the one side with the real things that wealth has to offer in culture, in learning, in art, philosophy and religion" while still maintaining contact "with the pulsating heart of the common man." It was this role of the middle class, the "solvent for many of the social and industrial ills of life," that Kingsley House sought to play.[34]

This idealization of middle-class life is all the more striking given the fact that discontent with their constricted role in the genteel family was a prime motive for many of the women who joined the settlement movement. Addams's portrait of the well-educated "young lady," especially, seems to add up to a complaint, in Lasch's words, "against middle-class culture in general."[35] In fact, some of these young women did view themselves as rebelling against their genteel upbringing. But this apparently was a transitory phenomenon.

As early as 1900, Vida D. Scudder of Denison House in Boston could reminisce about once wishing to leave behind "a good many of the comforts and conventions of life." "We desired," she wrote, "to live with

more simplicity" and "felt an impulse" to share the "bad air, over-crowding, and hard manual labor" that were "the lot of great numbers of our
brethren," but she added, "in decorous and mitigated form. . . . We carried
it out, a little." Then, "we were young and sentimental. . . ." Within a
few years, all had changed. ". . . from the point of view of comfort and
beauty, community life is seldom more agreeably ordered than in our
attractive houses. . . ." So, although residents still wished to give "their
strength and life to the neighborhood," "the other motive, almost equally
strong in early times, of self-identification with the life and conditions
of the poor, has shrunk to a vanishing point."[36]

That the romantic impulse to share the life of the poor should be so
short-lived is not surprising. "Bad air, over-crowding, and hard manual
labor" pall rather quickly. Besides the intrinsic disagreeableness of these
conditions, the settlement worker's own sense of mission drove her back
toward middle-class culture. For what, after all, was the "strength and
life" she wished to give to the neighborhood? Was not Addams correct
when she defined the settlement as "an attempt to relieve, at the same
time, the overaccumulation at one end of society and the destitution at
the other . . ."? She was not speaking of wealth. The settlement assumes
"that this overaccumulation and destitution is most sorely felt in the
things that pertain to social and educational privileges."[37] Settlements,
in other words, offered women a career opportunity *within* the parameters
of the genteel tradition. As Barbara Welter has pointed out, the "cult of
true womanhood" emphasized that women fulfilled themselves as pro-
tectresses of home and hearth, as guardians of children, as preservers of
culture. From these roles derived women's higher moral characters.[38]
Many women, of course, rebelled against this narrow stereotype,[39] but
many others found ways to use it for their own purposes. Women entering teaching or the new profession of nursing could argue they were
merely adapting their traditional roles to changing circumstances. So too
suffragists could claim that the higher moral character of women voters
would reform the corruption of politics. In this way the stereotype became an argument for giving women the vote.[40] In a similar way, the
settlement, saturated in the rhetoric of family and homelife, comported
very nicely with the genteel vision of women.

The leading role played by women in the movement, then, accentuated
a fundamental ethnocentrism already present in the settlements. Residents felt they had "something" to give to, or share with, the immigrant

working class. That "something" was, in Woods's words, a "pointed fitness for imparting to the immigrants a wider and higher range of wants
in his domestic and social life. . . ."[41] Despite the cultural judgment contained in expressions like "wider," "higher," "cultural destitution,"
"social and educational privileges," some historians have argued that the
settlement movement was not "built on the assumption that the upper
class had a responsibility to help the needy. . . ."[42] Instead they point
to the settlement pioneers' many positive comments about the value of
immigrant cultures to make the case that settlement workers approached
their neighbors as equals. Even though the pioneers deserve full credit for
their conscientious efforts to appreciate the Old World heritages of their
clients, the basic rationale of the movement precluded any sort of cultural
egalitarianism.[43] "We must," said William H. Kelley, of East Side House,
"stand for better things physically, intellectually, socially, morally, and
religiously than our neighbors, or they will take from us all that we have."[44]

This generalized, cultural sense of superiority was a necessary element
in the identification of Christianity with middle-class values. The Commons, in Chicago, for example, defined itself as a "family," "a group of
persons, more or less blessed with the privileges of what the world calls
culture, who choose to live where they seem to be most needed, rather
than where the neighborhood is supposed to offer the most of social privilege or prestige."[45]

Cultural blessedness, a secularized version of middle-class Protestantism, was the theme settlement workers returned to again and again when
they wished to explain their sense of mission to the immigrant. Archibald
A. Hill, head resident of Neighborhood House, in Louisville, described
"the intellectual barrenness" of the lives of his neighbors. They had come
"from countries where they have absolutely no educational advantages."
Moreover, they had "received a downward thrust from behind in the form
of a bad heredity" and were further pushed down by society "in the shape
of a wretched environment." Accepting middle-class standards as its new
gospel, Neighborhood House struggled "to bring these people to the cool,
fresh air of the intellectual and moral uplands."[46] Or, as Robert A. Woods
put it, "the settlement represents a shaft sent down to a certain stratum
of society."[47]

There was much in this missionary ideal that facilitated the transition
to professionalism; but in order to appreciate this it is necessary to recall
that although present-day social experts pride themselves upon the "value-

free" character of their studies, the first generation of social workers and
social scientists made no such distinction between morals and facts. Davis
falls into this anachronistic trap when he characterizes early settlement
studies as "hardly objective" because "they often made moral judgements
about what they saw."[48] In fact, the connection between these moral
judgments and the rise of social expertise in America is clear and important.

The connecting link can be found in the doctrines of the Social Gospel.
Graham Taylor, for example, urged that "To make society Christian there
must be a science of Christian society." This was to be a "new science"
for the "old 'kingdom.' "[49] Like other Social Gospellers,[50] Taylor feared
the churches were "in danger of being regarded as institutions of the
Bourgeois class and the self-appointed and accepted executors of its
residuary estate." To "bridge" the "tremendous gulf between the churches
and the mass of people" was Taylor's lifelong mission.[51] It led him to make
The Commons a laboratory

> to discover, demonstrate and interpret needs; to initiate,
> try out, test and approve efforts and agencies to meet these
> needs; to ascertain the facts and causes of deterioration and
> supply the conditions or apply the forces which will prevent
> or remedy it; to promote the ideals of progress and help cor-
> relate all the personal and public resources available for their
> realization.[52]

Woods was another who saw sociology as the theology of industrial
America. Because the settlements provided for "patient experimental
action, guided by an acquaintance with the facts that is both extended and
minute" it also gave "scope to a certain sense of moral adventure."[53]
Willis Breckenridge Holcombe, of East Side House, asked "is it not time
to recognize that sociology and philosophy and theology have need of a
laboratory as well as physics and biology and medicine?"[54] This casual
linking of sociology, philosophy, and theology was such a commonplace
of early settlement discourse that some workers were moved to protest.
Jane Elizabeth Robbins, head worker of the New York College Settlement, felt that "so much is said about sociological study and the investigation of the problems of the day that it is sometimes necessary to remind
ourselves that our first duty is to be 'a kind of a sister' to the boys and
girls, and a helpful friend to the whole neighborhood."[55]

Yet her successor, Elizabeth S. Williams, wrote that the worker seeking to be such a "sister" or "friend" "must soon feel that his work is infinitesimal compared to the need, and that something more far-reaching is necessary to remove the evils of which he gradually becomes aware."[56] Faced with the futility of befriending a minute fraction of their neighbors, settlement workers early realized that they could justify their activities only in the guise of expertise. Vida D. Scudder noted in 1900 that the "informal relations of the earlier days," the "often futile, bewildered, but loving efforts of more or less helpless amateurs to discover the means of making their spirit of love effective under strange and unknown conditions," were "yielding fast to the well-organized activities of a set of experts."[57] This had always been the goal for the College Settlements Association. "The education of our college women" was its "one great mission," for "in the awakened intelligence and consecration of the cultured class lies, after all, the most serious promise for the success of that great movement towards social reconstruction."[58]

The point is a crucial one. The settlements existed quite as much to serve the worker as the neighbor. This went far beyond meeting the "subjective necessity" of genteel young ladies by providing them with a romantic opportunity for "real life." The romance died quickly as Jean Gurney Fine, of the New York College Settlement, lamented. Within a year, "the picturesqueness had vanished, and the dirt seemed dirtier and the vice more revolting."[59] The lasting opportunity the settlements provided was training for a career in social expertise. As Charles C. Cooper of Kingsley House phrased it, "the social settlement should be the experimental station whereby social experiments are tried out and their worth determined." Then "the municipality, or society through other agencies, should undertake the work."[60]

The settlement worker saw himself, in the words of George A. Bellamy, head resident of the Hiram House in Cleveland, as "the pioneer in developing redemptive and remedial forces in society." The settlement should, according to this conception, be permanently committed to no activity other than research. "As soon as it can demonstrate and create public opinion, which shall take over the activities, it should be relieved of such financial and personal responsibilities as is entailed in the management of such activities."[61] Similarly, the College Settlements Association used as the rationale for their fellowship program the claim that "the settlement serves as a sociological laboratory."[62]

All of this, said Woods, meant "the development of the practical expert."[63] With the rise of the expert we may close our discussion of moti-
vation. A secularized but missionary sense of vocation, a romantic desire
to break free of genteel conventions, the attractions of a professional
career, and, doubtless, a host of subsidiary considerations sufficed to
bring a segment of the young, well-educated middle class into the settlements. Once there they encountered a growing professionalism that directed
their activities into the new fields of social expertise and into what historians label "reform." Every settlement worker, argued Elizabeth S.
Williams, "may not have the time or the ability to carry on a crusade,
but through the faithful discharge of his duties he has gained information
which may be used in inciting others to action, and which is invaluable
as campaign material."[64] Professional activity led, that is, to social action.
The social action, in turn, reflected both the experts' professionalism and
their middle-class background, status, and connections.

The various exigencies of their sense of mission had led social experts
to imbue middle-class culture with a sacred character. Their professional
needs and interests also led them to identify as much with the old middle
and upper classes as with the new immigrant proletariat. Experts usually
expressed these links positively, as the settlement's ability to mediate
class differences. John Lovejoy Elliot wrote that "the purpose of the
settlement is to act as an intermediary" linking "the employer and the
union," "the citizen and the state."[65] Or, in Taylor's formulation, settlements "interpreted" men to each other "across the lines of industrial
cleavage and class antagonism."[66] There was more to this rhetoric than
the ideal of brotherhood, more too than transplanting middle-class culture
in the slums.

For settlements, of course, were not self-supporting. Among the life
members of Kingsley House in Pittsburgh (those who had contributed
$1,000 or more by 1911), were three Carnegies, four Fricks, and five
Mellons.[67] It is not surprising that its resident director, Charles C. Cooper,
could predict in 1913 that "the day is rapidly coming when the *business
interests will demand, for business reasons, the solution of social problems.*"[68]

This should not suggest that settlements did not typically insist on
operational autonomy from their boards of trustees. Most head residents,
like George A. Bellamy of Hiram House, Cleveland, did "not believe that
any ordinary Board of Trustees can equip itself sufficiently well to take

authority of action regarding the policy of settlements."[69] But the financial situation required settlements to approach class divisions as interpreters and intermediaries and guaranteed their immunity from any species of radicalism.

The political situation, as settlement workers viewed it, also drew them toward the middle and upper classes. They could be nonpartisan, but not apolitical. As experts, their proposals for new governmental bureaus and agencies necessarily led them into the political arena. There they met a serious competitor, the machine politician. He too believed in neighborhood organization. He too sought to acculturate immigrants; he too provided social services and usually on a scale that beggared the settlement's resources.[70] Settlement worker and ward boss could, at times, cooperate;[71] but their ideas for filling municipal positions, civil service examinations versus patronage, were diametrically opposed.

Competition coincided with the middle-class background of the experts[72] to lead them to the cause of municipal reform. Their strategy was to combine, in Woods's words, their own constituency of "intelligent voters," members of the settlements' men's clubs, with "the trade-union constituency, which is increasingly independent of mere party lines in municipal elections" and so grasp the balance of power.[73] Because the strategy presupposed two parties more or less evenly matched, it rarely worked in the inner-city wards, where the machine usually had no significant competition.[74] In city-wide elections the strategy meant joining the "Goo-Goos," the good-government campaigns of the middle and upper classes.[75] Here the settlements, said Woods, "have a distinct mission,—to stand for a form of municipal government which will be not merely negatively incorrupt . . . but judiciously progressive in such a way as to serve actual public needs. . . ."[76]

The expert, as professional reformer, thus sought to attach his programs to the cause of good government. This goes a long way toward explaining what Allen Davis labeled the settlement workers' "idealistic belief that if people could be told the truth reform would follow naturally." More was involved. Experts were in search of a political base. The one that was available, for the most part, was business-sponsored municipal reform. Some experts, at least, had a very lively awareness that reform did not, in such circumstances, follow naturally from telling people the truth. As Woods put it, "the most serious weakness of the democratic form of government" was "that it has not yet learned sufficiently to trust the ex-

pert. . . ." His own idealistic belief was in expertise. The expert was "the
man who by heredity and training has the physical energy, intellectual
grasp, and moral power effectively to handle groups and masses of
men. . . ."[77]

NOTES

1. Allen F. Davis, *Spearheads for Reform: The Social Settlements
and the Progressive Movement, 1890-1914* (New York: Oxford University
Press, 1967), chap. 2 and notes. All biographical information is drawn
from this source unless otherwise specified.

2. Davis cautions that although his data should "by no means . . . be
interpreted as a scientific sample," he does think he studied "a representative group of settlement workers in the progressive era." Strictly
speaking, his is no sample at all. He compiled statistics for *each* person
he could locate information on. Nor, as pointed out in the text, is there
a basis for calling this group "representative" of any larger group. Actually,
what Davis put together is preferable to any sample, representative or
other. In statistical terms, what he has is a "universe," that is, all of the
people of a certain type for whom he could find information. As a result,
there is no margin of error. His findings are entirely reliable for the group
he studied (ibid., p. 265, n. 4).

3. Ibid., pp. xiii-xiv.

4. This is far from the usual view. Davis argues that professionalization did not get under way until after 1914 when certain unspecified
"trends within the broad field of social work . . . put more emphasis on
professional standing and less on social action" (ibid., p. xv). His interpretation presumes an opposition between "professional standing" and "social
action" that is highly questionable. As we shall see, those who pursued
careers in social expertise often demanded new programs. Without such
programs, such as factory inspection departments, tenement house commissions, child labor bureaus, experts would have had few professional
opportunities. Hence the first generation of experts were professional
believers in social action.

5. *Hull House Maps and Papers* (New York, 1895).

6. *Proceedings* of the National Conference of Charities and Corrections (1894), pp. 313-20.

7. See Charles H. Cooley, "Settlement Fellowships and the University,"
The Commons 5 (October 1900): 1-2.

8. Quoted in Davis, *Spearheads for Reform,* p. 29.

9. The Chicago School of Civics and Philanthropy, associated with

The Commons settlement house, opened in 1903 as the Social Science Center for Practical Training in Philanthropic and Social Work. The New York School of Philanthropy and the Harvard-Simmons School for Social Workers both inaugurated programs in 1904. The St. Louis School of Philanthropy, part of Washington University, began in 1908, and the Pennsylvania School of Social Service opened in 1910. See Louise C. Wade, *Graham Taylor: Pioneer for Social Justice, 1851-1938* (Chicago: University of Chicago Press, 1964), pp. 164-82; Elizabeth G. Meier, *A History of the New York School of Social Work* (New York: Columbia University Press, 1954), chaps. 1, 2; and Kenneth L. Mark, *Delayed by Fire: Being the Early History of Simmons College* (Concord, N.H., 1945), pp. 121-25.

10. See *Proceedings* of the National Conference of Charities and Corrections (1896, 1904).

11. Roy Lubove used the year 1900; see *The Professional Altruist: The Emergence of Social Work as a Career, 1880-1930* (Cambridge, Mass.: Harvard University Press, 1965). It is also used by Nathan Irvin Huggins, *Protestants Against Poverty: Boston's Charities, 1870-1900* (Westport, Conn.: Greenwood Press, 1971), chap. 5.

12. See Gilbert Barnes, *The Anti-slavery Impulse, 1830-1844* (New York, 1933), pp. 153-60.

13. Barbara Welter, "The Feminization of American Religion, 1800-1860," in William H. O'Neill, ed., *Insights and Parallels: Problems and Issues of American Social History* (Minneapolis: Burgess Pub. Co., 1973), pp. 305-31.

14. Jane Addams, *Twenty Years at Hull-House* (New York, 1910), p. 94.

15. Ibid., pp. 50, 49. She also claimed "other motives which I believe make toward the Settlement are the result of a certain renaissance going forward in Christianity" (ibid., p. 95).

16. See Lubove, *Professional Altruist*, p. 23: "The work of the friendly visitor in the nineteenth century was sanctioned by an organization established to eliminate pauperism and dependency; *her* motives. . . ." See also, ibid., chap. 1.

17. Addams, *Twenty Years at Hull-House, p. 94.*

18. The best general account is Henry May, *The Protestant Response to Industrial America* (New York: Octagon Books, 1963). See also the documents in Robert Cross, ed., *The Church and the City* (Indianapolis: Bobbs-Merrill, 1967).

19. See Cross, *The Church and the City*, pp. 55-95.

20. Louise C. Wade, *Graham Taylor: Pioneer for Social Justice, 1851-1938.*

21. Eleanor Woods, *Robert Woods, Champion of Democracy,* (Boston, 1929).

22. Davis, *Spearheads for Reform,* p. 27. See also pp. 13-17, 27-29, for additional examples.

23. Arthur C. Holden, *The Settlement Idea: A Vision of Social Justice* (New York, 1922), pp. 138, 137.

24. See Robert A. Woods and Albert J. Kennedy, eds., *Handbook of Settlements* (New York, 1911), which lists religious affiliation (if any) and all settlements providing religious instruction. Many of the latter might better be considered missions.

25. Paul U. Kellogg, "Social Settlements," *Encyclopedia of the Social Sciences,* 14: 158.

26. Circular No. 1, October 9, 1891, quoted in Woods and Kennedy, eds., *Handbook of Settlements,* p. 125.

27. Robert A. Woods, *University Settlements: Their Point and Drift,* pamphlet in NFS, Folder: 597 (1899), p. 10.

28. The East Side House, New York City, *First Annual Report* of the resident manager (Willis Breckenridge Holcombe), 1892. In NFS, Folder: 415.

29. *Second Annual Report* (1893) NFS, Folder: 415.

30. Woods and Kennedy, eds., *Handbook of Settlements,* pp. 197-98.

31. Edward T. Devine, *Social Work* (New York, 1927), p. 35.

32. Mary Kingsburg Simkhovitch, "A Settlement Catechism" (New York, n.d.), UNH, Folder: 1.

33. See Chapter 3.

34. The Kingsley Association, *Year Book,* 1916. (Pittsburgh), *Report* of Charles C. Cooper, Resident Director, pp. 46-47, NFS, Folder: 510.

35. Christopher Lasch, *The New Radicalism, 1889-1963: The Intellectual as a Social Type* (New York: Knopf, 1965), p. 13. In his introduction, Lasch relates "her sense of kinship with the 'other half' of humanity" to the intellectuals' "estrangement from the middle class . . ."(p. xv).

36. Vida D. Scudder, "Settlements Past and Future," pamphlet in *Denison House College Settlement, Report for 1900* (Boston) in NFS, Folder: 325. Denison House was founded December 27, 1892. Woods and Kennedy, eds., *Handbook of Settlements,* pp. 109-11. So Scudder's account refers to a seven-year period.

37. Addams, *Twenty Years at Hull-House,* p. 98.

38. Barbara Welter, "The Cult of True Womanhood: 1820-1860," *American Quarterly* 18 (Summer 1966): 151-74.

39. Charlotte Perkins Gilman is a prime example. See her *Women &*

Economics: The Economic Factor Between Men and Women as a Factor in Social Evolution, Carl Degler, ed. (1898, rpt., New York: Harper & Row, 1966.)

40. See, Eleanor Flexner, *Century of Struggle: The Woman's Rights Movement in the United States* (New York: Atheneum, 1968); Aileen S. Kraditor, *The Ideas of the Woman Suffrage Movement, 1890-1920* (Garden City, N.Y.: Doubleday & Co., 1971); and William L. O'Neill, *Everyone Was Brave: The Rise and Fall of Feminism in America* (Chicago: Quadrangle, 1969).

41. Woods, *University Settlements,* p. 14.

42. Davis, *Spearheads for Reform,* p. 19.

43. For a brief but insightful discussion of this point, see Paul Boyer, *Urban Masses and Moral Order in America, 1820-1920* (Cambridge, Mass.: Harvard University Press, 1978), pp. 155-58.

44. *Thirteenth Annual Report* of the East Side House (New York, 1905), William H. Kelly, Secretary and Headworker, p. 10, NFS, Folder: 415.

45. Quoted in *Chicago Commons: A Social Settlement,* pamphlet (Chicago, 1899), in NFS, Folder: 284.

46. Archibald A. Hill (Head Resident), *Neighborhood House and Its Work* (Louisville, Ky., 1898), pp. 22-23. Pamphlet in NFS, Folder: 320. Neighborhood House was maintained by the Jewish Federated Charities. Woods and Kennedy, eds., *Handbook of Settlements,* pp. 88-89.

47. Woods, *University Settlements,* p. 12. On page 10 he also notes, "The settlement comes in contact with its 'parish' by means of an ascending scale of clubs which is organized so as to meet the needs of all ages and both sexes."

48. Davis, *Spearheads for Reform,* p. 172. The consistent use of this standard would relegate the works of E. A. Ross, Franklin Giddings, Charles Cooley, and others to the position of protosociology. Presumably the rise of social science in America would then date from Talcott Parsons's translations of Max Weber.

49. Graham Taylor, "The Social Function of the Church," *Friends Quarterly Examiner* (January 1904): 9. Reprint in NFS, Folder: 284.

50. See, for example, Walter Rauschenbusch, *Christianity and the Social Crisis* (New York, 1907).

51. Taylor, "The Social Function of the Church," pp. 10, 7.

52. *Chicago Commons: 1894-1911* (Chicago, n.d.), pamphlet in NFS, Folder: 284.

53. Woods, *University Settlements,* pp. 6, 4.

54. *First Annual Report* (1892), p. 13.

55. *Fifth Annual Report* of the College Settlements Association (Philadelphia, 1894), p. 17 in NFS, Folder: 412.

56. *Seventeenth Annual Report* (New York, 1906), p. 5 in NFS, Folder: 412.

57. Scudder, "Settlements Past and Future," p. 3.

58. *Second Annual Report,* report of the electoral board (Adaline Emerson Thompson, Vida Dutton Scudder, Bertha Hazard), p. 7 in NFS, Folder: 412. The phrase "consecration of the cultured class" aptly captures the fusion of religion and middle-class values.

59. Ibid., report of the New York Settlement, pp. 13-14.

60. The Kingsley Association, *Year Book* (1914), p. 40 in NFS, Folder: 510.

61. George A. Bellamy to Graham Taylor, April 17, 1915, in NFS, Folder: 549. Bellamy founded Hiram House in 1896. Woods and Kennedy, eds., *Handbook of Settlements,* pp. 256-57.

62. Katherine Coman, "The Settlement Fellowships," *Fourteenth Annual Report* (Philadelphia, 1903), p. 25 in NFS, Folder: 412.

63. Woods, *University Settlements,* p. 17. "Considering that a great part of the toil of science consists in securing the most favorable conditions for investigation and experiment, the settlement must be admitted to have significant prospects as a laboratory and experimental station in one of the most important fields of economic science" (p. 16).

64. *Seventeenth Annual Report* of the College Settlements Association, p. 5.

65. John L. Elliot to Graham Taylor, May 5, 1915, in NFS, Folder: 131. Elliot was connected with Hudson Guild in New York City.

66. Graham Taylor, *Chicago Commons: A Social Center for Civic Cooperation* (December 1904), pamphlet in NFS, Folder: 284.

67. NFS, Folders: 509-11, Kingsley House, 1911-54. The 1915 *Year Book* notes as contributions to constructing and endowing a Convalescent Rest at Valencia, Pa.: Andrew Carnegie, $50,000; A. W. and R. B. Mellon, $25,000.

68. The Kingsley Association, *Year Book,* 1913, p. 17 in NFS, Folder: 510. Italics in original. Settlement ties to the business community were commonplace. J. P. Morgan, for example, was vice-president of East Side Settlement, in New York City, NFS, Folders: 415-17. So too the trustees of Chicago Commons included business executives, a member of the Board of Trade, and a member of the Civic Federation. *Chicago Commons: A Social Settlement* (March 1899), p. 15. Pamphlet in NFS, Folder: 284.

69. George A. Bellamy to Graham Taylor, April 17, 1915.

70. See Jane Addams, "The Alderman's Pull," *Commons* 2 (March 1898), for a rueful discussion of this.

71. See Davis, *Spearheads for Reform* (pp. 148-51), for the example of James "Honorable Jim" Donovan and Robert A. Woods in Boston's Ninth Ward.

72. See Lincoln Steffens, *The Autobiography of Lincoln Steffens* (New York, 1931), and Frederick Howe, *Confessions of a Reformer* (New York, 1925), for classic statements of the middle-class distaste for the corruption of urban politics.

73. Woods, *University Settlements,* p. 13.

74. One settlement that did have success was Graham Taylor's Chicago Commons in that city's Seventeenth Ward. See *Chicago Commons: A Social Settlement,* pp. 32-33, and *Chicago Commons: A Social Center for Civic Co-operation,* p. 8. See Davis, *Spearheads for Reform,* pp. 148-69, for failures in Boston, New York, Philadelphia, and other cities.

75. For the overall failure of the "Goo-Goos," Lincoln Steffens's *Autobiography* is still the best analysis. See also, William Riordan, *Plunkitt of Tammany Hall* (New York, 1963), especially "Reformers Only a Morning Glory," pp. 17-20.

76. Woods, *University Settlements,* p. 13.

77. Robert A. Woods, "Democracy: A New Unfolding of Human Power," reprinted from *Studies in Philosophy and Psychology: A Commemorative Volume Dedicated to Professor Charles E. Garman of Amherst College* (Boston, 1906), p. 83.

chapter 2

Expertise in the Making: The Pittsburgh Survey, 1907-09

Expertise required, in the first instance, detailed, systematic knowledge of social conditions. But even though the settlement and the organized charity society fostered professionalism, even though their residents and workers came more and more to think of themselves as experts, there was, as of 1906, no American counterpart to Charles Booth's massive study of London[1] and, therefore, no authoritative body of knowledge about industrial America. Carroll Wright, first as commissioner of the Massachusetts Bureau of Statistics of Labor and later as U.S. commissioner of labor, had, as early as 1875, begun to produce a model series of studies of industrial conditions, and he deserves much of the credit for first demonstrating the value of accurate social statistics.[2] Despite his efforts, however, much of what passed for knowledge among the experts was fragmentary and impressionistic.[3] Charity societies and settlement houses, as we have seen, strove mightily to gather reliable information. Their staffs met annually at the National Conference of Charities and Corrections to swap experiences. Nonetheless, their work was uncoordinated and limited in crucial ways. Settlements rarely ventured beyond their immediate neighborhoods; charity societies were preoccupied with ameliorating the immediate needs of the poor.[4]

Experts could hope to realize their ambitious programs of rationally directed social change only if they could overcome these limitations. Recognizing this, the central council of the New York Charity Organization Society established, in 1905, a National Publication Committee "to get at the facts of social conditions and to put those facts before the public in ways that will count." Specifically, the committee was to initiate "important pieces of social investigation not undertaken by any existing organization." The society's journal, *Charities and the Commons,* later to become the *Survey,* would publicize the findings.[5]

Edward T. Devine, then the editor of *Charities and the Commons* and one of the founders of professional social work, led a ten-month investigation into housing conditions in Washington, D.C. His report was sent to congressmen, civic leagues, newspapers, and magazines and led to some concrete, if limited, reforms. Congress established a juvenile court, passed a bill for the condemnation of insanitary housing that had been pending for nine years, and President Roosevelt appointed a Homes Commission to recommend ways of upgrading the capital's housing stock.

Encouraged by this success, the publication committee accepted the invitation of Alice B. Montgomery, the chief probation officer of the Alleghany County Juvenile Court, to make a similar study of Pittsburgh. The committee solicited the aid of William H. Matthew, the head worker at Kingsley settlement. He, in turn, induced Mayor George W. Guthrie, H. D. W. English, president of the local chamber of commerce, and Justice Joseph Buffington, of the circuit court, to act as references. The Pittsburgh Survey began in the winter of 1907 with a $1,000 grant from the committee and some $350 in local contributions. The bulk of the financing, some $26,500, came from the newly founded Russell Sage Foundation.[6]

The Survey[7] is a storehouse of information concerning the impact of industrialization upon living and working conditions.[8] It is also a record of the people who undertook this unprecedented investigation. As such, it forms an important chapter in the history of the new professional middle class whose careers started in settlement houses, charity organization societies, and universities and who later moved into governmental investigative and regulatory commissions, private foundations, additional surveys, and professional social work agencies. Fundamental to such a pattern of career development was an emerging technology of measuring and mediating social change familiar to us as social engineering.

The social engineers had first to identify the nature of an America that had suddenly become industrial, urban, and polyglot. Pittsburgh, with its mills and mines, congested central city, and enormous immigrant population, displayed these phenomena in their starkest forms. Similarly, the Pittsburgh Survey exemplified the elements of the new expertise, the kinds of institutions willing to support it, and the reforming ideology it sponsored. Because it allows us to study both the experts' perception of the new industrial America and their emerging ideological commitment to scientifically managed change, the Survey is a particularly resonant instance of expertise in the making.

What we must keep in focus is the dialectical relationship the staff of the Survey had with their subject matter. They had come to Pittsburgh to investigate just those phenomena that had made their careers possible while their careers involved just such an investigation. What they found to be true of Pittsburgh, in other words, was thereby true, in some sense, for themselves. For Pittsburgh was a microcosm of the new industrial America. "We felt," said Survey director, Paul U. Kellogg, who subsequently edited the *Survey* for over thirty years, "that Pittsburgh bore somewhat the same relation industrially to the country at large that Washington did politically."[9] Pittsburgh symbolized the future, *their* future, because their professions consisted of identifying and controlling the social forces that made Pittsburgh what it was. Thus both their descriptions and prescriptions have an ideological as well as an intellectual referent. This does not call into question the accuracy of their observations. Their professional careers depended upon accuracy, but they also depended upon demonstrating the necessity for social engineering.

Social engineering is an exact designation for this ideology. The Survey's staff conceived of society as a machine and of themselves as mechanics. So they attempted to measure social mechanisms in much the same fashion as scientific managers administered the machinery of business— by a system of cost accounting. Kellogg, for example, thought that hospitals, schools, and municipal departments could measure their "units of labor and product" as exactly as steelmakers weighed their tonnage or bankers counted their dollars and cents. The Survey was itself, of course, an example of how this could be done. Kellogg claimed "that we projected our inductive research in Pittsburgh into such methods of social bookkeeping as would show something of the larger waste of human life and private means."[10] Social bookkeeping may seem a far cry from the cultural messianism that animated settlement workers. In fact, it is yet another facet of the middle-class character of expertise. Missionary zeal did pervade the Survey's staff, but they borrowed their techniques of investigation from another part of their cultural heritage: industrial capitalism.

The amount of research was enormous. Dozens of intensive studies filled six volumes, and a full discussion of the methodology employed in each would be a sizable task. Common to them all, however, was the technique suggested in Kellogg's description of the Survey as social bookkeeping, namely, counting. R. R. Wright's "One Hundred Negro Steel Workers," for instance, was a study of virtually all the black employees of the Carnegie Company's Clark Mills.[11]

Similarly, Crystal Eastman's study of industrial accidents involved an investigation of "a year's industrial fatalities and of three months' industrial injuries in Alleghany County, Pennsylvania."[12] Elizabeth Beardsley Butler based her study of working women on an investigation of 448 shops and factories. Each investigation included such details as the amount of ventilated air per cubic foot.[13]

Sampling techniques were not unknown to the survey staff. H. F. J. Porter's examination of "industrial hygiene" in Pittsburgh was limited to thirty-eight companies selected "as reflecting the general range of working conditions. . . ."[14] Still many of the staff relied on statistical overkill, piling up case after case. If statistically unjustified, exhaustive case studies probably made political sense. Speaking of Eastman's study, Kellogg pointed out that her investigation "eliminated any change of partiality." No employer could attempt to escape her indictment by claiming that she had unfairly concentrated on his plant. "Only the occurrence of a fatality in an industry during the period studied would bring it within view of the inquiry; only the nonoccurrence of a fatality would keep it out."[15]

According to Kellogg, the purpose of all this counting was threefold. One was "to clamp our facts in so that they cannot be shaken off and so that they will have national interest and, within the limits we consciously set for them, scientific value." The second was "to make the town real—to itself. . . ." This did not involve "goody goody preachment [sic] of what it ought to be" nor "sensational discoloration" nor even "a formidable array of rigid facts." Kellogg thought of the Survey's staff as "on the high seas" between "the census at one pole" and "yellow journalism at the other." The "standard ahead of us" was "piled up actuality." The third was to establish "relations" to "project" the Survey's "work into the future," that is, to organize "local initiative . . . to shoulder the responsibilities which the facts show to be obvious."[16]

What was most obvious, they found, was that Pittsburgh verged on chaos. John R. Commons, a professor of political economy at the Uni-

versity of Wisconsin and an advisor to Robert LaFollette, declaimed,
"First Prince, then Pauper; overwork, then under work; high wages, no
wages; millionaire, immigrant; militant unions, masterful employers;
marvelous business organization, amazing social disorganization. Such
are the contrasts of 'Pittsburgh the Powerful,' the 'Workshop of the
world!' "[17] These contrasts became the principal data about industrial
society, and accounting for them became the principal task of the Survey.

The brute fact of the city fascinated and repelled the Survey's staff.
America had been a predominantly agrarian society, and the virtues of
the land had always figured prominently in American social thought. Now
those virtues counted for naught, especially to the social engineer whose
professional commitments were perforce to the city. Kellogg was only
uttering a commonplace of the day when he observed that "in all history,
cities have never reproduced themselves. They draw on the country districts to replace the stock they burn out." But for him it was a commonplace fraught with opportunity as well as danger. "The mere fact of
aggregation" would make the old relationship impossible. A third and
more of the population were coming to live in cities. Therefore, "it becomes vitally important that city people live well, else the race lapses."
The opportunity resided in the implicit premise that it was the new professional who would teach the people to live well, for urban living in the
twentieth century would differ from earlier patterns. "The life to which
these people come," observed Kellogg, "is different from that known to
any previous generation" and their work "is not the work of their fathers."
For expert and nonexpert alike, American society had reached a turning
point in which the city and the homestead had exchanged roles: ". . . the
city is the frontier of today."[18]

The lure of the city rested upon its new industries, and the combination of new populations and new factories created both great wealth and
an unmanageable crush in the central city. This congestion, according to
Woods, "brings out, in a peculiarly acute way, the breakdown of many
branches of the social administration of the city. . . ." It led to inadequate
housing and roofing, to outbreaks of typhoid fever and tuberculosis, to
the crowding of machinery so close as to cause accidents and disease.[19]
It implied, moreover, the need for housing and health experts. The alternative was suggested by Edward T. Devine, who noted that living in Pittsburgh, as it was, was "very unfavorable, very disastrous."[20]

Complicating these conditions were the facts that a high percentage of the new Pittsburghers were also "new" immigrants and that the native American stock lacked precisely those qualities needed for successful urban living. Frederick Jackson Turner's description of the American national character inspired doubts about the future. The city, after all, was the "frontier of today"; and its challenges could not be met by those qualities developed in conquering the frontier of yesterday. "The physical conquest of the continent," wrote Kellogg, "spread out our people, and made great draughts on individual initiative." This had had numerous beneficial results, "but we are beginning to find, in our scattered forces, in our inadequate social machinery and in our ineptness at team play, that we have paid a price for those qualities."[21] Yet for the expert this price was the justification of his own enterprise whose virtues were a mirror image of society's failings. The staff of the Survey were engaged in a joint project to appraise Pittsburgh's social machinery and, for that purpose, had gathered together from all over the country.

In brief, summarized Kellogg, the city was overburdened "with the impractical task of serving one of these new, sudden, overtoppling aggregations of people which modern factories gather about them." Making matters worse were a "native stock" strong in the frontier virtues and an immigration that added "difference of race, tradition, and religion." All in all, "our lack of habits and media for collective action is a serious handicap."[22] Although the difficulties encountered by native Americans attempting to adapt to the demands of urban life seemed great, they were dwarfed by those met by the immigrant.

According to Alois B. Kuokol, secretary of the Slavonic Immigration Society, the alien had left the Old World seeking to escape from a surplus of labor. He came to the United States believing "tales of wealth gained by some bold pioneer and of the great opportunities in this country, confirmed and exaggerated by the crafty agents of transportation companies."[23] Once in Pittsburgh, the immigrant found himself on an economic treadmill. Woods argued that the "great and continuous" flow of unskilled, foreign labor "has made it comparatively easy for industrial captains to control industrial administration" and to eliminate the opportunity of "workingmen to organize in their own behalf."[24] The immigrant was an intractable obstacle to the rational ordering of society; the unions' experience in organizing him offered a case in point.

Sheer force of numbers, according to Commons and one of his graduate students, William M. Leiserson, forced the miners' union to take up the difficult task of organizing the immigrants. The mine workers had had to translate their constitution and other literature into Polish and Italian, to employ organizers who spoke those languages, and to lower initiation fees and dues. Even with all this, the task was never ending, for "when he [the immigrant] has learned his lesson, he hears of better conditions in other districts, goes west, and becomes a strong union man."[25] Meanwhile the union remained chronically weakened. Immigrant labor endangered the native stock in another respect. John A. Fitch, another of Commons's students, argued that there was a direct link between the alien's unfamiliarity with industrial conditions and the frequency of accidents. He described the Slav workman as likely to throw "the lives of all his fellows into jeopardy" because he knew nothing of machinery and little of English. Guided only by "an exasperated boss shouting unintelligible orders," he would run into danger as often as out of it.[26]

So far as the Survey's staff was concerned, the immigrant was a "primitive" who, according to Elizabeth Beardsley Butler, the assistant secretary of the Rand School, had "served apprenticeship neither to the life of the city nor to the standards of industrial work."[27] They saw him as a tragic figure but also, and for the same reasons, as a menace to himself and the native stock. He was a man with no industrial skills and no knowledge of trade unions, a man without even the ability to express himself coherently in the language of his new home. He was grist for the industrial mill. By necessity he lived in overcrowded tenements and became the unwitting victim and carrier of disease. His lack of familiarity with urban conditions made him an easy prey for unscrupulous employers, landlords, saloonkeepers, and petty grafters alike. On occasion he would stumble into crime. Some few of his number found their way into organized crime; but for the most part, according to James Forbes, the secretary and director of the National Association for Prevention of Mendicancy, the immigrants became the prostitutes, vagrants, drunks, and disturbers of the peace. They were the "inarticulate rank and file, whose burdens, being the heaviest, are naturally held to strictest accounting."[28]

The staff of the Survey did not see the immigrant as a contributor to the industrial plenty, but as a competitor who retarded the wages and working conditions of the native. In his capacity as citizen, he seemed to advance the interests of machine politicians alone. And as one who met the minimum social demands of order and livelihood with difficulty, and frequently with failure, he seemed to default entirely on his civic responsibilities. This view of the alien as an irrational and wasteful force suggested to Kellogg and others the need for a program of Americanization. As Kellogg posed the problem, "the community has a claim on the vigor and intelligence of its people, on their activity in civic affairs. . . ." At any time a serious claim, the rising international tensions produced a nationalistic fervor that made it seem vital. "Social excellence" required "a great body of Americans" trim of muscle and vigorous of mind, for they had to match the labor forces of the world "in leisure, health, and stability, in creative imagination, and joy of the game."[29] The task was only too clear. "Pittsburgh must build up an active, native citizenship or be merely an industrial department."[30]

Ethnic associations and national churches seemed to be the chief barriers to assimilation; for a native citizenship was to be made, not born. The Reverend Peter Roberts, of the Industrial Department of the International Young Men's Christian Association, even feared "that the home governments of these peoples foster the formation of organizations along racial lines." This suspicion was not common, but Roberts's other fears were. He though that the immigrants' "racial consciousness" would either "thrust its own concepts and ideals into the social elements around it and modify them" or "it will build around itself a wall which the customs and habits of the country will find difficulty in penetrating."[31] Either of these eventualities would have a disturbingly centrifugal impact upon the community. Both would dispense with the services of the social expert, for both offered alternative methods of adjustment that bypassed rationally controlled Americanization. As Woods expressed it, "The city's population, instead of finding an increasing social unity, has been increasingly sectionalized by the overwhelming influx of every type of immigrant." Woods took shelter behind a benign Darwinism, believing "a sort of natural selection" ensured that America would receive only the "enterprising spirits of every European nation and tribe" and that an exposure to the American way of life would fully assimilate these hardy souls. They would become "Americanized not by a tradition or other educational process than that of having the typical American experience in what still remains the heart of the country."[32]

Not everyone could share this facile optimism. For one thing, there was a troubling intimation that natural selection could only work itself out over geological time. But the very pace of industrialization precluded such a luxury. As Kellogg summarized the situation, when "each new peasantry leaves the soil, the history of the industrial revolution is repeated, but processes are accelerated and the experience of a generation is taken at a jump."[33] The crucial task was to gain time. With this in mind, Kellogg proposed to the National Conference of Charities and Corrections that immigrants be kept out of the industrial labor market for their first five years in this country. This would require a law prohibiting any immigrant, for this period of time, from accepting an industrial job that paid less than $2.50 or $3.00 a day, should he choose to work in heavy industries. Under this proposal the alien, rather than the employer, would be responsible; and "the immigrant knowing he could not command such a wage would enter agriculture or some other nonindustrial occupation." This, according to Kellogg, would establish an equilibrium, first over the labor market, and then over immigration itself.[34]

This curious solution, which would restrict immigrants but not immigration, reflected the ambiguous attitudes the social engineer had toward the alien. "My own feeling," said Kellogg, "is that immigrants bring us ideals, cultures, red blood—which are an asset for America or would be if we gave them a chance." The new immigrant was a problem, not because of a "cultural deficit, but because he brings to America a potential economic surplus above his wants which is exploited." Yet Kellogg's feelings went deeper than this. Implicit in his rhetoric is an image of the immigrant as a destructive force, a "tyranny which holds the common labor market in the hallow of its great, untrained, earth-bred hand."[35]

A similar ambiguity characterized the staff's reaction to the city and the new industry—and for the same reasons. They were the first generation to have grown up in an industrial society and the first to build their careers upon correcting its excesses. They could not reject the basic phenomena of the future. Yet, at the same time, they could not accept them uncritically. Consequently, they accepted the city but not the tenement, the alien but not the immigrant laborer, the industrial revolution but not laissez-faire capitalism. As for the last, there was not an "invisible hand" but only blind forces operative in the marketplace. As Edward A. Ross, of the University of Wisconsin and a founder of the American Sociological Society observed, "The papers presenting the findings of the Pittsburgh Survey showed how an industry like steel making projects conditions which the working population cannot in the least alter and to

which the family structure must conform." He described the convention
that heard these findings as feeling "that if industry in obedience to its
gravitation towards maximum profits, thus blindly dominates and de-
forms men and their most cherished institutions, it is high time industry
be brought under the control of the social will"[36]—a will informed and
guided by investigations like the Pittsburgh Survey.

This indictment of laissez faire rested on the idea that "its gravitation
toward maximum profit," of necessity made it inimical to the public good.
In fact, the achievement of maximum profits became *prima facie* evidence
that the employer was acting against the interests of society. Phrases such
as "the interests of society" have to be interpreted as ideological signa-
tures. Like every class contending for its interests, the new professionals
sought to speak for the whole of society. For example, John Fitch argued
that "a proper economic policy from the standpoint of the individual
may be absolutely uneconomic from the standpoint of society." An
obvious case in point was the lumber industry, which had lain waste the
American forests, and "if the man who wastes and destroys *natural* resources is a public enemy, what of the corporations that exploit human
resources?"[37]

The new social engineer necessarily rejected both laissez faire and
individualism. This process can be traced both intellectually and organ-
izationally. As an interim report of the Survey phrased it, philanthropy
had been limited to individuals, the sick, aged, homeless, and poverty-
stricken. The beginnings of the charity organization movement coincided
with the first attempts to work with entire families. Settlement houses
widened this concern to include whole neighborhoods, while the new profession of social work defined its responsibilities in terms of the entire
community.[38] In other words, what the early proponents of philanthropy
had thought of as the failings of particular individuals, the Survey's staff
had come to define in terms of social forces. No longer were poverty or
broken homes seen as challenges to the conscience of the more fortunate.
The Survey's staff had learned to think in terms of the needs and responsibilities of society as a whole.

The evils that came with industrialization, then, were not those of one
individual oppressing another. Fitch argued that a man "might consider
himself recompensed by high wages for long hours and lack of touch with
the world or for extreme danger," but "society is not thereby recompensed."[39] Work was a social act. Crystal Eastman, the secretary of the

New York State branch of the American Association for Labor Legislation, claimed that "work however individually managed and controlled,
however competitively bargained for, is a part of a great undertaking in
which society as a whole shares and by which it profits."[40] Unrestrained
capitalism imperiled society on two counts: First, it deprived the polity
of good citizens; and second, it controlled the terms of production ex-
clusively in management's interests. The blame fell on manufacturers
only to the extent of recognizing their role as the efficient causes of the
situation. Fundamentally, of course, the fault was society's.

Industrialism posed a problem of responsibility—a problem that individualistic ethical systems could neither comprehend nor resolve. What
was needed was a social ethic or ideology, an ideology that could con-
ceive of individuals acting in terms of their social roles. Its basis was a
distinction between man, as an individual, and man, as a member of
society. Kellogg addressed this distinction in his headnote to a report on
the "company homes" of the U.S. Steel Company. He wished to explain
why the corporation's houses had been investigated. Denying any special
animosity toward U.S. Steel, he insisted that "if industrial chairmen,
presidents and superintendents become landlords, they must bear the
responsibility of landlords. . . ." In assuming a social role, they became
accountable for fulfilling its obligations. And it was society they were
accountable to: ". . . only as the public holds them up to these responsibilities as stiffly as their shareholders hold them up to dividends, will
they be in a position to devise and carry out policies which, as individuals,
we may assume they would act upon."[41] The pivotal phrase in this is
"as individuals." Clearly, appeals to the consciences of the steel company's
officials were misplaced.

An ethic of social responsibility was easier to proclaim than to define.
American thought had been triumphantly individualistic, and the popularity of Spencerian notions had accentuated this emphasis. Spencer, in fact,
had had no idea of society at all; rather he had thought in terms of a
collection of individuals engaged in competition for the necessities of
life. In this competition those who most successfully adapted to the demands of their environment would win, that is, survive. The environment, moreover, could not be so manipulated or controlled as to permit
all to survive; and because there was no such entity as society, but only
an aggregation of individuals, there was nothing capable of pronouncing
upon the desirability of this competition. Instead the recognition of its

inevitability granted a certain sanction to it.[42] The emerging ideology of
the Survey's staff, in effect, had to repudiate "Social Darwinism." However, on an intellectual level they did not so much refute Spencerianism
as they permitted it to play havoc with their thought.

This effect can be clearly traced in the work of Fitch. He wrote a book-
length study of the skilled and semiskilled steelworkers, whom he described as a "picked body of men." In other words, "through a course
of natural selection the unfit have been eliminated and the survivors are
exceptionally capable and alert of mind, their wits sharpened by meeting
and solving difficulties." The difficulties in question, the selective environment, were the relatively limited number of skilled positions in the mills
and the increasing demands upon the endurance and dexterity of those
who held them. Fitch noted that "the standard of efficiency required and
maintained in the mill has grown along with the growth in tonnage. The
steel mills today offer an excellent demonstration of the theory of the
survival of the fittest." He knew, however, that there was nothing "natural"
about mill conditions. The employers created the standard of efficiency;
and, as Fitch pointed out, "by methods both direct and indirect, the workmen are stimulated or 'speeded up' to as rapid a pace as is possible." He
had blundered into a vicious circle as he alternatively excoriated the capitalists for exploiting the workers and explained wages and working conditions as a result of the natural competition among workers. He resolved
this confusion not by rejecting Spencerianism but by leaping into the
rhetoric of democracy and social responsibility. These, he claimed, were
the basic issues, and "with them in mind, the facts presented become a
question and a challenge."[43]

Along with natural selection, there survived a variety of racial and
ethnic inferiority explanations. Butler described Polish women as limited
in the range of their industrial activity "by trade indifference, as well as
by the stolid physical poise that cannot be speeded at the high pressure
to which an American girl will respond."[44] And Commons and Leiserson
contended that "it is among the teamsters that the Negro finds his con-
genial job. The factory is too confined, the work too monotonous; but
following his horses, he can see the sights and get paid for riding."[45]

Most of the staff of the Survey could not accept such explanations.
They had a vested, professional interest in demonstrating the feasibility
of intelligently directed social change. Racial and ethnic theories all implied a fatalism about the social structure and, as such, were as antagonistic

to their purposes as Spencerianism. The use of these types of rhetoric represented, in the first instance, a lag between their interests and the development of a vocabulary suitable for expressing them. A classic example of this phenomenon lies in their borrowings from the language of the Social Gospel.

We have already seen how settlement workers used the Social Gospel's critique of traditional evangelical Protestantism to create a secularized urban ministry. As sociology became a new theology, the expert assumed a social ministry. The Survey's staff were engaged in a similar process. The Social Gospel provided them with a means of discrediting individualistic morality. This was a necessary step, for as long as social problems could be attributed, plausibly, to the sum total of individual sins, reform would mean revival—not social engineering.

Frederic Almy, secretary of the Buffalo Charity Organization Society and the director of a subsequent survey of the conditions in that city, touched upon a common theme when he argued that "in the past the church has concerned itself more with individual than with social sins."[46] This meant, according to Fitch, "that the ministers sometimes deliver their heaviest blows against secondary evils while the prime wrongs, the ones that dry up the roots of the community life, may escape their wrath."[47]

Typical of America's industrial life, Pittsburgh was also typical of the national moral sense. The city suffered from what Woods described as a "double standard of civic morality," which was the joint product of its Calvinist background and its too-rapid growth as an industrial center. He claimed that there was "no city in the country, and probably none in the world, where a strict Sabbath and liquor legislation is more strenuously enforced." As a consequence, "unusually genial to those who do well, the citizens of Pittsburgh are summary and even relentless with those who would lower the outward moral decorum of the city." Furthermore, Pittsburghers assumed the "sanctity" of business operations even when they nullified "the precepts of religion." Thus they accepted the seven-day workweek in the steel mills, which "eventuated, in great sections of the population, in the gradual destruction of the religious sense." Pittsburghers were moral enough, but their morality was "too intense and therefore too restricted." The city was going through a kind of "moral adolescence."[48]

Moral maturity involved, above all, an acceptance of the ideal of social responsibility. Judged from this point of view, social engineering could seem but a practical extension of the Social Gospel. As Frederic Almy told the National Conference of Charities and Corrections, "modern social work is . . . also vitally religious. . . ." To succeed it had to "reach the hearts as well as the heads of the American people"; it had to "get itself adopted by the church in every hamlet and crossroads."[49] Nevertheless, the "essential religion" of social engineering differed markedly from that of the Social Gospel. The difference is due to secularization. As experts sought a nondoctrinal Christianity and a social definition of sin, they had little to guide them beyond their sense of the fundamental rightness of middle-class culture. So it is not surprising that they turned to industrial corporations for their model of effective social organization. The correspondences between social engineering and the new doctrine of Scientific Management were deep and significant.

Again and again, the Survey staff turned to the contrast between, in Commons's phrase, Pittsburgh's "marvelous business organization" and its "amazing social disorganization." The city's prosperity was the result of the first whereas the second was the price it had paid for it. Industrial organization had eliminated any "dependence on personality in the masses" and had given rise to a system that gave "large rewards for brain,— to overseers, managers, foremen, bosses, 'pushers,' and gang leaders" while applying "heavy pressure toward equality of wages among the restless, changing, competitive rank and file."[50] This narrow-sighted efficiency had contributed to the larger social disorder. Industry could use and then discard workers without fear of the consequences because of certain temporarily favorable conditions. As enumerated by Woods, the combination of a steady stream of fresh labor from southeastern Europe, an unlimited supply of natural resources, and an "insatiable demand of the world market" enabled industrial capitalism to reduce the bulk of its laboring forces to the "masses."[51]

Freed from having to develop and conserve a labor force, management took better care of its machinery than it did of its workers. H. F. J. Porter, a consulting industrial engineer and a former executive of Bethlehem Steel and Westinghouse-Nerst, as well as the founder of the Efficiency Society, reported for the Survey that "in view of the care which is taken of machinery, the lack of care of the 'human parts' of the plant as a going concern stand out prominently in the Pittsburgh situation." The effect of this neglect upon the individual worker was disastrous. Pittsburgh was well on its way toward becoming a city of invalids. In addition to those actually killed or crippled in work accidents, there were large numbers broken by the long hours and the relentless, increasing pace of the work. Porter compared human fatigue to metal fatigue. For both there was "a certain point" beyond which fatigue was cumulative and "the natural processes cannot restore the injury which has been produced. . . ."[52] Industry exploited labor by extorting from it the maximum short-term advantage. Fitch laconically remarked that "the steel workers are men of strong, sturdy constitutions; they must be, for when they begin to fail they cease to be steel workers."[53]

Most damning was the fact that this system was unnecessary, that is, wasteful. Porter protested that it should have been obvious to everyone "that more and better work can be done in the light than in the dark" and "that when people are comfortable they can give more and efficient service than when they feel hot or cold or stupid from bad air." Nevertheless, "few industrial managers with whom I talked in Pittsburgh in 1910 had grasped these self-evident facts."[54] No matter how much in the long-term interests of industry the principles of scientific management might be, it was the interests of society, ideologically conceived, that were uppermost in the minds of the Survey's staff. Industry, by virtue of its favored circumstances, might avoid the consequences of its own folly, but society had no such immunity. It could not replace its members as easily as industry recruited new workers. Kellogg argued that the community had a stake in this question: "How much citizenship does Pittsburgh get out of a man who works twelve hours a day?" What kind of father could he be?[55]

According to Butler, the real threat was to "racial vitality by the nervous exhaustion of the girl workers." She emphasized that "where there is such nervous loss its cost is not borne by the industry." These girls began work in their early teens and "most of the girls marry at twenty or twenty-one, just at the time when their [working] speed breaks." The result is "some of the cost is borne by the homes into which they go." The homes are "unfit," and "the children of these women are undervitalized."[56]

Victimized by laissez-faire capitalism, Pittsburgh was further penalized by its inadequate social machinery. As Kellogg saw it, the basic contrast between "Pittsburgh, the industrial center, and Pittsburgh, the community," lay in the "progressiveness and invention which have gone into the details of the one and not of the other." Cases in point were the "children's institutions which fail to respond to modern movements in education, hygiene and childplacing." Another was the system of alderman's courts, which "unsupervised and unshorn of their powers of petty persecution in city and mill town" compared with the modern municipal court system of Chicago "about as the open forges of King John's time compare with a Bessemer converter."[57]

The comparison is revealing. If Pittsburgh suffered from this comparison with Chicago, "our severest criticism" came from contrasting "the haphazard development" of Pittsburgh's social institutions to "the organic development of its business enterprises." The way to solve community problems, then, was not to copy the institutions developed in other urban areas. Instead "a responsible citizenship" would find "some of its most suggestive clues" in the "methods and scope of progressive industrial organizations." Problems associated with the municipal services offered in Pittsburgh were those of "a piece of governmental machinery built for a small town,—a new fly-wheel rigged up here, and a misfit set of gears clamped on there,"—suddenly having to function for a community of hundreds of thousands.[58]

So mechanistic a viewpoint made "efficiency" a watchword for the social engineers. Florence Kelley, secretary of the National Consumers' League, for example, argued that government should issue reports based on the pioneer studies of the Bureau of Municipal Research of New York City because "official reports are in themselves tests of efficiency."[59]

The experts' view of efficiency, of course, meant more than getting the most out of each tax dollar. City services might be made more efficient, said Kellogg, "while wage-earners and householders generally" continued to suffer "from another and more irreparable form of taxation." These taxes included outbreaks of typhoid fever and tuberculosis, long lists of those killed or injured in mills and mines, children deprived of education by child labor, and row upon row of overcrowded tenements. For these an accounting had also to be made, and that accounting required the professional services of the social engineer. Eastman's study of work accidents and Roberts's study of immigrants were "methods of social bookkeeping as would show something of the larger waste of human life and private means."[60]

Pittsburgh, then, was what America was to become; and social accounting was what the Survey's staff was to do. Roberts's study of immigrant groups became the basis for a series of similar ones undertaken, with him as supervisor, by the International Young Men's Christian Association. Lawrence Veiller's housing investigations developed into the National Housing Association while Eastman became the secretary of the Employer's Liability Commission of New York. Under a grant from the Cabot Fund, Fitch was able to extend his study of the steel industry to include conditions in Birmingham, Alabama, Lackawanna, New York, and Gary, Indiana. Devine became the chairman of the committee that lobbied for the creation of the Federal Industrial Relations Commission, and Commons became one of its initial members. Shelby M. Harrison, who supervised the graphic and statistical aspects of the Survey, became director of the Department of Surveys created by the Russell Sage Foundation. Finally, *Charities and The Commons,* by then the *Survey* under the editorial direction of Kellogg, and the Sage Foundation undertook a series of similar surveys of Topeka, Kansas, Springfield, Illinois, Syracuse, New York, and Birmingham, Alabama.[61]

Social engineering was more than a profession; it was also a perspective on the new industrial society and a vision of a more efficient and better future. This vision formed the *apologia* of a portion of a new professional middle class whose careers were premised upon the manageability of social change. Their interests were frequently enough urged with the fervor and universality of the Social Gospel; but they owed their existence, their model of the ideal society, and their technology of social accounting to industrial capitalism.

NOTES

1. Charles Booth, *Life and Labour of the People in London,* (London, 1889-1903), 17 vols.

2. See James Leiby, *Carroll Wright and Labor Reform* (Cambridge, Mass.: Harvard University Press, 1960).

3. An enlightening discussion of what was "known" is Robert Bremner, *From the Depths: The Discovery of Poverty in the United States* (New York: New York University Press, 1956). The best of the contemporary accounts was Robert Hunter, *Poverty* (New York, 1904).

4. I have no wish to deprecate the very sizable achievements of these agencies. Allen T. Davis, *Spearheads for Reform: The Social Settlements and the Progressive Movement, 1890-1914* (New York: Oxford University Press, 1967), and Clarke A. Chambers, *Seedtime of Reform: American Social Service and Social Action, 1918-1933* (Ann Arbor, Mich.: University

of Michigan Press, 1967), give spirited descriptions of them. I wish merely
to point out that, as institutions, they had certain limitations.

5. Paul U. Kellogg, "Field Work of the Pittsburgh Survey," Appendix
E in *The Pittsburgh District: Civic Frontage (The Pittsburgh Survey*, 6
vols., ed. Paul U. Kellogg, New York: Survey Associates, Inc., 1914), p.
495.

6. Ibid., pp. 496-98.

7. Published first in three special, monthly issues of *Charities and
The Commons,* beginning January 2, 1909, and then in Kellogg, ed.,
The Pittsburgh Survey, 6 vols. (New York: Charities Publication Commit-
tee; then Survey Associates, Inc., 1910-14).

8. It has become a standard source in urban history. See, for example, Roy Lubove, *Twentieth Century Pittsburgh: Government, Business,
and Environmental Change* (New York: Wiley, 1969), pp. 6-16, 19-60.

9. Kellogg, "Field Work of the Pittsburgh Survey," pp. 496-97.

10. Paul U. Kellogg, "Community and Workshop," in Paul U. Kellogg,
ed., *Wage-Earning Pittsburgh* (New York, 1914), p. 16.

11. R. R. Wright, "One Hundred Negro Steel Workers," in Kellogg,
ed., *Wage-Earning Pittsburgh,* pp. 96-110. The total number of blacks
working in the steel mills was 110, "all of whom were interviewed."
Wright then made an "intimate personal study" of 100 of them (p. 97).

12. Crystal Eastman, *Work-Accidents and the Law* (New York, 1910,
1916), p. 6.

13. Elizabeth Beardsley Butler, *Women and the Trades* (New York,
1909), pp. 80-81, 210.

14. H. F. J. Porter, "Industrial Hygiene of the Pittsburgh District," in
Kellogg, ed., *Wage-Earning Pittsburgh,* p. 217.

15. "Editor's Foreword," Eastman, *Work-Accidents and the Law,* p. vi.

16. Paul U. Kellogg, "The Pittsburgh Survey of the National Publication Committee of *Charities and The Commons," Charities and The Commons* 19 (March 7, 1908): 1668, 1669.

17. John R. Commons and William M. Leiserson, "The Wage-Earners
of Pittsburgh," in Kellogg, ed., *Wage-Earning Pittsburgh,* p. 119.

18. Paul U. Kellogg, "The Pittsburgh Survey," *Charities and The Commons* 21 (January 2, 1909): 522.

19. Robert A. Woods, "Pittsburgh: An Interpretation of Its Growth,"
Charities and The Commons 21 (January 2, 1909): 531.

20. Edward T. Devine, "Results of the Pittsburgh Survey," *American
Journal of Sociology* 14 (March 1909): 667.

21. Kellogg, "Community and Workshop," p. 4.

22. Ibid., pp. 4-5.

23. Alois B. Kuokol, "A Slav's a Man for a' That," in Kellogg, ed., *Wage-Earning Pittsburgh*, p. 62.

24. Woods, "Pittsburgh: An Interpretation of Its Growth," p. 530.

25. Commons and Leiserson, "The Wage-Earners of Pittsburgh," pp. 168-70.

26. John A. Fitch, *The Steel Workers* (New York: Charity Publication Committee, 1910), pp. 68-69.

27. Butler, *Women and the Trades*, p. 129.

28. James Forbes, "The Reverse Side," in Kellogg, ed., *Wage-Earning Pittsburgh*, pp. 368-69.

29. Kellogg, "Community and Workshop," pp. 27-28, 3-4.

30. Kellogg, "The Pittsburgh Survey," p. 529.

31. Peter Roberts, "The New Pittsburghers: Slavs and Kindred Immigrants in Pittsburgh," *Charities and The Commons* 21 (January 2, 1909): 549.

32. Woods, "Pittsburgh: An Interpretation of Its Growth," pp. 532, 528.

33. Kellogg, "The Pittsburgh Survey," p. 523.

34. Paul U. Kellogg, "The Minimum Wage and Immigrant Labor," *Proceedings* of the National Conference of Charities and Corrections (Fort Wayne, 1911), p. 165.

35. Ibid., pp. 166, 172, 171. For a fuller discussion of this plan, see Chapter 4.

36. E. A. Ross, "The Atlantic City Meetings," *Charities and The Commons* 21 (January 9, 1909): 664.

37. Fitch, *The Steel Workers*, p. 206. Italics in original.

38. Kellogg, "Field Work of the Pittsburgh Survey," p. 509.

39. Fitch, *The Steel Workers*, p. 242.

40. Eastman, *Work-Accidents and the Law*, p. 152.

41. Editor's note to F. Elizabeth Crowell, "Painter's Row: The United States Steel Corporation as a Pittsburgh Landlord," *Charities and The Commons* 21 (February 9, 1909): 899.

42. Herbert Spencer, *First Principles* (Philadelphia, 1880). See also Pitirim A. Sorokin, *Contemporary Sociological Theories Through the First Quarter of the Twentieth Century* (New York, 1928), pp. 3-62, 195-218, 309-56.

43. Fitch, *The Steel Workers*, pp. 20, 183, 184, 6.

44. Elizabeth Beardsley Butler, "The Working Women of Pittsburgh," *Charities and The Commons* 21 (January 2, 1909): 571.

45. Commons and Leiserson, "The Wage-Earners of Pittsburgh," p. 121.

46. Frederic Almy, "The Value of the Church to Social Workers," *Proceedings* of the National Conference of Charities and Corrections (1911), p. 258.

47. Fitch, *The Steel Workers,* p. 223.

48. Woods, "Pittsburgh: An Interpretation of Its Growth," as reprinted in Kellogg, ed., *Wage-Earning Pittsburgh,* p. 253.

49. Almy, "The Value of the Church to Social Workers," p. 255.

50. Commons and Leiserson, "The Wage-Earners of Pittsburgh," pp. 119, 117.

51. Woods, "Pittsburgh: An Interpretation of Its Growth," *Charities and The Commons,* 21 (January 2, 1909): 530.

52. Porter, "Industrial Hygiene of the Pittsburgh District," p. 253.

53. Fitch, *The Steel Workers,* p. 183.

54. Porter, "Industrial Hygiene of the Pittsburgh District," p. 223.

55. Kellogg, "Community and Workshop," pp. 27-28.

56. Butler, *Women and the Trades,* p. 95.

57. Kellogg, "Community and Workshop," pp. 12-13.

58. Ibid., pp. 7, 4-5.

59. Florence Kelley, "Factory Inspection in Pittsburgh," in Kellogg, ed., *Wage-Earning Pittsburgh,* p. 192. Kelley had been the first chief of factory inspection in Illinois.

60. Kellogg, "Community and Workshop," p. 16.

61. Kellogg, "Field Work of the Pittsburgh Survey," pp. 513-14.

chapter 3
Seeking Institutional Support: The Russell Sage Foundation

The Pittsburgh Survey marked an advance in both the scope and the sophistication of social expertise. It was easily the most ambitious undertaking to date of the new middle class; and it had been possible to carry out only because of the financial support of a new kind of institution, the general service foundation. Other available agencies of support—the settlements and charity societies, the slowly expanding number of local and state governmental agencies—lacked the resources to underwrite large-scale research or experimentation. The Russell Sage Foundation, which had underwritten both the investigations and publication of the Pittsburgh Survey, promised to remedy some of these deficiencies. Whether it would or not, however, depended upon the experts' success in influencing its grant decisions. So a study of foundation politics affords us an important opportunity to analyze expert attempts to control the institutions they depended upon for support. The fact that the Sage Foundation was the first of its kind made those attempts all the more important. If they succeeded, the development of expertise would be far smoother and more rapid.

It was thus with joy that social experts hailed the establishment of the Russell Sage Foundation in 1907. Two symposia[1] organized by *Charities and The Commons* provide evidence that they saw the foundation as vital to the development of their profession. The foundation came along, as Edward T. Devine, editor of *Charities,* put it, at "a fortunate moment in many respects." In what Devine called the "first duty," investigating social conditions, he wrote that the Sage trustees would "find ready to their hand existing agencies with which they can profitably cooperate." "Never," said Devine, "was there so large a number of trained and competent workers" worthy of support.[2] Graham Taylor, warden of the Chicago Commons settlement house, pointed out that the foundation could provide a "greater superstructure" for the professions, specifically "research and publication . . . together with practical yet technical training in all the arts of civic, social, and individual service."[3] The foundation was, according to Lee K. Frankel, the manager of the United Hebrew Charities of New York, a "wonderful opportunity . . . to bring the science of philanthropy on [sic] a level with other preventive sciences."[4]

A considerable degree of unanimity characterized the symposia. With one voice participants warned against using the fund for charity. Instead all focused upon the professional needs of the experts. Their recurrent themes were investigation, experimentation, training, and publicity. This consensus was perhaps most clearly expressed by Charles A. Ellwood, a professor of sociology at the University of Missouri. He noted that the social sciences lagged far behind the natural sciences.

> If the trustees of the Sage Foundation will in some measure
> reverse all this; if they will direct scientific energy to the
> problem of transforming the social environment; if they will
> have all adverse social conditions scientifically investigated;
> if they will aid in the establishment of chairs of sociology
> and philanthropy in our colleges and universities, and in the
> establishment of schools for the practical training of social
> workers; if they will promote the development of all the
> social arts and sciences, the Sage Foundation will become
> the most beneficient gift in the history of our race.[5]

Certainly the foundation's first project, financing the Pittsburgh Survey, lent substance to these hopes. Ironically, however, what turned out to be most prophetic in Ellwood's summary was his conditional syntax. "If the trustees . . ." was exactly the correct manner of discussing the foundation. Its charter embodied a significant legal innovation that gave unusual power to its trustees. Hitherto philanthropic endowments had been restricted to the uses enumerated in their charters, but New York State granted the Sage Foundation the right to hold and invest monies and to

use "the income thereof to the improvement of social and living conditions in the United States of America. It shall be within the purpose of
said corporation to use any means to that end which from time to time
shall seem expedient to its members or trustees. . . ."[6]

This elastic formula created a closed corporation entitled to elect its
own membership, which received the tax benefits and public prestige
accorded to religious and educational institutions without any accompanying limitations upon its activities other than the vague injunction to
improve social and living conditions. The foundation was not even enjoined
from engaging in profit-making ventures. The Sage Foundation and those
foundations, notably the Carnegie and Rockefeller, that possessed similar
charters were virtually free from legal restraint in the use of their enormous
resources. This became a matter of public controversy when the U.S.
Industrial Relations Commission investigated the role of the Rockefeller
Foundation in developing what became the "Rockefeller Plan" of company unionism after the Ludlow Massacre.[7]

George W. Kirchwey, the former dean of Columbia Law School, testified that

> the law under which such philanthropic institutions as the
> Rockefeller, Carnegie, and Sage Foundations were incorporat-
> ed would be held to be unconstitutional if the question was
> ever taken to the courts. The legislative acts which brought
> them into being . . . did not set forth clearly in the title the
> aims of the organizations.

However, if the constitutionality of their charters was suspect, the foundations were practically immune from legal challenges. As Kirchwey pointed
out, an aggrieved party would have to show injury from putatively educational or philanthropic activities in order to bring suit, a virtual impossi-
bility he believed. Events bore him out. There was, he said, "nothing in
the law to prohibit a corporation such as the Rockefeller Foundation
from conducting propaganda against trade unions. . . ." Nor could the
court dissolve it "if its funds were used in a campaign of education against
workmen's compensation or a widow's pension. . . ."[8]

What this meant for the social experts is clear. Until World War I temporarily opened up a number of federal positions, the Sage Foundation
was their principal national source of support. The future development
of social expertise was therefore largely dependent upon the goodwill of

a handful of key trustees. Commenting on this state of affairs, the noted sociologist Franklin H. Giddings observed that as "far as the law of the case is concerned, the income of the Sage Fund could one of these days be devoted to the propagation of either anarchism or socialism, free trade or protection, neo-Malthusianism or the patriarchal family." He thought it most unlikely that the foundation would support "any kind of moral or social radicalism." Far more likely, he thought, would be a profound conservatism.[9]

Here was the crux of the matter. The new middle class was dependent upon a venture of the old upper class. When Margaret Oliva Sage, widow of railroad and banking tycoon, Russell Sage, sought philanthropic uses for her huge fortune, she turned for advice to her legal counselor, Robert W. de Forest.[10] He was the scion of an old Hugenot family who, after study at Yale, Bonn, and Columbia, had joined the family firm of Weeks, Forster, and de Forest and entered upon a career as counsel to railroad, banking, and insurance companies. He was general counsel and vice-president of the Hackensack Water Company, a director of the Niagara Fire Insurance Company, and a trustee of the Hudson Trust Company, the New York Security and Trust Company, and other concerns. He was also the most prominent figure in the New York philanthropic world. He was a founder and first president of the Provident Loan Society, the first philanthropic pawnbrokery; chairman of the Tenement House Commission of New York of 1900; the president, since 1888, of the Charity Organization Society of New York; and president, in 1903, of the National Conference of Charities and Corrections.

De Forest advised Mrs. Sage against committing herself to any "single form of social betterment." He told her that in view of the "constant change and shift of social conditions, and extension, or it may be contraction, of the sphere of government activity, the future may develop other and greater needs for philanthropic action than any which are now apparent." The foundation "should be sufficiently elastic in form and method to work in different ways at different times." He concluded that "its ultimate good will depend almost entirely upon how it is administered."[11]

In filling out the board of trustees, Mrs. Sage and her attorney vested control of the foundation in the hands of the New York aristocracy to which they both belonged. Joining them on the Executive Committee of the board were Helen M. Gould (the daughter of Jay Gould), Gertrude S. Rice, and Daniel Coit Gilman. Gould's[12] interest in benevolence began with the Spanish-American War when she donated $100,000 to the U.S.

government. She had then become an active member of the Women's National War Relief Association, helped nurse soldiers at Camp Wikoff, and given another $50,000 for medical supplies.

Gilman[13] had been president of the University of California, 1872-75, and then, until 1902, the first president of Johns Hopkins. From 1901 to 1904 he had been president of the Carnegie Institute in Washington. He too had been active in philanthropy, especially in connection with blacks, as president of the John F. Slater Fund for the Education of Freedmen and vice-president of the Peabody Educational Fund.

Rice was one of the founders of the Charity Organization Society of New York and an officer of the State Charities Aid Association of New York. In these activities she had cooperated extensively with de Forest and had been named to the board on his recommendation.[14]

The other trustees were Cleveland Hoadley Dodge,[15] member of Phelps, Dodge and Company and director of the New York Life Insurance and Trust Company and the National City Bank; Robert Curtis Ogden,[16] member of John Wanamaker's and president of the board of trustees of Hampton Institute, director of the Union Theological Seminary, trustee of Tuskeegee Institute, president of the Southern Education Board, the Conference for Education in the South, and the General Education Board; and Louisa Lee Schuyler,[17] daughter of an old Dutch family, founder of the State Charities Aid Association and of the Bellevue Hospital training school for nurses.

As a group the trustees were distinguished, wealthy, benevolent, and Protestant. With the possible exception of Gilman, none could be classed as an expert or a member of the new middle class. All but one (Gilman) were from New York City. All but one (Gilman again) possessed considerable personal fortunes. All had been involved in one or another form of organized charity. Gould, the youngest trustee, was thirty-nine. Mrs. Sage was the oldest—seventy-eight. The median age was over sixty. The board became even more homogeneous when Alfred Tredway White[18] replaced Gilman, who died in October 1908. White was a Brooklyn merchant who, in 1876, constructed some of the first model tenement houses. He had built more in 1877, 1878, and 1890. He was a director of the City and Suburban Homes Company and a trustee of Phipps Buildings, both builders of model tenements. He had served with de Forest on the Tenement House Commission of New York and was president of the Brooklyn Bureau of Charities.

It is not surprising that such a group should have been of one mind on most matters. In fact, the Trustee *Minutes* of the foundation do not show so much as a single formal vote on any matter through 1921. What the *Minutes* do show is a conservatism composed of equal measures of philanthropy and benevolent capitalism. Both were admirable qualities, perhaps; but neither augured well for the rapid development of expertise.

Philanthropy typically took the form of long-term grants or subsidies to the pet charities of the trustees. The most striking fact about Sage Foundation grants is the persistence of this pattern. Between 1907 and 1946[19] over $9 million was dispensed in grants. By 1921 nine recipients were receiving regular contributions that by 1946 would total over $5 million. In other words, well over half (55 percent) of the total went to a handful of projects chosen very early in the foundation's career. (See Table 1).

TABLE 1   Major Grants of the Russell Sage Foundation*

June 1907 to 1916—$355,100 to Charities Publication Committee of New York, COS.

June 1907 to 1943—$891,800 to State Charities Aid Association of New York

June 1907 to 1946—$1,079,471 to Charity Organization Society of New York City

June 1907 to 1917, 1926—$114,550 to National Association for the Study and Prevention of Tuberculosis

December 1908 to 1946—$350,133 to Brooklyn Bureau of Charities

March 1910 to 1936—$295,425 to National Housing Association

December 1914 to 1946—$141,653 to National Social Workers Exchange

April 1919 to 1946—$267,551 to National Conference on City Planning, American Civic Association and Federated Societies on Planning and Parks

October 1919 to 1946—$740,322 to American Association for Organizing Family Social Work

May 1921 to 1932—$1,186,768 to Regional Plan of New York and Its Environs

*Data drawn from *Russell Sage Foundation,* Appendix D, 2: 685-97.

In some of these cases trustees simply siphoned off foundation funds
to charities in which they were personally interested. De Forest was president of the Charity Organization Society of New York. It received
$1,079,471. Its publication committee received another $355,100, for
a total of almost one-sixth of the whole amount of $9 million. Schuyler
was the founder of the State Charities Association, which received
$891,800. White's Brooklyn Bureau of Charities (he was president) re-
ceived $350,133. These grants belong in the same category with Mrs.
Sage's bequest, in 1918, that the foundation oversee a bird sanctuary she
had established.[20]

Another pattern emerges from this table, one that socialist Morris
Hillquit labeled "philanthropic consolidation."[21] De Forest was a founder,
in 1904, of the National Association for the Study and Prevention of
Tuberculosis, which received $114,550 in grants. Another interlocking
directorate was between the foundation and the National Housing Association (NHA), which received $295,425. The president of NHA was
de Forest; its treasurer was John M. Glenn, who was director of the Sage
Foundation. Glenn, de Forest, and White were all members of its board
of directors.

The Sage Foundation, in short, was part of a system of interlocking
directorates and trusteeships that linked charity societies, the Red Cross,[22]
and other social and health agencies into an eastern philanthropic establishment. Any would-be social expert seeking support would be well advised to cultivate one of this small band of aristocrats.

A sufficiently critical reading of Glenn's[23] official description of the
process of making grant decisions leads to the same conclusion: "No
staff of investigators was employed. No application blank was prepared.
No imposing array of documents was collected." Instead of formal procedures for application,

> the director himself [Glenn] found out all he could about
> each proposal . . . chiefly by talking with the proposers
> and persons whose advice he valued and [by] examining
> work already done by the agency; discussed it with the vice-
> president [de Forest] and any members of the Board of
> Trustees especially interested who were within reach; made
> up his own mind about it; and prepared a concise statement
> of pertinent facts for the Executive Committee. . . .[24]

In other words, grant decisions were informal, based upon personal contact, upon the advice of people close to Glenn, and upon the reactions
of the trustees. "In their general point of view for the Foundation the
Trustees were exceptionally harmonious. On most questions brought before them in these early years, several of them were likely to have personal
knowledge."[25]

One consequence of this centralized, aristocratic control was that no
one whose proposal differed markedly from the programs of the charity
societies could expect much support. The foundation's official history
notes, without a trace of irony: "The Foundation's policy in dealing with
grantees had much in common with current charity organization principles
for helping families: individual treatment, based on knowledge of circumstances; avoidance of 'pauperization'; aid toward self-support."[26]

None of this meant that the foundation could not undertake many useful programs. Nor did it mean that those experts who did receive grants
were unworthy. Rather it defined a political situation. As long as experts
and trustees agreed as to what merited support, all would be well. When
they disagreed, the trustees' view would prevail. Disagreement was not
long in coming. It arose over the second element of trustee conservatism,
their commitment to benevolent capitalism. Specifically, it arose over the
foundation's decision to build a "model" community at Forest Hills in
New York City.

Although philanthropic investment had few charms for the experts,
it held a fatal attraction for the trustees, particularly for de Forest and
White, who had been active in model businesses like the Provident Loan
Society and the City and Suburban Homes Company before joining the
Foundation. In fact, de Forest's earliest memorandum to Margaret Sage
on "suggestions for a possible Sage Foundation" emphasized several such
projects. One involved "tenements in the city and small houses in the
suburbs—for the working classes on a business basis, or for semi-dependent
families on a semi-charitable basis." Others were for a chain of retail stores
to sell the necessities of life to "the poorer classes" at cost plus a reasonable profit of 6 percent and for industrial insurance for "the working
classes" again at cost plus 6 percent.[27] Overall he proposed that the foundation be able to invest up to one-half of its capital funds in ventures of
this sort provided they yielded a profit of at least 3 percent.

Mrs. Sage apparently had her doubt about this. She said, in her letter
of gift, April 19, 1907:

> I have had some hesitation as to whether the Foundation
> should be able to make investments for social betterment
> which themselves produce income, as for instance small
> houses or tenements. . . . I realize that investments for
> social betterment, even if producing some income, may not
> produce a percentage as large as that produced by bonds . . .
> and that the income of the Foundation might be therefore
> diminished by such investments.

Finally, though, she relented saying "if I fail to give the Foundation powers
in this respect it may be unable to initiate or establish important agencies
or institutions."[28]

Thus even before the formal incorporation of the foundation, and the
outpouring of expert advice in the *Charities* symposia, de Forest already
saw a broad field for good works in benevolent capitalism. Further he
had won the consent, with some hesitations, of Mrs. Sage. She had fur-
nished the foundation with the requisite authority, although she limited
the investment of capital funds to one quarter rather than the one-half
suggested by de Forest.[29]

Philanthropic investment took several forms. When the Charity Organization Society of New York established the National Employment Exchange in early 1909, the foundation subscribed $19,000 of its working
capital. By 1913, the foundation had invested $94,500 in the capital stock
of the Chattel Loan Society of New York and $500,000 in Provident
Loan Society Certificates.[30] All of these ventures were de Forest-sponsored
model businesses; that is, all attempted to attack social evils—the padrone
system, the extortionate pawnbrokeries, the high-interest loan companies—
by providing comparable services honestly and economically. All were designed to yield a "reasonable" return. The assumption behind such enterprises was that capitalism could reform itself, that businessmen seeing
that profits could be made without chicane would abandon it.

This was an assumption expert opinion did not share. Nonetheless,
the best advice of leading housing authorities was unable to dissuade the
foundation from undertaking what was perhaps the largest venture in
philanthropic capitalism to that date, the Russell Sage Homes Company,
which attempted to regenerate the real estate market in New York City
by constructing Forest Hills Gardens. This project was to be an extension
of the model tenement movement as de Forest's initial announcement
in the pages of the *Survey* made clear.

> The subject on which the Foundation is at the moment
> placing great emphasis is the housing of the working classes.
> It is not proposing to duplicate the model tenements build-
> ing of Phipps Houses, or the City and Suburban Homes
> Company [White's enterprises], in Manhattan or Brooklyn,
> but is giving serious attention to suburban housing.[31]

This flew in the face of expert opinion. Lawrence Veiller, the leading
housing authority in the United States,[32] argued that housing demonstrations called forth only other demonstrations. He pointed out that, by
1910, "efforts of philanthropically inclined persons" had resulted in 25
groups of model tenements in Manhattan housing 17,940 people. "Over
the same period unconverted builders had put up 27,100 tenements
housing over one million people." To Veiller,

> the great objection to the building of model tenements as
> a solution of the housing problem is that it means, as a rule,
> the complete diversion of the interest, energy and financial
> support of benevolent people who genuinely desire to im-
> prove the condition of the poor away from lines of effort
> that are fundamentally corrective towards those that are
> merely palliative.

His own program was emphatic. "Until adequate restrictive legislation has
been passed and the certainty of its enforcement secured, there should
be no talk of any other form of effort in housing reform."[33]

"Adequate restrictive legislation," Veiller's Model Tenement Law, was
adopted in New York State in 1901 following the recommendations of
the Tenement House Commission of 1900. The secretary of that commission was Veiller; its chairman was de Forest. When a reform administration in New York City appointed de Forest tenement house commissioner,
he named Veiller as his deputy. The lesson Veiller drew from this experience was that in the period 1901-08, "philanthropy has provided but
seven-tenths of one percent of the improved living conditions while
99 3/10 percent has been provided by the speculative builder restrained
and controlled by wise legislation."[34] The lesson drawn by de Forest was
that "investment philanthropy" ought to be a major activity of the
Russell Sage Foundation.

It must be emphasized that this criticism was not directed at the foundation by an unknown. Veiller and de Forest had worked closely together
for a number of years. Furthermore the foundation itself recognized
Veiller's preeminence in his field. His book, *Housing Reform,* from which
these strictures have been taken, was published by the Russell Sage Foundation. It contains a highly laudatory introduction by de Forest. At the
very time the foundation was rejecting his advice, it was generously supporting Veiller's proposal for a National Housing Association.[35] If there
was an expert in the country who could have influenced the foundation's
policy, it was Veiller. He failed.[36]

Given his financial dependence on the foundation, his public criticism
of Forest Hills Gardens had to be veiled. Nonetheless, Veiller presented
his audience at the First National Housing Conference with a remarkably
accurate sketch of the project's prospects. He conceded that "the garden-
city movement is a most important one. Every effort should be made to
encourage and develop it." "But," he cautioned,

> for my part I feel clear that it is unwise for those who are
> taking up housing reform as a new problem [that is, the
> Sage Foundation] to allow their attention to be diverted
> from the fundamental and primary necessities of decent
> housing for the poorest elements of the community by the
> attractiveness of what must necessarily, for many years to
> come, be development for the better-paid members of the
> community, and essentially a suburban or rural one.

Instead the foundation should support city planning "which vitally affects
the housing problem and should be given closest attention."[37]

Veiller was correct in suggesting that the first casualty of the great enterprise would be the working class. The original proposals had called for
housing for the "lower classes" including "semi-dependent families." By
November 1910 de Forest announced that Forest Hills Gardens were to
be "for persons of modest means, who could pay from twenty-five dollars
a month upward in the purchase of a home."[38] The income groups to be
served continued upward in fact. When the first homes went on sale in
1915, they ranged in price from $10,265 and $10,516 to $22,057 and
$31,933.[39] At the bottom price range, therefore, at least $50 per month
would be required; that is, approximately 75 percent of the average work-

ingman's salary. Forest Hills Gardens were, as Veiller predicted, to house
the well-to-do.

The reason for this is easily surmised. Forest Hills Gardens embodied
incompatible purposes. On the one hand, said de Forest, the endeavor "is
a business investment of the Russell Sage Foundation. It will be conducted
on strictly business principles for a fair profit. . . . In its business purpose
Forest Hills Gardens does not differ materially from other Long Island
real estate enterprises." On the other hand, de Forest hastened to add that
"a distinct educational purpose exists." If successful, "the Sage Foundation will accomplish several objects. It will provide more healthful and
more attractive homes to many people. It will demonstrate that more
tasteful surroundings and open spaces pay in suburban development and
thereby encourage imitation. It will encourage economical methods of
marketing land." And, of course, "it will secure an attractive income for
the Foundation."[40]

This attempt to combine progress and 6 percent—in short, to solve the
riddle of American capitalism—meant making the progress dependent
upon the 6 percent. Grosvenor Atterbury, Forest Hills Garden's chief
architect, sought to explain the situation to the "many . . . doubtless . . .
disappointed to find that the first housing demonstration to be made by
the Russell Sage Foundation will not reach the so-called laboring man, or
even the lower-paid mechanic. . . ." He pointed out that

> while the Russell Sage Foundation is primarily seeking to
> make its housing demonstration especially applicable to
> dwellings of low cost and rentals, it is essential to the
> financial success of the enterprise that the size and quality
> of the houses be suited to the value of the property upon
> which they are placed. Any attempt to put up and market
> a type of building unsuited to the land would be to violate
> the first principles of successful housing development.

Echoing de Forest's theme that the foundation must behave like other
Long Island real estate operators, Atterbury felt that

> if by reason of certain rather unusual conditions pertaining
> to operations conducted by the Russell Sage Foundation such
> an attempt could be successfully started, its educational value,

as in all probability also its ultimate financial value as an investment for the individual purchaser, would inevitably suffer. The equation is fundamentally an economic one.[41]

In suiting "the size and quality of the houses" to "the value of the property," the foundation committed itself to building a "model" community for the affluent. In this it clearly succeeded. Forest Hills Gardens were built on a 200-acre site in the borough of Queens. At one end, facing the Long Island Railroad station was the Forest Hills Inn and a series of shops. The layout of the streets and several small parks was designed by Frederick Law Olmstead. The houses were scattered, some standing singly, others clustered in groups, along the tree-shaded streets. Off to one side was the famous, and exclusive, West Side Tennis Club.[42] For more than sixty years now, Forest Hills Gardens has been one of the most desirable, and most expensive, residential areas in New York City.

Market conditions, in other words, tempered benevolence even if philanthropy could not redeem investment. The educational value of the enterprise would be wasted, Atterbury had admitted, unless the foundation achieved its results "in the face of conditions no more favorable than ordinarily met with in other land development. . . ."[43] Conditions dictated middle- and upper-income housing. Thus a project intended to show that attractive suburban housing could be made available to the working classes demonstrated instead that such housing was for the affluent.

In February 1922 the foundation finally unloaded its interest in the Sage Foundation Homes Company—at a loss of $350,000—to a syndicate headed by John M. Demarest, the manager of the company, and composed mainly of residents of Forest Hills Gardens. De Forest did his best to disguise the magnitude of the failure by claiming that the foundation had carried the project "to substantial completion" and accomplished every purpose "save only the hope of making it successful from a mere business point of view. . . ."[44] Unhappily the "mere" business point of view was fundamental. The other purposes had depended upon it, and they too were frustrated. No "garden city" movement swept the country. For that matter Forest Hills Gardens did little to transform its own immediate neighborhood—at least in ways anticipated or desired by the foundation.

Forest Hills did become a desirable residential area; but other real-estate developers adopted neither the foundation's architectural standards nor, crucially, its business practices. A particularly galling example was Gardens Apartments, Inc., whose properties benefited by their proximity

to Forest Hills Gardens and by their similar name. In March 1920 Gardens
Apartments, Inc., announced an across-the-board rent increase of 200 percent! Suits and summonses followed in great profusion capped in October
by mass eviction proceedings.[45] If there was a lesson in all this, it was
hardly the foundation's "educational design."

If the foundation suffered from this benevolent debacle, the bigger
losers were those experts dependent upon it for support. Forest Hills
Gardens was the "albatross" of the Russell Sage Foundation for its first
fourteen years. It occupied some $4 million of its $10 million principal
for much of that time, thereby reducing its income by a minimum of
$180,000 a year as the foundation earned an average of 4.5 percent on
its other investments at this time.[46]

Counting the $350,000 loss in the final sale of 1922, the total loss
could scarcely have been much less than $1.5 million. To the experts seek-
ing support, moreover, the loss was much more severe than these figures
indicate.

In 1907 the foundation received $458,080 on its $10 million principal,
which was invested primarily in railroad bonds and mortgages on midtown
Manhattan properties. Capital investments in land and development at
Forest Hills gradually reduced these earnings (see Table 2).

TABLE 2   Income of the Russell Sage Foundation*

YEAR	INCOME	DECLINE IN INCOME**
1909	$460,000	—
1910	435,000	$ 25,000
1911	416,000	44,000
1912	346,000	114,000
1913	267,000	193,000

*Data are from Financial Reports, Trustee *Minutes,* 1: 170 (October 30, 1911),
  1: 203 (October 28, 1912), and 1: 252 (October 27, 1913). All numbers have
  been rounded off to the nearest thousand.

**The year 1909 is used as the base year.

By 1913 just over $4 million of the foundation's principal had been
diverted to the Sage Foundation Homes Company, and its income was
down 42 percent from 1909. A severe financial squeeze became inevitable.
The fiscal year 1914-15 saw a deficit of $31,000 incurred because John

Glenn managed to convince the trustees that "further reductions in grants or direct work would check important measures that had been in progress for some time, and would force a reduction in salaries or the discharge of employees at a time when it is impossible to find new places. . . ."[47]

All grants, however, were reduced by at least 33 1/3 percent, and no obligation for support longer than three months was assumed.[48] By 1915, some of the financial pressure was relieved through the sale of some of the houses and land at Forest Hills; but income was still severely limited, and grants were available only on a six-month basis.[49]

The foundation made no new grants between 1914 and 1919. It created no new departments or divisions for its own direct work between 1912 and 1924.[50] Overall it seems reasonable to conclude that the investment in Forest Hills Gardens necessitated a 40 percent reduction in the foundation's activities for the period 1912-21. The period of greatest scarcity was 1914-17, and the measure of this is the limiting of grants to three- or six-month periods as well as the complete elimination of new grants.[51]

Although the Russell Sage Foundation more than justified its existence by sponsoring many valuable programs, both at this time and later,[52] its early history displays a pattern of institutional control that experts would encounter again and again. Foundation policy was set by a small band of benevolent aristocrats who also controlled settlement houses, charity societies, health and educational associations, and the Red Cross. Moreover, this control was far from nominal. As a result, expertise developed only as fast as the available means of support allowed and only in directions approved by the rich and powerful.

NOTES

1. "The Russell Sage Foundation: Its Social Value and Importance— Views of Some of Those Actually Engaged in Social Work," *Charities and The Commons* 17 (March 23, 1907): 1079-85, and "What University Men Think of the Russell Sage Foundation: Suggestions in Large Part from the Chairs of Economics, Sociology and Political Economy," *Charities and The Commons* 18 (May 11, 1907): 186-91.

2. Edward T. Devine, "Social Forces: A Foreword Fortnightly by the Editor," *Charities and The Commons* 17 (March 23, 1907): 1071-72.

3. "The Russell Sage Foundation: Its Social Value and Importance," p. 1081.

4. Ibid., p. 1082.

5. "What University Men Think of the Russell Sage Foundation," p. 187.

6. Copy of charter in Russell Sage Foundation, Trustee *Minutes,* vol. 1

7. U.S., Industrial Relations Commissions, *Industrial Relations* (Washington, D.C., 1916), 9: 8215-29.

8. Ibid., pp. 8219, 8220. See also *New York Times,* February 5, 1915.

9. Franklin H. Giddings, "The Danger in Charitable Trusts," *Van Norden Magazine* (June 1907), quoted in John M. Glenn, Lilian Brandt, F. Emerson Andrews, *Russell Sage Foundation, 1907-1946,* 2 vols. (New York, 1946), 1: 17. This is the official history written by members of the foundation's staff. Waldemar A. Nielsen's recent authoritative study, *The Big Foundations,* A Twentieth Century Fund Study (New York: Columbia University Press, 1972), substantiates Giddings's forebodings. Nielson characterizes the 100 largest foundations as "overwhelmingly passive, conservative, and anchored to the *status quo*" (p. 406).

10. *Dictionary of American Biography* (cited hereafter as DAB), 21: 286. See also Glenn *et al., Russell Sage Foundation,* 1: 4-6.

11. Quoted in *Russell Sage Foundation,* 1: 7.

12. *National Cyclopaedia of American Biography,* 13: 523.

13. *DAB,* 7: 299.

14. Glenn *et al., Russell Sage Foundation,* 1: 9.

15. Ibid.

16. *DAB,* 8: 641.

17. See Walter I. Trattner, "Louisa Lee Schuyler and the Founding of the State Charities Aid Association," *New York Historical Society Quarterly* 51 (July 1967).

18. *DAB,* 20: 86. Nielsen finds that typical trustees today are between fifty and seventy years of age, college educated, of British or northern European origin, Protestant, Republican in politics, and residing in the east. "The biggest single group are businessmen, followed by lawyers . . ." (*The Big Foundations,* p. 315). The Sage Foundation's original board of trustees deviated from this pattern only in the number of women trustees.

19. This is the period covered in Glenn *et al., Russell Sage Foundation,* Appendix D, 2: 685-97. Some grants can be followed through the Trustee *Minutes,* but others were referred to an executive committee whose records have not been preserved. So *Russell Sage Foundation* is the most complete source.

20. Ibid., 1: 270.

21. U.S., Industrial Relations, *Industrial Relations,* 9: 8264. See also *New York Times,* February 5, 1915.

22. During World War I, Cleveland Hoadley Dodge was chairman of the War Finance Committee of the American Red Cross. See "The Red Cross Civilian Relief Plan: Organization of the Chapters and a Great Campaign for Money," *Survey* 38 (May 19, 1917): 162-64.

23. He was a Baltimore attorney who had given up his law practice

for philanthropy. Before becoming director of the Sage Foundation, he had been president, Supervisors of City Charities, Baltimore (Glenn *et al., Russell Sage Foundation,* 1: 21).

24. Ibid., 1: 29.

25. Ibid.

26. Ibid., 1: 46.

27. Robert W. de Forest to Margaret Oliva Sage, December 10, 1906. Quoted in ibid., 1: 7.

28. Trustee *Minutes,* 1: 13-14.

29. Later on January 19, 1911, the authorization was restored to one-half. Ibid., 1: 14.

30. Financial Report, October 27, 1913, ibid., 1: 252.

31. Robert W. de Forest, "The Initial Activities of the Russell Sage Foundation," *Survey* 22 (April 13, 1909): 74.

32. Roy Lubove, in *The Progressives and the Slums: Tenement House Reform in New York City, 1890-1917* (Pittsburgh: University of Pittsburgh Press, 1962), entitles one chapter "The Age of Veiller," pp. 151-84.

33. Lawrence Veiller, *Housing Reform* (New York, 1910), pp. 69-70.

34. Ibid., p. 70.

35. Trustee *Minutes,* 1: 95 (October 25, 1909), and 1: 105 (December 10, 1910). See also Table 1.

36. Lubove noted in *The Progressives and the Slums* that there was some antagonism between Veiller and de Forest. Lubove, although he interviewed Veiller, was unable to determine whether this was based upon conflicting personalities or differing views on housing reform.

37. Lawrence Veiller, "A Programme of Housing Reform," reprinted from *Proceedings* of the First National Housing Conference (1910?) in *National Housing Association Publications,* no. 16 (New York? 1910?), unpaginated pamphlet. The last piece of advice, to concentrate upon city planning, was finally adopted in 1921. See Table 1.

38. "Garden City Platted by Russell Sage Foundation," *Survey* 25 (November 26, 1910): 309.

39. Trustee *Minutes,* 1: 330 (October 25, 1915).

40. "Garden City Platted," pp. 309, 310.

41. Grosvenor Atterbury, "Forest Hills Gardens: A Study and Demonstration in Town Planning and Home Building Undertaken by the Russell Sage Foundation at Forest Hills, Long Island," *Survey* 25 (January 7, 1911): 565.

42. See Glenn *et al., Russell Sage Foundation,* 1: 49-51. The General Plan, reproduced from *New York Regional Survey,* vol. 7, is on p. 50.

43. Atterbury, "Forest Hills Gardens," p. 563.

44. Quoted in Glenn *et al., Russell Sage Foundation,* 1: 272.

45. See *New York Times* (March-October 1920).

46. See Mrs. Sage's Letter of Gift, Trustee *Minutes,* 1: 16, List of Securities and Property.

47. Ibid., 1: 306 (October 26, 1914).

48. Ibid.

49. Ibid., 1: 318 (March 29, 1915).

50. Glenn *et al., Russell Sage Foundation,* 1: 55.

51. The loss involved in the changed character of the grants to short-term projects cannot be measured in dollars, but ought to be part of a final accounting from the point of view of the experts.

52. These are cataloged in Glenn *et al., The Russell Sage Foundation.* See also Chapter 2.

PART II:
The Quest for Power

Introduction

Social engineering emerged, in the years preceding World War I, as a series of related and self-conscious professions. The engineers themselves had started out in the 1890s in the settlements and charity organizations, where they had fused their religious impulse to serve the less fortunate with their middle-class ambition for professional status. The resulting amalgam was not without its ironies. Women like Jane Addams dedicated part of their lives to bringing to the immigrant poor the selfsame genteel conventions they had found so suffocating in their own lives. Thorstin Veblen, a jaundiced but acute observer, pointed this out with ill-concealed distaste. Settlements and charities were, he wrote, "of a quasi-religious or pseudo-religious character." Part of the "solicitude" of the "good people who go out to humanize the poor" was "directed to enhance the industrial efficiency of the poor," but it was "no less consistently directed to the inculcation, by precept and example, of certain punctilios of upper-class propriety in manners and customs." The new professionals were "commonly persons of exemplary life and gifted with a tenacious insistence on ceremonial cleanness in the various items of their daily consumption." With his customary sarcasm, Veblen found the "cultural or civilizing efficiency of this inculcation" was "scarcely to be overrated; nor is its economic value to the individual who acquires these higher and more reputable ideals inconsiderable."[1]

Veblen, the son of Norwegian immigrants, had personal reasons for disliking the gentility of the native American middle class. In fact, much

of his adult life consisted of collisions with the upholders of "propriety
in manners and customs" in higher education.[2] And so, he cannot have
the final word about the new professionals. Certainly, as Allen Davis and
others have shown, the settlements and charity societies did more than
"inculcate punctilios" or "enhance the industrial efficiency of the poor."
Just as certainly, however, Veblen, as both a second-generation immigrant and a social scientist situated in Chicago during the early years of
Hull House and The Commons, was able to see aspects of these new institutions missed by later, more sympathetic, historians. Particularly important for our purposes are his insights into their "quasi-religious"
emphasis on the genteel tradition and into their admiration of industrial
efficiency.

This ideological mixture is precisely what characterized the Pittsburgh
Survey as well. The social accountants who undertook that study were
able, for the first time, to examine systematically the effects of modernization; and they completed their project confident not only of the effectiveness of their new techniques of social investigation but also of their own
ability to manage rationally the whole range of social change brought on
by the industrial revolution. The techniques, while statistically somewhat
crude, had indeed proved their worth. Subsequent generations of scholars
have attested to the reliability of the Survey's data. More problematic
was the engineers' faith in themselves. That rested, to a large extent, on
the optimistic belief that the tenets of the Social Gospel and the techniques of Scientific Management automatically complemented each other.
Brotherhood, they were sure, was not only right—it was also efficient.
A measure of Veblen's corrosive skepticism might have served to temper
their too facile confidence.

Experts had used the occasion of the Survey to claim a major role for
themselves as social planners. But their reach greatly exceeded their grasp.
They could translate their ambitions into programs only through the support of key institutions, such as the Russell Sage Foundation. Experts
needed the foundation; they did not, however, control it. Forest Hills
Gardens demonstrated that a board of trustees, drawn from the financial
and philanthropic elite, could have definite ideas of its own about how
to meet the problems of industrial society. Some of these trustee projects
accorded a major role to the engineers; some did not. Thus the Sage
Foundation underwrote the Pittsburgh Survey for $26,500; it also in-
vested some $4 million in Forest Hills Gardens and hundreds of thousands

of dollars more in other benevolent enterprises that did not require the experts' services.

Such, at least, is the picture suggested by these first case studies. Caution is necessary of course. It would be a mistake to reach any dogmatic conclusions from such limited data. Still caution need not prevent us from recognizing the significance of what we have found. For the settlement house was, in the early twentieth century, the most important recruitment center for experts; the Survey was the most important social investigation undertaken before the war; and the Sage Foundation was, in the same years, the most important single source of support for the new professionals. We have, in other words, been looking at the main line of the professional development of social engineering; and this supplies a certain presumption in favor of our findings. And what we have found, so far, does not bear out the general scholarly view of the importance of social expertise in the twentieth century. Nor does it support the view that the possession of a special competence was equivalent to holding a position of power as Talcott Parsons has suggested.

Far from revolutionizing twentieth-century politics, as Robert Wiebe has hypothesized, experts faced a political situation they did not create and could only marginally control. On the local level this meant that they had little choice but to join in the good-government campaigns of business-minded municipal reformers. In an institutional context it meant that experts had to persuade a philanthropic elite, composed of strong-minded and experienced individuals like Robert W. de Forest, to finance their programs. This was no easy assignment, for people like de Forest not only held the purse strings, they also had quite definite proposals of their own. On the national level it meant that expert fortunes were tied to those of Theodore Roosevelt's 1912 campaign.[3] His defeat and, more critically, his decision to abandon third-party politics left the experts without a base in national politics.

Overall, however, their situation was by no means bleak. The settlement and charity movements were both prospering. State and municipal progressives were slowly creating a network of investigatory and regulatory agencies in which engineers could develop their expertise. The federal government also had made some progress in the same direction as the examples of the Industrial and Immigration Commissions make clear. Experts, that is, were slowly but steadily making a place for themselves in the new social order. There was nothing revolutionary in their advancing status, but they could take some satisfaction in the distance traveled.

Here matters stood when war broke out in August 1914. The United States of course managed to stay out of the conflict until April 1917. The effects of the war, however, were felt much earlier. Relatively little has been written about the war's impact on the development of social expertise, and what has been written has been preoccupied with the question of how the war jeopardized or sustained various "reforms."[4] The following chapters, then, represent a new venture. They deal with the new professionals' efforts to influence social planning in the areas of Americanization, wartime mobilization, postwar reconstruction, and antiradicalism. These areas are especially pertinent because they clearly illustrate the general strategy experts followed in trying to effect social policy and promote their own professional careers. Together they will allow us to make a preliminary estimate of the impact of the war on the development of expertise. If these four cases yield a consistent pattern, we shall have a reasonable basis for generalization.

Because so little is known of the domestic impact of the war, it is necessary to sketch a general interpretation of it and of the relations of the four topics to it. These sketches all presume a departure from the historians' normal scheme of periodization, because they treat the years 1915-24 as a coherent era in American politics and society. Thinking of these years as a "period" will help us to make sense of the more detailed case studies, but it obviously makes claims about the American past that these studies cannot validate by themselves. It therefore makes most sense to regard these four cases as probes, discrete shafts of light that will enable us to see some things with tolerable clarity. But, it has been necessary to hypothesize about the rest.

The war had a decisive effect upon the development of social expertise. It not only enormously broadened the scope of governmental activity and thus offered experts new sources of support and a new arena in which to campaign for their programs, but it also made matters previously ignored by nonexperts, such as immigrant assimilation, burning questions of public policy. Experts, in these new circumstances, sought to promote their proposals as scientific responses to war-related emergencies. The war offered opportunity and experts sought to seize it. Their success would depend, as it had before the war, on their ability to influence the programs of key institutions. The question for us, as a consequence, is whether the pattern of elite control and expert subservience we found in the case of the Sage Foundation, also held for the federal bureaus of Education and Naturalizaiton, the Committee on Public Information (the Creel committee, the Wilson administration's official propaganda agency), the Council of National Defense, the American Red Cross, the War Camp Community Services, and other key agencies.

Before getting down to cases it is necessary first to say something about the war years themselves. Traditionally, historians have dealt with them as a hiatus between the Progressive era and the "normalcy" of the 1920s.[5] And this reflects the profession's tendency to organize its studies around wars, reform movements, and economic depressions. So we usually think of progressivism as ending with the war, the war leading to a period of business ascendancy that was ended only by the Great Depression, and a new version of the cycle beginning with the New Deal.

This scheme is sensible enough, but its virtually axiomatic use obscures an important sequence in American social and political history that we can label the first Americanism era.[6] This era began with the Americanization and preparedness campaigns of the prewar years, continued through the espionage and sedition prosecutions of the war years, reached a kind of climax during the Red Scare of 1919-20, witnessed the postwar "American Plan" campaign of company unionism, and culminated in the Immigration Restriction Act of 1924. The essential continuity of these events is evident as soon as they are listed together, but they have been traditionally studied singly and, therefore, viewed as isolated exceptions to the general pattern of American history.[7] Far from being exceptional, these events conformed to the dominant political pattern of the war years.

Most important for our purposes was the impact of Americanism upon federal authority. The best place to begin our discussion of this is with Randolph Bourne's 1919 essay "The State." John Dos Passos has left us with a vivid portrait of Bourne and his essay:

> This little sparrowlike man
> a tiny twisted unscared ghost in a black cloak
> always in pain and ailing,
> put a pebble in his sling
> and hit Goliath in the forehead with it.
> *War,* he wrote, *is the health of the state.*
>   . . .
>
> If any man has a ghost
> Bourne has a ghost,
> a tiny twisted unscared ghost in a black cloak

hopping along the grimy old brick and brownstone
streets still left in downtown New York,
crying out in a shrill soundless giggle:
War is the health of the state.[8]

In peacetime, Bourne argued, the government had claimed to be nothing
more than the machinery for carrying on the public business. This matter-
of-fact view allowed, even required, a healthy suspicion of both government and politicians. "Government is obviously composed of common
and unsanctified men, and is thus a legitimate object of criticism and
even contempt."[9]

War, however, changed popular attitudes according to Bourne. The
government was transformed into "the state." The state was more than
the instrumentality of government; it was, or claimed to be, the symbol
of all cultural and civic virtues. Far from being an object of contempt,
it demanded reverence. What had once been criticism or suspicion became, in wartime, sedition and disloyalty. War produced fear, and the
state provided safety. Ordinary civic loyalty thereby acquired a critical
quotient of panic and became militant patriotism.[10]

The cult of the state rested on more than changes in attitude. The war
brought opportunity. Profiteers could testify to this, albeit unwillingly.
So could young men with unanticipated careers as officers and gentle-
men. So could social engineers who rushed off to Washington to contribute
their expertise to the war effort. Businessmen, whose efforts at coordina-
tion had been subjected to the intermittent harassment of antitrust actions,
suddenly received federal sanction. The American Federation of Labor
(AFL) found itself the recognized bargaining agent in industry after
industry by virtue of governmental decree.

If state-sponsored mobilization afforded opportunities, so did the
emotional atmosphere of the war. Local businessmen found that by
organizing defense societies or security leagues they could become the
arbiters of the permissible in their communities. They could hound the
International Workers of the World (IWW) practically out of existence,
jail socialists, smoke out "radical" teachers and ministers, and otherwise
guarantee that their towns would follow the lead of the "respectable"
people.[11] Their wives could become social leaders through Liberty Bond
campaigns or Red Cross activities. Not least of all, ambitious politicians
found they could build careers on denunciations of "hyphenates,"
aliens, and "Huns."

In brief, the war proved itself in the land of opportunity. There seemed to many no reason for surrendering the advantages it brought just because the Armistice had been signed. For one thing, the cult of the state had been promulgated too effectively for it to die in a day. For another, too many had benefited from the exercise of authority their identification with the national cause had brought. The defense societies, for example, had no desire to disband. Instead they were joined in the field by the newly organized American Legion, whose uniformed patriotism permitted a political career parallel to that of the Grand Army of the Republic.[12] Businessmen had no desire to return to simulating competition. On the contrary, they launched a major campaign against unionism, the "American Plan."[13] Nor did politicians want to relinquish so popular an issue.

Almost providentially the October revolution in Russia granted the cult of the state a new rationale. "Bolshevik" replaced "Hun," and the communization of women succeeded the rape of Belgium as sensational headline material; but the atrocity stories, the tales of sabotage, the suspicion of "hyphenates," and the campaign for "100 percent Americanism" all continued unabated. The substitutions were easily made. Wartime propaganda had set the stage by portraying the Bolsheviks as German agents treacherously bent upon forsaking the Eastern Front; stories of Lenin crossing German-held territory in the famous sealed train highlighted accounts of Russia's separate peace agreement of 1918. This theme would be played with innumerable variations in the postwar days. A *New York Times* headline sounded one possibility:

> Germans Exploit Attacks on Wilson / Are Aided by
> Bolsheviki; Sinn Feiners, and Some Americans in Propa-
> ganda / Use Switzerland As Base / Speeches of Hostile
> Senators and Newspaper Criticisms Are Actively Circulated.[14]

In addition to warmed-over propaganda, those seeking to perpetuate the politics of patriotism made use of the outbreak of civil war in the Soviet Union to distinguish between good Russians and evil Bolsheviki. The rescue of the Czech Legion in central Siberia served as a pretext for intervention.[15]

In the U.S. Senate the Overman committee smoothly shifted its investigation from German sabotage and espionage to "Red-inspired" domestic radicalism. A. Mitchell Palmer, the self-proclaimed "Fighting Quaker," bid for the presidency by hunting "Reds"; and J. Edgar Hoover began his unique career by organizing the Palmer raids. Opportunity still knocked. Seattle's mayor, Ole Hanson, gained national prominence and a lucrative career on the lecture circuit from his opposition to the Seattle general strike of 1919. Governor Calvin Coolidge did even better. His telegram condemning the Boston police strike of 1919 made him a national hero and contributed to his nomination for the vice-presidency on Harding's ticket.

Liberals in general, and social experts in particular, joined in the chorus. The standard liberal version of anticommunism was fully enunciated by the *Survey* as early as February 1, 1919. On that date it hailed the famine relief bill of 1919 as "the only way" of fighting bolshevism—"by feeding the starving masses of eastern Europe and thus reducing the popular support of merely disruptive and destructive political movements."[16] This undoubtedly expressed a sincere conviction. It was also, however, an attempt by experts to translate popular fears into support for their programs. This was their characteristic strategy in the years 1915-24, applied to wartime mobilization, postwar reconstruction, antiradicalism, and Americanization alike. Like other elements in the population, in other words, experts sought to seize the opportunities presented by the Americanism era.

Generally speaking, expert Americanism was unsuccessful. What these new experts had failed to realize was that the politics of patriotism inevitably undercut the rationale for their programs precisely to the extent that it oversimplified issues. Experts can only hope to exercise influence when problems are thought to be complex. When Theodore Roosevelt, for example, reduced the whole question of ethnic pluralism to the single, burning issue of loyalty to the state in his 1916 run for the Republican nomination, he was helping to create a political climate in which experts would have difficulty catching their breath. If repression and restriction were grotesquely oversimplified reactions to cultural diversity, it was equally true that educational programs of Americanization were foolishly elaborate responses to disloyalty. Experts could not have it both ways; yet this is precisely what they sought to accomplish.

The following chapters then recount the experts' efforts to present their programs as "scientific" versions of nativism, patriotism, and antiradicalism. As was the case with the preceding case studies, we shall survey expert opinion, identify some of the crucial institutional settings in which experts sought power, describe the other interests they were competing with, and venture a tentative judgment of their relative success or failure.

We shall consider Americanization first because experts had long claimed they possessed a special fitness for promoting assimilation. These claims, as we have seen, date back to the early days of the settlement movement. Because they do, Americanization affords a particularly good opportunity to gauge the impact of the war upon already existing expert proposals.

Americanization may well be the least studied major social movement in American history. More than thirty states passed laws requiring Americanization programs; hundreds of chambers of commerce organized English and civics classes in thousands of factories; more than 3,000 school boards initiated similar classes; unions, particularly the United Mine Workers, encouraged their members to learn English and take out naturalization papers; philanthropic organizations, such as the Young Men's and Young Women's Christian Associations (YMCA, YWCA), began programs in hundreds of communities; and, as one might suspect, patriotic organizations—from the Daughters and Sons of the American Revolution to the American Legion—entered the field. If experts were going to exert a "revolutionary" influence, or anything even remotely like one, on American society, then here was one of their major opportunities. And experts certainly saw it as such.

Although experts could claim several decades of experience in working with immigrants, neither they nor anyone else had had to deal with the social dislocations that accompanied modern warfare. Yet even here experts did claim a special competence based upon their experience with the social problems occasioned by industrialization. Here again was a major area in which experts sought to influence social policy.

Wartime mobilization promised to meet their long-standing need for governmental support. It promised, in fact, to redeem expert losses in the Bull Moose campaign of 1912. The promise proved greater than the reality, and experts managed to exercise little control over mobilization. They were not immediately disheartened, however, for they could explain away their lack of success in terms of what they came to view as the "abnormal" conditions of war. They could, and did, pin their hopes for power on what they fondly believed would be a major program of domestic "reconstruction" which was to follow the war. These hopes rested upon the Wilson administration's willingness to promote a broad restructuring of American society, and they were quickly frustrated once it became apparent that Wilson was content to allow domestic conditions to return to the status quo ante bellum.

The final case study, on the experts during the Red Scare in New York

State, examines the consequences of their failure to gain positions of power during the war years. The New York experience is especially revealing for several reasons. One is that it foreshadows the New Deal alliance between experts and machine politicians. Experts in New York were, as late as 1917, still firmly allied with "good government" movements and resolutely opposed to Tammany Hall. They discovered in the immediate postwar years, however, that their fortunes were bound up with those of Tammany Hall's. They launched a joint campaign for the repeal of various Red Scare-inspired legislation. This new alliance, formed around the figure of Alfred E. Smith, marks an end to the early history of social engineering and, thus, a fitting end to this history.

New York is an apt choice to study the impact of the Red Scare on expertise for other reasons as well. It was a center, perhaps *the* center, of social engineering. It was also the place where the Red Scare assumed its most virulent form. So the New York experience is paradigmatic, not in the sense that it is typical of what happened elsewhere, but in the sense that the historical developments we have been tracing were most fully articulated there. If experts were to learn from experience, it was New York they would have to turn to.

NOTES

1. Thorstin Veblen, *The Theory of the Leisure Class* (New York, 1934), pp. 399, 344-45.

2. See David Riesman, *Thorstin Veblen: A Critical Interpretation* (New York: Scribner's, 1953).

3. See Allen F. Davis, *Spearheads for Reform: The Social Settlements and the Progressive Movement, 1890-1914* (New York: Oxford University Press, 1967), chap. 10, "The Progressive Crusade."

4. See Arthur Link, "What Happened to the Progressive Movement in the 1920's?" *American Historical Review* 44 (July 1959): 833-51; Allen F. Davis, "Welfare, Reform and World War I," *American Quarterly* 19 (Fall 1967): 516-33.

5. An important first attempt to find continuities between the war and the Harding-Coolidge administration is Burl Noggle, *Into the Twenties: The United States from Armistice to Normalcy* (Urbana, Ill.: University of Illinois Press, 1974).

6. The second Americanism era accompanied World War II.

7. Edward Hartmann's *The Movement to Americanize the Immigrant* (New York, 1948) follows the career of the National Americaniza-

tion Committee and so closes with 1921 when the NAC papers end. On the other hand, the Restriction Act of 1924 was, in effect, the definitive Americanization measure. Similarly, Robert K. Murray's *Red Scare: A Study in National Hysteria, 1919-1920* (New York: McGraw-Hill, 1964) does not refer to wartime antiradicalism or the "American Plan" of antitrade unionism. H. C. Petersen and Gilbert Fite's *Opponents of War, 1917-1918* (Seattle, Wash.: University of Washington Press, 1957) is limited strictly to those years.

8. John Dos Passos, *Nineteen Nineteen* (New York, 1946), pp. 90-91.

9. "The State," in Carl Resek, ed., *War and the Intellectuals, Collected Essays [of Randolph Bourne] 1915-1919* (New York: Harper & Row, 1964), pp. 71, 65.

10. Ibid., pp. 65-104.

11. For examples, see Petersen and Fite, *Opponents of War,* and Chapters 5 and 6.

12. See Murray, *Red Scare,* pp. 87-90.

13. See Irving Bernstein, *The Lean Years: A History of the American Worker, 1920-1933* (Boston: Little, Brown and Co., 1960), pp. 146 ff.

14. *New York Times,* June 1, 1919.

15. See Christopher Lasch, *The American Liberals and the Russian Revolution* (New York: McGraw-Hill, 1962), pp. 158-89.

16. "The Famine Relief Bill," *Survey* 41 (February 1, 1919): 632. The Wilson administration, as might be expected, led the way. See Franklin K. Lane [secretary of interior], "What Americanism Means: Why We Need Not Fear Revolution," *Forum* 62 (September 1919): 370-71, and Josephus Daniels [secretary of the navy], "Above All—Patriotism! A Seven-Point Remedy for Our Hectic After-War Fever," *Forum* 63 (March 1920): 298-306.

chapter 4
Prelude to Americanization: Experts and Immigrants in Prewar America

Modern American society took shape in the decades before 1920. More precisely, the census of that year recorded the high points of three of the main indices of modernization. After 1920, the percentage of industrial workers in the labor force would level off, even decline somewhat; after it, too, the movement of people to the cities would begin to give way to suburbanization; and, because of the Restriction Acts of 1921 and 1924, the foreign-born would begin to decline as a percentage of the total population during the 1920s. By 1920, in other words, the United States was as industrial, urban, and pluralistic as it would ever be. And, contrary to popular tracts like *Future Shock,* the transitions to "postmodern" society have proved far less traumatic than those that shook America between the presidencies of Lincoln and Harding.

Experts were united in the claim that their new techniques would enable society to manage rationally the "shocks" of modernization. Experts had had, however, only limited opportunities to put their new ideas to work. The enormous expansion of governmental activity—on every level— occasioned by the prospect and the reality of war seemed, at the time, to change this. War, despite its horror, promised welfare. This was so because the war seemed to be a mandate for social activism. The United States could be an international power only if domestic weaknesses were overcome. Thus Walter Lippmann's vision of "mastery" shone with special brilliance in 1917 and 1918.

The campaigns to formulate a national immigrant policy are particularly important instances of the experts' efforts to realize the promise the war seemed to hold. One reason is that concern with the problems faced by immigrants, and an accompanying desire to share the blessings of middle-class gentility with these culturally "destitute" neighbors, supplied much of the original impetus behind the decision of many young people to seek careers as experts. This concern had, if anything, deepened over the years. As a result, by studying how experts sought to direct policy in this area we are following their own sense of what was important.

Then too the coming of the war sharply altered the way the "immigrant problem" was popularly defined. And the changes, from racial and/or economic definitions to ones that laid greater stress on cultural factors, were ones that seemed to enhance the experts' prospects of exercising real influence, because experts had tended to formulate the issue in those terms all along.[1]

Appropriate in terms of both the priorities and the prospects of the experts, the "immigrant problem" is also a good case to study in terms of the impact of the war on social issues. Not only did the war redefine the "immigrant problem," it also gave it an urgency that it had seemed to lack in peacetime. Before the war, despite pressure from groups ranging from the settlements to the Immigration Restriction League, the United States had drifted along without an immigration policy. The war would change that. Because of it there would be a policy, and experts would do their utmost to shape it.

Before we can assess the strategies experts adopted during the war years, we must first examine more systematically how experts thought about the immigrant. Although their settlement roots predisposed them to a position we can call (in distinction to cultural pluralism) cultural hegemony, experts were far from being of one mind on the subject. Both racial and economic theories of immigration claimed many proponents. Racial, economic, and cultural views all led to different kinds of solutions of the immigrant "problem," and we need to look at these prewar policy recommendations. Finally, we must also see what roles experts actually played in the prewar national debate over what to do about immigration.

Although the immigration problem evoked a dazzling array of theories, it is possible to discern three general approaches or orientations from which experts generally began. These were racial, economic, and cultural.[2] We shall first note some of the more salient characteristics of each, and then concentrate not only on how they differed from each other but also on how each displayed certain *internal* tensions or contradictions, for it is these that afford the most suggestive clues as to how popular nativism influenced scientific thinking.

The racialist orientation was most fully developed in the eugenics movement, virtually all of the ideas of which can be found in popular form in the works of Madison Grant. His *Passing of the Great Race* (1916), in fact, became a kind of textbook for racialists. For our purposes, however, it is more useful to focus on the works of Edward A. Ross and Henry Pratt Fairchild, both professional sociologists who exercised considerable influence on their discipline, because our interest is in the range of scientific and expert opinion. Both Ross and Fairchild wrote extensively about immigration; both emphasized the racial factor; and both were incapable of accepting the full logic of the racial argument, as they derived it from Darwin, and so displayed in their writings certain tensions and contradictions that may reveal the extrascientific bases of their ideas.

Both men accepted the view of Francis Amasa Walker[3] that, after 1820, immigration from Europe had led to a decline in the birthrate of the native population. So, Fairchild argued, "the admission of millions of foreign laborers has not added to the working force," for "we have supplanted native laborers with foreigners." Fairchild found the explanation of this tragic development (as he saw it) in the theories of Thomas Malthus. The limits of population or, in civilized society, of family size were allegedly set "by the amount of advantages which are required to keep the family in the social stratum to which it belongs or to which the parents aspire. . . ." Native-born Americans, Fairchild believed, were "endued by nature and inheritance with American ideals and ambitions." When confronted with competition from aliens with lower standards of living, the native faced a cruel choice. He could either lower his own standard or else reduce his family size. According to Fairchild, he had chosen the latter horn of the dilemma. As a consequence, native Americans had fewer children and "we have a working class [of the foreign-born] but little higher in the scale of education than that of the most illiterate country of Europe."[4]

Ross's version of the "race suicide" thesis was perhaps more influential than Fairchild's because, although most of Fairchild's writings appeared in professional journals, the editor of the popular *Century* magazine serialized Ross's book, *The Old World in the New,* in twelve installments.[5] Like Fairchild, Ross turned Darwin upside down. Their premise was, of course, that the European peoples constituted competitive racial stocks. From this a Darwinist would seemingly have had to draw a series of conclusions profoundly disquieting to the belief in Anglo-Saxon superiority. Competition for limited foodstuffs would favor a group with a lower standard of living. Furthermore, fecundity could never be "excessive," (the word Ross and others most used when referring to the birthrate among the foreign-born). It was instead the fundamental measure of "fitness." Sterility (the word Ross most used in describing the native-born), on the other hand, marked approaching extinction.[6] The "Great Race," the "fittest" in Darwinian terms, could not pass away. The "survival of the fittest" was a tautology; whoever survived was, by that very fact, the fittest. But the "Great Race" could not, in these terms, be Anglo-Saxon.

Ross inverted Darwinism because he could not accept the ability to propagate as the fundamental measure of "fitness." His attitudes, and those of others who shared his views,[7] were evidentally shaped by an application of entrepreneurial moral codes to sexual mores. Believers in this ethic of deferred gratification, of thrift, of fear of bankruptcy (impotence) were profoundly affronted by the notion that fecundity equaled fitness. They stared into Fairchild's terrible dilemma: Lower the standard of living or limit family size. As Ross put it, "the competition of low standard immigrants is the root cause of the mysterious sterility of Americans," and the end result would be "extinction."[8]

Demography haunted nonracists as well. Over a decade before Ross's articles in the *Century,* President Charles W. Eliot, of Harvard, expressed alarm in his annual presidential report that the Harvard man was not reproducing himself. He was, Eliot decided, postponing marriage until too late in life. He felt undergraduates should enter college sooner and graduate earlier, giving themselves more time to establish careers and raise larger families. Meanwhile Eliot felt Harvard would have to recruit promising young men of lower-class origin to replenish the aristocracy.[9] Of the proposed remedies only the last proved successful. Young men proved uninterested in either shortening their college careers or enlarging their families. As Fairchild noted, "the higher the social class, the smaller ... the average family."[10] Here, in a nutshell, was the anomaly of the racial approach. The category of "high" social class was supposed to correspond to "high" racial attributes. But the strategies of deferred gratification, including sexual gratification, that led to economic success led to racial failure. Biological and cultural currencies proved nonconvertible.

In other words, the native-born bourgeoisie expressed its sexual mores in terms of savings and projected its repressed desires to "spend" onto the southern and eastern European immigrant.[11] To their horror and fascination, sexual improvidence seemed paradoxically to guarantee racial solvency. The horror was all too real. Ross wrote of "the Caliban type" and asserted "the fact" that from 10 to 20 per cent of all immigrants were "hirsute, low-browed, big-faced persons of obviously low mentality. . . . clearly they belong in skins, in wattled huts at the close of the great ice age." Evolution was turning upside down. Here were these "oxlike men," "descendants of those *who always stayed behind*," pushing the native American aside.[12]

The racial argument, in sum, owed as much to Victorian proprieties and middle-class, white Anglo-Saxon Protestant ethnocentrism as it did to Darwinian theory. In fact, it owed more. The racism of Ross, Fairchild, and others resembled that described by Joseph Conrad in *The Heart of Darkness*. Anglo-Saxons were projecting those desires of their own that they had learned to reject as "dark" or evil or depraved onto a dark-complected, strange people.[13] There is, in this connection, no lack of evidence that Ross and his fellow racial theorists regarded eastern and southern Europeans as nonwhite. He quoted, for example, a physician in his article on "Racial Consequences of Immigration" to the effect that " 'The Slavs are immune to certain kinds of dirt. They can stand what would kill a white man.' " And in blaming capitalists in search of cheap labor for America's immigration problem, Ross commented: "Once before captains of industry took a hand in making this people. Colonial planters imported Africans."[14]

Surely there was more to this sort of Victorian racism than frustrated sexuality. John Higham has argued that these "allegations of a racial peril in the new immigration rationalized an underlying concern about cultural homogeneity." What racialists really feared was that "immigration was undermining the unity of American culture and threatening the accustomed dominance of a white Protestant people of northern European descent." Higham is almost certainly correct in this. There is little doubt that the differences a Ross or a Fairchild attributed to race we would attribute to cultural diversity. And there is little doubt that racialist fears were cultural in origin. But it does not follow therefore that "the science of the day, together with America's traditional susceptibility to race feelings, made the language of race an impelling vehicle for thinking and talking about culture."[15] The fact of the matter is that the language of race made thinking and talking about culture virtually impossible because it systematically obscured the role of the environment in shaping behavior and because it confused history with heredity. An example may make this plain.

   In 1920, Vernon Kellogg, an official with the War Relief Administration, set out the racialist program of assimilation with admirable clarity. For him the issue was the preservation in the United States of "the characteristics of the white race taken as a whole." This meant that "any serious attempt" had to begin with anthropological and biological research. "The Commissioner of Immigration should be an anthropologist exercising authority conferred on him by a Congress of biologists." For Kellogg, and for racial theorists in general, the presence of diverse ethnic groups in America did not produce a clash of loyalties or a confrontation of cultures. These were epiphenomena. Primary was a war of germ plasms in which the scientific community was to serve as a kind of general staff.

>   To help out in Americanizing the germ plasm already in our
>   country, in the way we want it Americanized, there should
>   be a Commissioner of Americanization who should know
>   more about the laws of heredity than about pedagogy or
>   civics. And he should have the authority to prevent the per-
>   petuation of obviously bad and dangerous germ plasm by
>   mixture with good. Don't call this eugenics; call it scientific
>   Americanization.[16]

As Vernon Kellogg noted, a cultural definition of the immigrant problem led to "pedagogy or civics," that is, English and citizenship classes. A racial definition led to a very different solution.

   Racialism tapped cultural misgivings then, even if it did not express them. It may also have tapped a general reaction against the impersonality of modern life. Oscar Handlin has theorized that the rootlessness of American life bred a compensating desire for community, which men sought to satisfy by excluding strangers. "It was as if only by creating an antagonist upon whom all the hatred and fear within them [the native-born] could be expended, could they find a communion of the unexcluded that would summon up their capacities and longings for love."[17] Higham, as we have seen, places less emphasis upon the immigrant as scapegoat and focuses instead upon the actual dangers of cultural diversity. According to him, the nativist longed less for love than for homogeneity. Both theses, however, assume a will-to-wholeness behind the nativist crusades. And there is little reason to doubt that nativism, at bottom, was provoked by the sheer fact of difference. But because the longing for love and the distrust of difference underlay all forms of nativism, they tell us comparatively little about its racial form. For that we need to turn to the specific fears and fantasies that Darwinism enabled Ross and his cohorts to express. And these are largely sexual.[18]

Racial theories, despite the patina of scientific respectability they borrowed from evolutionary biology, scarcely monopolized expert thinking about immigration. One reason, quite apart from the intellectual inadequacies of the racial orientation, is that experts were seeking a definition of the "immigrant problem" which would require their skills as part of the solution. The most influential alternative, in the prewar period, was the economic orientation. This was the preponderant point of view taken in the Dillingham Immigration Commission's *Reports* of 1911 although it inconsistently also used racial categories.[19] Created by Congress in 1907, the commission was a temporizing response to demands for restriction. The delay, of course, permitted continued immigration; but it was nonetheless a victory for restrictionists, who dominated its membership.[20] This fact makes the *Reports* a singularly unreliable source—if one is interested in the study of immigration.[21] If, however, one is interested in the uses of social science, the *Reports* are very useful.

As presented by the commission, the economic orientation viewed the immigrant "problem" as one of unskilled, unattached transient males who undersold native Americans in the labor market. These "birds of passage" thereby lowered the general standard of living even as they raised their own. They then returned to their native lands with whatever savings they had accumulated.[22] Overlaying this dollars-and-cents argument was a series of invidious distinctions, presented in elaborate if spurious detail, between "old" and "new" immigrants.[23] It is these latter that are the commission's chief claim to notoriety. Our interests, however, are not in how the commission systematically libeled the "new" immigration so much as in how experts sought to use economic theories to define the "immigrant problem." For this purpose the *Reports* present a problem because of the key role played by politicians like Senator Dillingham in drafting them. Far better is a scholarly work, *The Immigration Problem,*[24] written by two social scientists instrumental in the commission's investigations. Jeremiah W. Jenks was professor of government and director of the Division of Public Affairs at New York University; he had been a member of the commission. W. Jett Lauck was a former associate professor of economics and politics at Washington and Lee University; he had directed the commission's industrial investigations. They claimed the strictest scientific objectivity for their work. They were "not advocates, but interpreters of facts" who "until about the time the investigation was completed . . . had not formulated in their own minds any definite policy which they believed Government should follow."[25] So, they wrapped their conclusions in the mantle of disinterested science. Moreover, their subsequent careers display strong commitments to trade unionism and industrial democracy. They both served, for example, as expert witnesses on behalf of the workers before a Senate committee investigating the Passaic Textile Strike of 1926. Many of the strikers were new immigrants, and the strike itself was led by a Communist-affiliated "united front" committee.[26]

Yet, even given their liberal, perhaps radical, sympathies, Jenks and Lauck approached the immigration question from a conservative, even Sumnerian perspective. They argued that the government and institutions "in any country" were "not merely the government 'that the people deserve,' but the only government that under the circumstances is then possible," and concluded that the new immigrants were dangerous because they were different: "The imposing of new institutions from outside could hardly fail to be detrimental, however good such institutions might have been in the home country." As was noted earlier, this rejection of difference per se is the one common feature of nativist thought, whatever its theoretical orientation. The racialist Henry Pratt Fairchild, for instance, also wrote that "The United States demands assimilation of the immigrant not because he is less wise, or less intelligent, or less good than the American, or inferior in any respect, but because he is different."[27] This glorification of the status quo is so out of keeping with Jenks and Lauck's reform sympathies that it suggests that what their elaborate statistical studies really measure is not the economic dimensions of immigration but the social distance the authors saw, and wished to maintain, between the middle-class WASP American and the new immigrant. As they put it, "certain marked characteristics of the immigrants . . . emphasize strongly the fact that the new immigration differs much more radically in type from the earlier American residents than did the old. . . ."[28]

What did they mean? First we must note that the categories they use—age and sex ratios, literacy, city versus country residence, and occupation—have little to do with politics, very little to do with culture, and nothing to do with loyalty to America. Economic nativism, in other words, was no more a language for talking about culture than was race. The economists' categories did concern *when* the new immigrants arrived, and Jenks and Lauck decisively biased their studies by comparing the latest stages of the old immigration with the early stages of the new. An example may serve to indicate the kind of distortion that necessarily resulted. Jenks and Lauck found that, between 1899 and 1909, 36.7 percent of the newcomers from southern and eastern Europe were common laborers compared with only 17.7 percent of those from northern and western Europe; for the same years they found a comparable discrepancy in the proportion of skilled immigrants, 8.9 percent as opposed to 19.5 percent. These differences in skill formed part of the evidence for their conclusion that the "new" immigrants undersold native American laborers. But the authors did not point out that the countries of northern and western Europe were largely industrialized by the late nineteenth century, or that skill levels reflected the level of economic development in the home country. Nor did they use comparable data from the 1840s or 1850s for the old immigrant groups.[29]

Despite this systematic bias, the data Jenks and Lauck collected showed the new immigrants to be *more* desirable than either the old immigration or the native population in a number of respects. They were healthier, less subject to "diseases that seem to be allied with moral weakness [alcoholism, venereal disease] ," less likely to seek or need charity, and less liable to commit crimes.[30] Frequently, however, the authors presented their data in a confusing or misleading way. They said, for example, "that certain aliens are more inclined toward insanity than are native-born Americans," and they related this, "in a measure at least, to racial or national tendencies." If one consults the table containing these statistics, one learns that the "certain aliens" were most often members of the old immigration, particularly the Irish. Jenks and Lauck did not state this, and allowed the unwary reader to assume that new immigrants were meant.[31] Sometimes they made assertions, based upon no data whatsoever, that recall the lurid imaginings of E. A. Ross. Witness their discussion of the "social evil":

> It is, of course, impossible to discuss in detail the evil results of this traffic in immigrants. Suffice it to say that it has materially heightened the gross evils of prostitution. Unnatural practices are brought largely from continental Europe; the fiendish work of the procurers or pimps is largely done by aliens or immigrants; diseases are spread more widely among guilty or innocent; even the ancient vice of the use of men and boys for immoral purposes is coming from abroad.

They claimed all of this despite their own data which showed, as they admitted, that a "very large proportion" of prostitutes were American-born and that "new" immigrants had lower levels of venereal disease than did natives. And they admitted grudgingly that "at the present time there is no serious danger to be apprehended immediately from the social defects of the immigrants."[32] Note the elaborate qualifiers that surround this exoneration of the newcomers. "At the present time" there is "no serious danger" to be apprehended "immediately" from the "defects" of the immigrants. What defects? Their own statistics showed that the immigrants had relatively few social defects, especially when compared with native-born Americans.

The main point in this attempt to disentangle the tissue of fact, myth, and stereotype that formed the economic orientation is to show that it was deeply divided against itself. The principal charge in the economic case against unrestricted immigration was that the newcomers' low standard of living lowered wages. As Jenks and Lauck put it:

It can hardly be doubted that the low standard of living, the
illiteracy, the absence of industrial training, and the tracta-
bility and lack of aggressiveness of the southern and eastern
Europeans in our industrial communities, constitute a menace
to the native Americans and wage-earners from Great Britain
and northern Europe.

Here again the authors reached a conclusion that belied their own evidence. Indeed, "one of the most striking facts" they found was that a
comparison of the earnings of various "races" in different industries
showed "that earning ability is more the outcome of industrial opportunity than of racial efficiency and progress." This "striking fact" was
buried in the middle of a paragraph in the middle of a chapter devoted
to data showing the lower wages of new immigrants. New immigrants
did earn less, on the average, than the native-born. The question was
whether this resulted from their own low standards or from their need
to take whatever work was available no matter how low paying. Jenks
and Lauck espoused the first explanation, but their data supported the
second. As they summarized their findings, "there is no evidence to show
that the employment of southern and eastern European wage-earners has
caused a direct lowering of wages or an extension in the hours of work
in mines or industrial establishments." Where then was the menace? Wages
and working conditions, it turned out, reflected "industrial opportunity,"
that is, market conditions, and not the standard of living or "tracta-
bility" of the workers. In this context, Jenks and Lauck finally turned
to the market to explain economic conditions. They argued that the
"large supply" of immigrant labor had retarded the *increase* in wages
that would otherwise have occurred. Their "conclusion of greatest significance" was "that the point of complete saturation has already been
reached in the employment of recent immigrants in mining and manufactur-
ing establishments."[33]

The most noteworthy feature of the economic approach was this re-
luctance to explain the immigrant labor question in terms of supply and
demand. Why should this have been so? The law of supply and demand,
after all, was the most basic theorem in the science of economics. And it
led, in this case, to the simplest and most adequate explanation of the
available data. Massive immigration unquestionably increased the labor
force, at least over the short run, and therefore may well, as Jenks and

Lauck argued, have retarded wage increases. Here surely was a reasonable basis for concern over unrestricted immigration. But it was a basis that applied to "old" and "new" immigrants alike, and this is what made it unacceptable to thinkers like Jenks and Lauck. For all of their discussion of the "saturation" of the industrial labor market—a highly problematical assertion that assumed that the "rapid expansion" of the American economy would not continue—they were eager for increased immigration, but from northern and western Europe:

> . . . unless there is a limitation placed upon the inexhaustible supply of cheap foreign labor of low standards and aspirations which is now coming to this country, it is perfectly clear that the American wage-earner can not hope to participate properly in the results of our industrial progress. Moreover, altho [sic] the present rate of increase in the supply of unskilled labor would be lessened by a restriction of immigration, it can not be questioned that the higher wages and better standards of living which would be the logical outcome, would attract to our shore skilled and highly trained workmen from northern and western Europe who, under present conditions, have ceased to immigrate to the United States.[34]

Fairchild and Ross, for all of their borrowing from evolutionary theory, rejected the basic Darwinian definition of "fitness" because it failed to comport with their notion of the "Great Race." In similar fashion, Jenks and Lauck rejected supply and demand in favor of a standard-of-living argument discredited by their own investigations. In both cases the reason was the same.[35] A rigorous application of either Darwinian or economic theories would discredit the alleged superiority of northern and western Europeans and their American descendants.

Although racial and economic theories had their roots in a desire for cultural wholeness, users of them systematically obscured or denied the importance of cultural considerations. Cultural theorists attempted to express these concerns directly but had little success in gaining a hearing until the war. There were two main schools of cultural theorists. The first consisted of the pluralists. They have undoubtedly had the greatest long-range influence and therefore have gained the lion's share of scholarly attention.[36] At the time, however, they were less significant than those that might be called cultural hegemonists. Pluralists argued for the desirability of cultural and ethnic diversity. Such differences, they believed, enriched American democracy. Hegemonists, on the other hand, defined assimilation as the progressive elimination of undesirable ethnic characteristics. This was the dominant point of view of the social and settlement workers who frequently defined the settlement house as a missionary outpost. Robert A. Woods of South End House, Boston, gave a typical version of this claim as early as 1899:

> In its pointed fitness for imparting to the immigrant a wider
> and higher range of wants in his domestic and social life, and
> stimulating him to the accomplishment of his new desires,
> the settlement becomes a distinctly important means toward
> true Americanism.[37]

The distinction between cultural pluralists and hegemonists is an important one. Failure to draw it has led several historians to put settlement and social workers in the pluralist camp.[38] Yet their ethnocentric stance created important affinities between their position and those of the racial and economic theorists.

Hegemonists had first to gain a hearing, no easy task given the popularity of the racial and economic orientations. One of the first to try was Paul U. Kellogg, who had previously directed the Pittsburgh Survey and then become editor of the *Survey*. The publication of the preliminary abstracts of the Dillingham commission allowed him to propose an immigrant labor tariff. Kellogg firmly rejected the various distinctions between "old" and "new" immigrants and seemed, rhetorically at least, to take a pluralist position. "My own feeling," he wrote, "is that immigrants bring us ideals, cultures, red blood—which are an asset for America or would be if we gave them a chance." His point of view was that of a worried native American: "We suffer not because the immigrant comes with cultural deficits, but because he brings to America a potential economic surplus above his wants which is exploited." How do *we* (that is, native-born Americans) suffer? The immigrant (known as a "greener") with no "funds to stake him in the new country, ignorant of the language and to a great extent of knowledge of industrial opportunities among us, unaccustomed, perhaps, to work for pay, with labor agents egging him on and the fear of hunger dogging him if he delays," makes a "bad employment bargain." The description is not unsympathetic, but the limits of Kellogg's sympathy were quickly reached. For if, he continued, the bad employment bargain affected only the "greener," it would be no problem. "But multiply that greener by a hundred thousand and you have a force more powerful to affect the wages of an industry than congress and all legislatures." Multiply that hundred thousand "over and over and you have the tyranny which holds the common labor market in the hollow of its great, untrained, earth-bred hand." The result was a "silent, un-angry, inexorable undermining of the American basis of living."[39] Immigrants, taken as individuals, were victims of industrial conditions and were to be commiserated with. Taken together, however, they assumed monstrous proportions in Kellogg's mind; they held the labor market in their "great, untrained, earth-bred hand."

Nightmares of giants aside, there was a nice irony in Kellogg's argument. Whereas the economists of the Dillingham commission blamed low wages on the newcomers' general backwardness and sought relief in a literacy test, here was a culturalist who, arguing that backwardness was remedial, blamed low wages on an oversupply of industrial labor and sought to regulate that by one of the most curious restrictionist schemes of the era. Kellogg proposed that no immigrant engaged in industrial employment be permitted to earn less than $2.50 or $3 per day for a period of five years after his arrival. If he earned less, the penalty would be deportation. Because the immigrant, and not the employer, would be liable, Kellogg felt that he would enter agriculture or some other nonindustrial pursuit.[40]

The proposal had no influence on the commission's recommendations, nor was it incorporated into the political debates over restriction. In fact, it and all other culturalist arguments were absent from volume 41 of the *Reports,* which was devoted to statements by advocates and opponents of restriction.[41] Kellogg, however, was able to use his position as editor of the *Survey* to keep his idea alive in professional circles, where it generated an interesting debate that reveals much about the way in which social and settlement workers thought about the immigration question.[42] One booster was Father John Ryan, a spokesman for liberal Catholicism, who felt it was "a very fascinating suggestion" that had "the merit of going straight to the root of the immigration problem." Even more enthusiastic was Frederic Almy, the secretary of the Buffalo (New York) Charity Organization Society. Almy described himself as "tempted" by

Kellogg's "alluring and audacious suggestion." His support was based upon doubts as to the effectiveness of a literacy test as a means of screening immigration. "Educated raw material [that is, literate immigrants] is less raw, and so easier to digest, but what we are after is the best raw material." Serenely unaware of his cannibalistic image, Almy declared that "we would rather have the very best meats and do the cooking after we get them. A little cooking often keeps us from recognizing bad meat."[43]

Industrial America, in this view, would continue to gobble up common labor; but meanwhile a kind of pure food law was needed. Almy was exceptional only in the carelessness of his metaphors. Kellogg had, for example, quoted him in making his original case: " 'Safe living [for immigrants] does not mean comfortable living. It means safe for the rest of us.' "[44] The need to protect native-born Americans from a distasteful immigrant population was a common theme of social and settlement workers, and this was true even of those who went furthest to aid and comfort their immigrant neighbors. Lillian Wald, the founder of the "House on Henry Street," was one of the most selfless of the new experts; yet even she objected to Kellogg's plan on the grounds that it would create "a privileged class and that consisting of the alien laboring man." She thought that although the proposal was designed to discourage immigration, it was likely to have the opposite effect, because "immigrants would regard it as a safeguard against their exploitation."[45] It was not, in this view, the immigrant who needed protection; or, more precisely, it was the native-born who needed protection first.

While it was designed to make immigration more palatable, Kellogg's scheme had a serious defect from a professional point of view. Like other restrictionist measures, its implementation would not require the services of social experts. Other expert proposals were designed to remedy this oversight. Their objective was to prevent immigrants from assimilating on their own terms. Charles W. Blanpied, the immigration secretary of the Young Men's Christian Association in San Francisco, posed the issue sharply. "There are," he claimed, "two classes of assimilative processes." The superior one, "which a better class of society stands for," was that sponsored by agencies like his own. It was a "protective program" that stood guard "against graft and chicanery." The other was "the great nether world, or as we call it, the slum." It featured "the open door of the saloon, districts of vice and of idleness," and other "unwholesome" attractions. It was, nonetheless, Blanpied confessed, a place of "intense democracy, to reach which requires no struggle whatever and needs only a lack of application on the part of the new arrival to attain better things."[46]

The jibe about the "intense democracy" of the slum was probably aimed at the machine politician, a figure with a certain expertise of his own when it came to assimilation. Even E. A. Ross paused long enough in his racial fantasizing to bemoan how the "Tims" bossed the "Guiseppes." His central thesis was that "for all their fine Celtic traits, these Irish immigrants had neither the temperament nor the training to make a success of popular government." And when the "Guiseppes" remained unbossed, it was because they remained unnaturalized. "No doubt the country is better off for their not voting." Even so, labor, Ross realized, was underenfranchised as a consequence. His solution to the machine's control of the saloon and the ethnic vote was to "bore from within." Within months that phrase would be reserved for the activities (largely imaginary) of alien spies and saboteurs. But in January 1914, Ross could use it to describe social settlements, "the quick intelligence of the immigrant Hebrew," stricter naturalization procedures, and restriction of immigration.[47]

Here we have a clear statement of the class bias of the professional social expert. The ward boss, after all, was a competitor. He, in fact, was the pioneer in social work because he "was the discoverer of the fact that the ordinary immigrant is a very poor, ignorant, and helpless man" and had used this discovery to control votes by doing "many things that the social settlement does for nothing."[48] There is a scarcely veiled resentment that the politician did social work more effectively than the social worker in this grudging admission.

The most ambitious plan for taking assimilation out of the hands of the immigrant and the politician, perhaps, was offered by Graham Taylor, who had founded The Commons settlement in Chicago and who served on the editorial board of the *Survey*. He called for "a country-wide co-operation between official and voluntary agencies" to implement a three-point program: "To receive, distribute and locate immigrants; to protect their persons and property from exploitation and abuse; to inform and train them for citizenship." This proposal affords us an opportunity to determine what the social engineer meant by assimilation. It was synonymous with training for citizenship, and Taylor discussed it as a genuine technology. "Standardized and uniform information, curriculum and text books for instruction in the methods of our government and for training all new voters in voting are the surest solvents of our internal immigration problems." The instruction should be undertaken with "the joint efforts of boards of education and immigration bureaus."[49]

Here matters stood before the war. To the expert the immigrant existed first and foremost as a "problem." Only in the second instance could he be seen as having problems. Both racial theorizing and standard-of-living arguments were popular positions, and both, despite flaws made glaring by the cool light of hindsight, were scientifically respectable. But neither allowed the expert to express his own cultural anxieties, and neither offered much opportunity for the exercise of his professional skills. Cultural hegemony had neither of these deficiencies. One of Blanpied's colleagues at the San Francisco YMCA, Frank B. Lenz, urged that the "education of the immigrant adult should begin on shipboard. . . . Trained social workers appointed by civil service examination should be selected to do this work."[50] In attempting to arrogate to themselves the solution of what Taylor called the country's "internal immigration problems," the cultural hegemonists seemed to be preaching a gospel of moderation that has stood them in good stead with historians.[51] While racial and economic theorists were insulting the heredity of southern and eastern Europeans, while corporations and political machines were exploiting their labor and votes, experts like Taylor or Blanpied were seeking to "protect" them.

It was not altogether clear, however, what this protection might entail. It could have included some form of restriction, probably tied to the needs of the labor market for unskilled hands. It certainly included "assimilation" and "training for citizenship." But what did those terms mean? Experts tended to define them in terms of *who* should do the training (themselves), *how* the instructors should be chosen (civil service examinations), and *when* training ought to begin (as soon as possible). The content of this training presumably would be filled in later. The existing settlement programs do provide some idea of what the newcomers were expected to assimilate.

Settlements ran a rich variety of programs for immigrants ranging from sewing to English classes, and all served, to a lesser or greater degree, to interpret, in the words of College Settlement of New York head worker Elizabeth S. Williams, "American customs and ideals." Her settlement laid "great emphasis" upon the obligations of citizenship, recognizing "that its immigrant neighbors need especial training for their duties as future voters, and possibly lawmakers. . . ."[52] Behind the rhetoric lay efforts, largely token, to offer the benefits of self-government to the settlement's clientele. One head worker, William H. Kelley, admitted that he tried "to make the East Side House [of New York City] as nearly self-governing as the contemporaneous existence of a Board of Managers, a contributing public, a large number of more or less order-loving people, and a head-worker with nerves would permit."[53] Self-government under these cir-cumstances did not amount to much, as Kelley's self-deprecating sense of humor enabled him to confess.

It is difficult to avoid the judgment that assimilation in this context meant little more than the kinds of cultural missionary work described in Chapter 1. Most experts, as cultural hegemonists, assumed that the white, Protestant culture of the middle class was superior to any that the immigrant might derive from his native land or develop here. Indeed, one of the standard claims made in behalf of the settlements was that they permitted "large numbers of persons possessing the advantages of life" to develop "a sounder and more constraining sense of social service" by working with their cultural inferiors.[54] It was the experts' mission to pro-vide the newcomers with the advantages they already possessed themselves.

Cultural hegemonists, then, did have an institutional base in the settle-ments and charity societies; but they were unable to translate that into effective political influence. This briefly but radically changed after 1916 when the prospect of war raised the issue of immigrant loyalty, and the whole question of cultural assimilation emerged as a national concern. Then the "hyphenate" issue engendered political demands that went far beyond the experts' rather vague plans for uplifting immigrants to "American standards." How did the social engineers respond to this new situation? Were they able to convert the new national awareness into sup-port for their own programs? Or did politically generated demands for "100 percent Americanism" supply a new content for expert schemes of assimilation? Certainly a survey of the ethnocultural roots of prewar social expertise would predispose one to the latter alternative. An analysis of expert attempts to influence policy indicates that they tended to accommodate these political pressures and tried to present their programs as "scientific," and therefore more efficient, versions of "100 percent Americanism." As the engineers retreated from assimilation to American-ization, moreover, they surrendered the rationale for their own efforts. Expertise, after all, makes a plausible case for itself only when problems are thought to be complex; but the campaign for "100 percent Americanism" radically simplified the question of ethnic diversity, reducing it, in fact, to the question of potential disloyalty. Unfortunately for the experts, the logic of the loyalty issue tended to lead to sedition laws, deportation proceedings, and restriction. Experts had to struggle with this even as they sought to exploit the national concern over diversity.

NOTES

1. One handy measurement of the absence of a nonprofessional audience, before the war, for cultural definitions of the "immigrant problem" is the absence, before 1915, of any entries in *The Reader's Guide to Periodical Literature* under "Americanization." Articles listed under "Americanism" all dealt with the linguistic peculiarities of American English.

2. With the exception of race, these categories do not coincide with the "patterns of American nativism" identified by John Higham. Higham's patterns are derived from an analysis of the content of nativist writings. The categories here are based on an analysis of scientific orientation. In this regard, I will refer to as "scientific" whatever the social scientists of the period claimed had scientific validity. In this I am following the usage of Thomas S. Kuhn. See his *The Structure of Scientific Revolutions* (Chicago: University of Chicago Press, 1970). I have avoided referring to these orientations as "paradigms" because that term is more properly reserved for theories that have gained consensus. As we shall see, experts tended to adopt several of these approaches, despite their contradictions, because, as Kuhn points out, the lack of consensus invites eclecticism.

3. See John Higham, *Strangers in the Land* (New Brunswick, N.J.: Rutgers University Press, 1955), pp. 142-49; Thomas Gossett, *Race: The History of an Idea in America* (Dallas, Tex.: Southern Methodist University Press, 1963), pp. 302-4.

4. Henry Pratt Fairchild, "The Paradox of Immigration," *The American Journal of Sociology* 17 (September 1911): 256, 262, 263, 260, 263; see also Fairchild, *Immigration* (New York, 1925); "Restriction of Immigration," *American Journal of Sociology* 17 (March 1912): 634-46; "Literacy Test and Its Making," *Quarterly Journal of Economics* 31 (May 1917): 447-60; "Distribution of Immigrants," *Yale Review* 16 (November 1907): 296-310; "The Ultimate Basis of Immigration," *Annals of the American Academy* 93 (January 1921): 198-201; and *The Melting-Pot Mistake* (Boston, 1926).

5. The articles appeared from November 1913 through October 1914. Ross had the dubious distinction of coining the phrase "race suicide." See his "The Causes of Race Superiority," *Annals of the American*

Academy (July 1901): 67-89. See also *Standing Room Only?* (New York, 1927).

6. See Charles Darwin, *The Origin of Species* (1872; reprint ed., New York: Collier Books, 1962), especially pp. 90-137.

7. For examples, see John R. Commons, *Races and Immigrants in America* (1920 rprt., New York: A. M. Kelley, 1967); W. B. Bailey, "The Bird of Passage," *American Journal of Sociology* 18 (November 1912): 391-97; Sidney L. Gulick, "Immigration Policy," *Journal of Heredity* 7 (December 1916): 546-52; and G. P. Madge, "Menace to the English Race and to Its Traditions by Present Emigration and Immigration," *Eugenics Review* 11 (January 1920): 202-12.

8. E. A. Ross, "Racial Consequences of Immigration," *Century* 65 (February 1914): 621, 622.

9. Charles W. Eliot, *President's Report* (for 1901-02) (Cambridge, Mass., 1903), pp. 31-32.

10. Fairchild, "The Paradox of Immigration," p. 261.

11. Steven Marcus, *The Other Victorians: A Study of Sexuality and Pornography in Mid-nineteenth Century England* (New York: Basic Books, 1966), notes that "to spend" was the nineteenth-century equivalent of "to come" as a slang term for sexual climax, and discusses the analogy between semen and money it implies.

12. Ross, "Racial Consequences of Immigration," p. 615. Italics in the original. Some portions of the liberal press favorably reviewed Ross's articles. The *Nation*, for example, called the articles "well-fortified by fact" and "not unsympathetic in spirit." *Nation* 48 (March 26, 1914): 320.

13. Joseph Conrad, *Heart of Darkness* (1899; reprint ed., New York, 1960); Winthrop D. Jordan, *White Over Black* (Chapel Hill, N.C.: University of North Carolina Press, 1968) is a scholarly presentation of the same thesis with regard to "American Attitudes Toward the Negro, 1550-1812."

14. Ross, "Racial Consequences of Immigration," pp. 618, 616.

15. John Higham, "The Politics of Immigration Restriction," in *Send These to Me: Jews and Other Immigrants in Urban America* (New York: Atheneum, 1975), p. 47.

16. Vernon Kellogg, "Race and Americanization," *Yale Review* 10 (July 1920): 732, 734, 740.

17. Oscar Handlin, *Race and Nationality in American Life* (Boston: Little, Brown and Co., 1957), pp. 164-65.

18. For contemporary critiques of their "science," see Franz Boas, "This Nordic Nonsense," *Forum* 74 (October 1925): 502-11; Herbert A. Miller, "The Myth of Superiority," *National Conference of Social Work* (1923): 502-4; "Race Pride and Race Prejudice," *Nation* 120 (June 3,

1925): 622; Robert Ezra Park, "The Basis of Race Prejudice," *Annals of The American Academy* 140 (November 1928): 11-20; and William I. Thomas, "The Psychology of Race Prejudice," *American Journal of Sociology* 9 (March 1904): 593-611.

19. *Reports of the Immigration Commission,* 42 vols. (Washington, D.C., 1911). The inconsistency lay in the fact that, as we have seen, the racial theorists held that immigrants *replaced* natives in the labor market so that, to the extent that wages and other conditions of work were set by supply and demand, they could have *no* long-range effect on the labor market. The economic approach, on the other hand, assumed immigration *increased* the supply of labor. Logically the two orientations excluded each other, but this did not prevent the commission from utilizing both. Ross, who borrowed heavily from the commission's data, was equally inconsistent. See "The Old World in the New: Economic Consequences of Immigration," *Century* 65 (November 1913): 30-34. The commission further confused matters by defining "race" in terms of language and geography. *Abstracts Of Reports of the Immigration Commission,* vol. 1, p. 17.

20. See Higham, *Strangers in the Land,* pp. 188-89.

21. See Oscar Handlin's pioneering critique, "Old Immigrants and New," in *Race and Nationality in American Life;* see also Maldwyn Allen Jones, *American Immigration* (Chicago: University of Chicago Press, 1960), chap. 7.

22. *Abstracts of Reports,* 1: 1-4, 12, 13-20.

23. Ibid., especially pp. 13-14.

24. Jeremiah W. Jenks and W. Jett Lauck, *The Immigration Problem: A Study of American Immigration Conditions and Needs,* 4th ed., revised and enlarged (New York, 1917).

25. Ibid., p. xx.

26. See the documents collected in Paul Murphy *et al.,* eds., *The Passaic Textile Strike of 1927* (Belmont, Calif.: Wadsworth Pub., Co., 1974).

27. Jenks and Lauck, *The Immigration Problem,* pp. 24-25; Fairchild, *The Melting-Pot Mistake,* p. 176.

28. Jenks and Lauck, *The Immigration Problem,* p. 26.

29. Ibid., p. 30.

30. Ibid., pp. 28, 47, 50, 53-56.

31. Ibid., pp. 49, 51.

32. Ibid., pp. 66-67, 64, 47, 68.

33. Ibid., pp. 78, 198ff.; 202, 158, 207, 210.

34. Ibid., p. 212.

35. The commission *Reports* and *The Immigrant Problem* are the definitive statements of the economic orientation. There were numerous

restatements and variations. See Ross, "The Old World in the New: Economic Consequences of Immigration"; Bailey, "The Bird of Passage"; W. J. Lauck, "The Real Significance of Recent Immigration," *North American Review* 195 (February 1912): 201-11; T. W. Page, "Causes of Eastern European Immigration to the United States," *Journal of Political Economy* 19 (October 1911): 679-93. For a pro-immigrant critique, see Isaac A. Hourwich, "Economic Aspects of Immigration," *Political Science Quarterly* 26 (December 1911): 615-42; and *Immigration and Labor: The Economic Aspect of European Immigration to the United States* (New York, 1922).

36. See David A. Hollinger, "Ethnic Diversity, Cosmopolitanism and the Emergence of the American Liberal Intelligensia," *American Quarterly* 27 (May 1975): 133-51; Milton M. Gordon, *Assimilation in American Life* (New York: Oxford University Press, 1964); and John Higham, "Ethnic Pluralism in Modern American Thought," in Higham, *Send These to Me*, pp. 196-230. The most notable pluralist writings include: Horace M. Kallen, *Culture and Democracy in the United States: Studies in the Group Psychology of the American Peoples* (New York, 1924); Isaac B. Berkson, *Theories of Americanization: A Critical Study with Special Reference to the Jewish Group* (New York, 1920); Julius Drachsler, *Democracy and Assimilation: The Blending of Immigrant Heritages in America* (New York, 1920); Grace Abbott, *The Immigrant and the Community* (New York, 1917); Randolph Bourne, "Trans-national America," in Carl Resek, ed., *War and the Intellectuals; Collected Essays, 1915-1919* (New York: Harper & Row, 1964), pp. 107-23. The most important institutional support for the pluralist position was provided by the Carnegie Corporation's Americanization Studies, of which the most important is W. I. Thomas, *Old World Traits Transplanted* (New York, 1921), attributed to Robert E. Park and Herbert A. Miller. The director of the studies was Allen T. Burns; see his "Address," *Proceedings*, Americanization Conference (of the Bureau of Education, Department of the Interior) (1919), p. 291.

37. Robert A. Woods, *University Settlements: Their Point and Drift* (1899), pamphlet in National Federation of Settlements Papers, University of Minnesota Social Welfare History Archives, Folder: 591, p. 14. For numerous other examples, see Chapter 1.

38. See Allen F. Davis, *Spearheads for Reform: The Social Settlements and the Progressive Movement, 1890-1914* (New York: Oxford University Press, 1967), pp. 46-50; Higham *Strangers in The Land*, 236; and Robert L. Buroker, "From Voluntary Association to Welfare State: The Illinois Immigrants' Protective League, 1908-1926," *Journal of American History* 58 (December 1971): 643-60.

39. Paul U. Kellogg, "The Minimum Wage and Immigrant Labor,"

Proceedings, National Conference of Charities and Corrections (1911), pp. 171, 171-72.

40. Ibid., p. 165.

41. Dillingham commission, *Statements and Recommendations Submitted by Societies and Organizations Interested in the Subject of Immigration.* Another measure is a symposium on "What Is Americanism" conducted by the *American Journal of Sociology* in early 1915. The editors questioned 250 "representatives of every type of group . . . which may be reckoned as consciously contributing to our public opinion" except politicians. Only E. A. Ross even mentioned immigrants, and he did so in racial terms. *American Journal of Sociology,* 50 (January, March 1915): 433-36, 471.

42. See Paul U. Kellogg, "An Immigrant Labor Tariff," *Survey* 25 (January 7, 1911): 529-31; and a symposium, "Minimum Wage and Immigration Restriction," *Survey* 25 (February 4, 1911): 789-92.

43. "Minimum Wage and Immigration Restriction," pp. 789, 791.

44. Kellogg, "The Minimum Wage and Immigrant Labor," p. 168.

45. "Minimum Wage and Immigration Restriction," pp. 791-92.

46. "Report of [the] Special Immigration Survey of the Pacific Coast," *Proceedings,* National Conference of Charities and Corrections (1913), p. 66.

47. E. A. Ross, "Immigrants in Politics: The Political Consequences of Immigration," *Century* 65 (January 1914).

48. Ibid., p. 395. See also Jane Addams, "Why the Ward Boss Rules," *Outlook* 58 (April 2, 1898): 879-82, reprinted in Christopher Lasch, ed., *The Social Thought of Jane Addams* (Indianapolis: Bobbs-Merrill, 1965), pp. 126-33. For the ward boss' point of view, see William Riordan, *Plunkitt of Tammany Hall* (New York: Dutton, 1963).

49. Graham Taylor, "Distribution and Assimilation of Immigrants" (report of the committee), *Proceedings,* National Conference of Charities and Corrections (1912), pp. 31, 35, 34.

50. Frank B. Lenz, "The Education of the Immigrant: Education of Immigrant Adults and Evening Schools for Foreigners," *Educational Review* 51 (May 1916): 469.

51. See Davis, *Spearheads for Reform,* and Higham, *Strangers in the Land.*

52. *Twenty-third Annual Report* of the College Settlement; Report of Headworker, 1912. NFS papers, Folder: 413.

53. *Thirteenth Annual Report* of the East Side House, 1905. NFS papers, Folder: 415.

54. Woods, *University Settlements,* p. 61.

chapter 5

The Techniques of Patriotism: From Assimilation to Americanization

What is needed is a law that will define certain principles for the guidance
of decisions, that will set up the requisite machinery for getting the needed
facts; and that will provide an agency for evaluating those facts and for
applying the principles in the light of the facts, so that the immigration
allowed may be steadily adjusted to the ever changing economic, industrial
and social conditions.[1]

So wrote Henry W. Jessup, the chairman of the National Committee for
Constructive Immigration Legislation, which he, Franklin H. Giddings,
Charles Stelze, and other prominent social experts formed during World
War I. The style of their proposal is unmistakably that of social engineering. They wanted a pragmatic, flexible policy geared to changing economic
and social conditions. They wanted to determine the "facts" and admit
the number and type of immigrants the "facts" justified. But although
the committee spoke of the indispensability of "patient, scientific investigation,"[2] the legislation they offered required immediate action based
upon open, and admitted, ignorance. Their bill called for an "Immigration
Board" composed of the secretaries of state, labor, commerce, interior,
agriculture, and a sixth member appointed by the president to establish
annual immigration quotas for various "ethnic groups." The board's first
duty would be to "define and interpret the term 'ethnic group,' taking
into consideration questions of race, mother-tongue affiliation, nationality,
and such other relationships as tend to constitute group unity."[3]

The committee acknowledged, in other words, that it was not even sure what ethnic groups were. Nonetheless, it proposed their "scientific" regulation. Its members admitted that the board's early decisions, those taken before the "facts" were known, might prove arbitrary (not to say unjust), for "we are not quite certain yet how successful we have been with the more recent immigration—that from southern, central and eastern Europe." Nonetheless, the committee asserted "some peoples become assimilated sooner than others" although it was not "quite certain" who they might be. Such niggling doubts did not keep it from proposing quotas that would have barred all immigration from Asia and favored "old" European immigrants over "new" by a ratio of 3.6 to 1. These initial decisions, the committee members knew, "will bring results; results will influence decisions," but this self-perpetuating process was no vicious circle, not to their minds. "Gradually, as the years pass in the administration of the law we will accumulate both knowledge and wisdom. This is indeed the whole method of human progress."[4]

Despite its extended litany to the blessed attributes of expertise, this particular piece of "constructive legislation" actually amounted to a roundabout way of doing what the Restriction Acts of 1921 and 1924 did more straightforwardly: exclude nonwhites and discriminate against "new" immigrants. Not surprisingly, it was not adopted. In these and in several other respects it typified the experts' attempts to influence national immigration policy. The experts typically accepted popular nativist definitions of the "immigrant problem." They routinely promoted their own fitness to solve this problem even though they usually admitted there was little if any scientific information available. That, supposedly, would be generated in the process of implementing their solution. Generally, they failed to achieve any long-range success. This chapter examines how this melancholy situation came about.

Until 1916 much had been written, but very little had happened. Congress twice passed the literacy test for immigrants recommended by the Dillingham commission, but Presidents Taft and Wilson had both vetoed it. Meanwhile, cultural hegemonists, who advocated a policy of assimilation, could not even point to the near success of the sort racialists and economic theorists had had with the literacy test. The closest the cultural hegemonists had come was when they had managed to write the social welfare plank of the Progressive party platform of 1912.[5] Assimilation, however, was not a major issue in that campaign; and Woodrow Wilson's election meant that discussions of scientific assimilation were once again relegated to the professional conferences.

The danger of war, and then the war itself, accomplished what the experts had been unable to do. The two largest ethnic minorities, the Germans and the Irish, quickly demonstrated an interest in American foreign relations that Anglophiles found close to treasonous. Clearly their loyalties were "hyphenated." Clearly too, from the pro-British point of view, the United States was threatened with "Balkanization" as ethnic groups banded together in ghetto neighborhoods, read their foreign-language press, and in general isolated themselves from "American" life. Worse still, immigrants and their children gave every sign of retaining their "Old-World" political loyalties. Who was to say that these permanent aliens were not already engaged in espionage and/or sabotage? The prospect of war turned, in other words, the normal distrust natives felt toward immigrants into a searing suspiciousness that resembled paranoia.

Something of this sort was no doubt inevitable in a society as ethnically diverse as that of the United States. But the antihyphenism of the war years took on an added virulence because of the overheated rhetoric of the 1916 presidential campaign. Early in the year Woodrow Wilson had tried to reassure native Americans that the danger of immigrants dividing their allegiance between the United States and their native countries was "now passed and overcome." Theodore Roosevelt, however, made loyalty a key issue in his run for the Republican presidential nomination. He told visitors to his home at Oyster Bay not to offer him their support unless they were "prepared to say that every citizen of this country has got to be pro-United States first, last, and all the time, and not pro-anything else at all. . . ."[6] Roosevelt did not get the nomination, but his freewheeling use of the explosive loyalty issue set the tone for the general election. He suggested in Detroit, for example, that Henry Ford's pacifist campaign was "one of the most sinister developments of the last twenty-two months." To thunderous applause he charged that "a section of the professional German-Americans has joined the pacifists in the effort to keep America helpless." This was "moral treason to the American commonwealth." The *Literary Digest*'s press sample indicated broad support for Roosevelt's attacks.[7]

Wilson was not about to allow an old and bitter rival to monopolize so popular an issue. Accordingly, at the president's dictation, the Democratic platform declared "the supreme issue" to be "the indivisibility and coherent strength of the nation." It charged that there were "conspiracies" to advance "the interests of foreign countries" and condemned "as subversive of this nation's unity" every organization "that has for its object the advancement of the interest of a foreign Power, whether such object is promoted by intimidating the Government, a political party, or representatives of the people. . . ."[8]

As the campaign heated up, so did the antihyphen rhetoric. Both parties congratulated themselves on their own Americanism and suggested that the other was secretly appealing for the German-American vote, although neither bothered to explain how such an appeal could be shared with millions of voters and still remain secret. Both parties denied that citizens of German or Irish or eastern European extraction had any right to influence American foreign policy, and neither would entertain the notion that Anglo-Americans were hyphens in their own right. Roosevelt, campaigning for Hughes in Maine, denounced as "a foul and evil thing" any attempt to organize American citizens along "politico-racial" lines. Such ethnic associations were, he proclaimed in his favorite phrase, "moral treason to the Republic."[9]

Wilson won this competition with a melodramatic telegram exchange in October. Jeremiah A. O'Leary, of the American Truth Society, cabled the president charging him with being "pro-British," with "truckling to the British Empire," and with establishing a "dictatorship over Congress." Wilson sternly replied that "I would feel deeply mortified to have you or anyone like you vote for me. Since you have access to many disloyal Americans and I have not, I will ask you to convey this message to them." The *Literary Digest* found "widespread approval" in the press for this "stinging retort."[10] Wilson had come a long way from his statement, early in the year, that the danger of alien disloyalty had passed.

There is no precise way of measuring the impact of the loyalty issue in the campaign; nor can we gauge with any exactitude the contribution its antihyphenism made to the national mood when war came a few months later. Some antialien sentiment was inevitable in any event. But the politicians of 1916 stepped away from the opportunity to reassure Americans about each other and made worse an already dangerous situation.

Only the small band of cultural pluralists among the experts sought to warn against this turn of events. One spokesperson was Grace Abbott, of the Chicago-based Immigrant Protection League. She urged social experts not to join in "the tyranny of this sort of Americanization." The "fostering of our national egotism," she wrote, "would increase our racial prejudice, our fear of the 'inferior peoples' who are coming to 'dilute the old American stock' and to 'destroy the old American ideals.' " Rather than join in the politician's antihyphenate campaign, Abbott beseeched social experts to promote a "democracy of internationalism." This was a view having an obvious appeal to immigrants. Israel Friedlaender, who held the chair of Biblical Literature at the Jewish Theological Seminary of America, for example, called for a "constructive" Americanization that would encourage the immigrant Jew "to recreate for himself his former environment." And Edward A. Steiner, a Carpathian by birth, called for a "truly international" American civilization.[11]

Most experts, of course, had no intention of permitting immigrants to Americanize themselves. They hoped rather to convert the new national concern into support for their own programs just as, in 1917, they would hope to channel war-inspired hysteria into enthusiasm for reform.[12] And, in both cases, their spokesperson was John Dewey. Addressing the National Education Association in 1916, Dewey distinguished between two kinds of nationalisms. One, which he strongly endorsed, was a "unity of feeling and aim, a freedom of intercourse" that would replace the "earlier local isolations, suspicions, jealousies and hatreds" of an ethnically diverse America. This "real Americanism" rejected outright any adaptation made by immigrants in terms of their own cultural heritages. Dewey pronounced it a "dangerous thing . . . for each [ethnic] factor to isolate itself, to try to live off its past, and then to attempt to impose itself intact upon the other elements, or, at least, to keep itself intact and thus refuse to accept what other cultures have to offer. . . ." So much for a "democracy of internationalism."

Dewey stigmatized the other sort of nationalism as "a sense of unity within a charmed area . . . accompanied by dislike, by hostility, to all without." Many "influential and well-meaning persons" were attempting "to foster the growth of an inclusive nationalism by appealing to our fears, our suspicions, our jealousies, and our latent hatreds." In the face of "every hysterical wave of emotion, and of every subtle appeal of sinister class interest," Dewey called upon the public school teachers, "the consecrated servants of democratic ideas," to hold fast.[13]

It was perhaps second nature to Dewey, a logician of the first rank, to meet the growing national phobia toward aliens by making a distinction, but it was a utopian rather than a pragmatic procedure. Dewey's typology of nationalisms was similar to the position he took over the issue of American entry into the war. There he distinguished between force and violence. The war, he argued, was unavoidable because the misuse of force by Germany (in Dewey's language, violence) could only be met by force. Therefore, he held, those pacifists who indiscriminately condemned all uses of force were trying to resist the irresistible in the name of an abstract ideal. Worse, by taking a position of blanket opposition, they were avoiding their real moral responsibility, which was to humanize the American military effort by holding it to President Wilson's goals.[14]

So too Dewey argued that the "nationalizing" of American education—and of American life—for Dewey would never make *that* distinction—was inevitable. It was therefore essential that the experts, in this case the teachers, "the consecrated servants of democratic ideas," rather than the professional patriots be in charge. But the first rule of pragmatic discourse is that only those distinctions that actually *make* a difference truly express a difference. Making a difference, in this context, meant translating Dewey's distinctions into public policy, but this was just what Dewey had failed to explicate. In both cases what was involved was access to certain key institutions such as the Bureaus of education and naturalization, the Committee on Public Information, and the Council of National Defense, not to mention state and local boards of education. Were there experts in positions to influence these bodies? If there were, would they be willing or able to implement Dewey's suggestions?[15]

To answer these questions we shall look at several experts, or groups of experts, who sought to give some direction to the burgeoning Americanization movement. The first was Frances Kellor, a New York attorney, former settlement worker, and, in 1916, the secretary of the National Americanization Committee (NAC), which was, by far, the most important private organization active in the movement. In 1907 a group of New England businessmen formed the North American Civic League for Immigrants (NACL), an organization dedicated to changing "the unskilled inefficient immigrant into the skilled worker and efficient citizen."[16] Three years later the league joined with the New York State Immigration Commission, whose secretary was Frances A. Kellor, to form the New York Committee of the NACL. This body too was composed of industrialists and financiers.[17] Also in 1910, Kellor became the chief investigator of the New York State Bureau of Industries and Immigration. She did not, however, sever her connections with the business-oriented NACL. She apparently saw no conflict of interest, although as chief investigator she might well have to examine the activities of NACL members. In 1911, New Jersey created a similar bureau of immigration. Because the legislature appropriated no funds to operate it, the league's newly renamed New York-New Jersey Committee stepped in to provide them and to extend its governmental connections.[18]

By this time, the New York-New Jersey Committee was larger and more active than its parent, and it was not long before it separated from the NACL. In 1914, under its new name, the Committee for Immigrants in America, it expanded still further by providing the funds for a Division of Immigrant Education in the federal Bureau of Education.[19] In the days before the war, the division devoted most of its efforts to promoting factory classes in English and civics for alien workers. Its appeal, as its director, H. H. Wheaton, noted, was to employers and emphasized "practical considerations, such as increased efficiency, dimunition of accidents, and reduction of the cost of supervision, rather than a desire to engage in welfare work for employees."[20] It was guided, in other words, by the same purposes that had led to the founding of the NACL.

A new opportunity arose in 1915. The Bureau of Naturalization persuaded the mayor of Philadelphia to hold a public reception honoring his city's newly naturalized citizens. The mayor agreed; and on May 10, 1915, President Wilson came to commend the new Americans and to deliver his "Too Proud to Fight" speech. To take advantage of the resulting publicity the committee organized the National Americanization Day Committee and persuaded Frederick C. Howe, commissioner of immigration at Ellis Island, to write to mayors all over the country urging them to make July 4, 1915, Americanization Day in their communities.[21] This campaign proved so effective that the committee stayed in existence, calling itself the National Americanization Committee (NAC).

The NAC/Committee for Immigrants continued its policy of growth through subsidization in 1917 when it underwrote the creation of the Immigration Committee of the U.S. Chamber of Commerce.[22] Although the original North American Civic League maintained an independent stance and some local chambers, unaffiliated with the U.S. Chamber of Commerce, sponsored Americanization drives in their communities, the

NAC had, by 1917, made itself the authoritative voice of the business community on the Americanization question. It had developed governmental connections that most interest groups usually only dream about. Kellor had become the spokeswoman for this network of committees, bureaus, and divisions. She was assistant to the chairman of the Committee on Immigration, vice-chairman of the Committee for Immigrants, and a member of the Executive Committee and later vice-chairman of the NAC.[23] As such she could influence public policy far more than Dewey. And, unhappily for Dewey's distinction between good and bad forms of nationalism, she had quite definite ideas of her own about what that policy ought to be.

Her prewar program was a combination of scientific management and cultural hegemony very much in harmony with the interests of her backers and the "new nationalism" of Theodore Roosevelt. She had, in fact, been active in the Progressive campaign of 1912; and in 1916 she began to advocate "industrial preparedness," a position obviously modeled on Roosevelt's call for military readiness. "Industrial preparedness" required the "unity of all peoples in America behind America's flag on American soil." It contained three elements. The first was the "elimination of the physical toll [on industrial workers] by such physical construction of the plant as will give the best possible conditions in light, air, freedom from dust, wash and lunch rooms and appliances for preventing and dealing with accidents." Second was "the elimination of production tolls by economy in administration, elimination of waste, etc., by the adoption of so-called efficiency methods." And third was "the elimination of citizenship tolls . . . by the adoption of methods which will conserve workmen and stabilize the labor market."[24]

These proposals, while toll-free, had a distinctively progressive ring. They suggested science and conservation and enlightened public policy; they suggested, in the terms popularized by Walter Lippmann, "mastery" instead of "drift." In detail, Kellor intended:

> to put English-speaking workmen in its [the American city's]
> factories, men able to understand orders and guard against
> accident; men able to grasp American industrial ideals, open
> to American influences and not subject only to strike agita-
> tors or foreign propagandists; to turn indifferent ignorant
> residents into understanding voters, participants in the laws

under which they reside; to make immigrant homes American homes and to carry the American standards of living
to the farthest corners of the community; to unite foreign-
born and native alike in enthusiastic loyalty to our national
ideals of liberty and justice.[25]

Here is a clear illustration of the conservative implications of much con-
ventional progressive rhetoric. "Conserve workmen" and "stabilize the
labor market" meant getting foreign-born workers to "understand orders,"
and "to grasp American industrial ideals" meant immunization against
"strike agitators or foreign propagandists." All of this was grouped under
the general rubrics of "unity" and "enthusiastic loyalty." John Higham
dates Kellor's "slip" from the concepts of the welfare state to those of
welfare capitalism at 1917 "once wartime apprehensions muted progressive aspirations." This, to judge from these 1916 articles, does not appear
to have been the case. Higham understates both the continuity of Kellor's
opinions and their congruence with the interests of her backers in the
NAC. At the same time, he exaggerates the difference between Roosevelt
progressives and welfare capitalists. Herbert Hoover, after all, had been
a Bull Mooser in 1912.[26]

If the war did not "mute" progressivism, it did highlight the repressive
side of social engineering. That side had always been present; the war
merely accentuated it. The NAC spared no effort to shape federal policy
toward immigrants during the war. Its subsidy of the Division of Immigrant Education in the Bureau of Education gave it a friend in Secretary
of the Interior Franklin K. Lane, whose department housed the bureau.
And it was Lane who first proposed to the Council of National Defense
that an advisory commission prepare recommendations on "the matter
of the alien and his relation to the war activities of the United States. . . ."
This commission's first act was to call "into conference representatives
of the National Americanization Committee and its affiliated organizations" to draw up a "War Policy for Aliens."[27]

In a joint memorandum, the NAC and its *alter ego,* the Committee for
Immigrants, painted a lurid picture of the immigrant menace. Thirteen
million newcomers lived apart from America's "national institutions and
life in colonies, camps, and quarters isolated from American control."
Neglected by the government, the immigrants were ignorant "of where
they are, what they are doing and of attitude [*sic*] toward America."

Moreover, "the inheritance of industrial injustices and unfavorable living conditions" decreased manpower and enabled "pacifists, agitators, and other anti-American groups to ferment [sic] unrest, dissatisfaction and disloyalty." Specifically, German agents were "retarding production, damaging property, endangering life . . ." while the IWW was "making active propaganda and headway among aliens friendly toward America." This all contributed to "the prevalence of industrial unrest, sabotage, strikes, riots, and other labor disturbances, not only in war industries but throughout the country." There was also, the memorandum warned, an "increase in fires, accidents, explosions and other damage to property in industry vital to the production of war materials." Worse still, "the control of industries by aliens and [the] anti-American influences in industries holding war contracts" delayed mobilization. Last but not least on the list of dangers was "the influence of some of the foreign-language press. . . ."[28]

The NAC was but one voice in a chorus of alarm. Senator Lee Overman (D., North Carolina), for example, defended the Espionage Act of 1917 as necessary to protect the nation from the 100,000 German spies he claimed were at work. The number was supplied, he said, by "creditable reports from secret-service men" passed on to him by the Department of Justice.[29]

So grave a situation demanded strong countermeasures, and the NAC was eager to suggest them. It advocated a four-point policy that included the surveillance of all aliens whether from enemy countries or not; "elimination of incentives of unrest, disorder and disloyalty"; the placing of enemy aliens on probation so they could work in nonwar industries and friendly aliens in the military of either the United States or their native countries; and, finally, provision of Americanization opportunities to all newcomers who wished to become citizens. To carry out this sweeping policy, the NAC urged the Council of National Defense to appoint a committee on Americanization. Laws would also be needed. Real estate owners would be required to register their tenants with the government semiannually. Immigrants would have to declare their intention of learning English and applying for citizenship or face deportation. A federal bureau would regulate private employment agencies, a measure presumably directed against the *padrone* system. Congress would fund the Division of Immigrant Education. Moreover, the council itself would regulate housing and working conditions, establish standards of industrial safety and public health, prohibit the soliciting of labor from war industries, and create a priority board for the allocation of labor. Finally, the council was to set up an Americanization program that would study and tighten citizenship requirements, secure the cooperation of ethnic societies in a war policy for aliens, and run English and civics classes for interned enemy aliens.[30]

The advisory commission consolidated most of these recommendations into a call for a special committee of "experts on immigration and alien conditions," which would coordinate federal Americanization efforts, formulate "a sound national policy," and prepare "recommendations for legislative action." Even in this milder, or at least vaguer, form, the NAC's war policy seemed "unwise" to the council, which held that it should not take "any special or extraordinary action apart from the normal and customary functions now exercised with reference to aliens by authorized agencies." The council voted to refer the report to the Bureau of Education and the Department of Labor, which contained the bureaus of naturalization and immigration, with the advice that "the alien question should continue to be handled along broad educational lines as heretofore, and that the direction of effort should be toward expediting normal processes."[31]

So sweeping a rejection normally would have meant that Kellor's proposal was a dead letter; but the NAC was not a normal interest group. It was instead the senior partner in a joint venture with the Bureau of Education to control federal Americanization policy, and the Council of National Defense had labeled the "alien question" an "educational" one. Thus, on December 13, 1917, the council did not hesitate to endorse "the efforts of the United States Bureau of Education" and to "request the cooperation of the State Councils of Defense and committees of public safety, [in] developing this educational policy." When the bureau subsequently submitted a proposal for the cooperation of the state councils, the national council routinely approved it. In doing so, it approved a number of NAC recommendations it had previously rejected.[32] Soon thirty-five state councils were operating Americanization bureaus along the suggested lines.

George Creel, chairman of the Committee on Public Information, recounted what the state councils' idea of Americanization was. During Liberty Loan drives, men from the councils would visit the homes of the foreign-born and "insist upon a statement of earnings, expenditures, savings, etc.," and then stipulated the contribution "dazed victims were expected to make." Anyone who protested this high-handed treatment was put down as a "slacker" or as disloyal. These then faced possible "expulsion from the community, personal ill treatment, or a pleasant little attention like painting the house yellow."[33] The NAC of course was not responsible for this patriotic hooliganism. On the other hand, by advocating the surveillance of all aliens and the deportation of those who did not become citizens, the NAC did contribute to the overall atmosphere that made gangsterism a measure of one's devotion to one's country.

Power over the national purse resides, according to the Constitution, with Congress. But, as we have seen, it was possible until the end of fiscal 1919 for private groups to fund public agencies. Thus bureaucrats, such as Interior Secretary Lane, could enter into "understandings" with private interests over matters affecting millions of citizens and immigrants alike. The activities of the Division of Immigrant Education had never been authorized by Congress, nor were they subject to congressional oversight. Even the Council of National Defense had no clear idea of what it had approved when it endorsed the Americanization activities of the Bureau of Education. The NAC had achieved, in short, a quasi-governmental status by the end of 1917. The scope of its activities was limited only by its own financial resources, which, while considerable, were already committed to a wide range of programs, and by the imagination of Kellor.[34] Kellor recognized only the sky as a limit.

By the early spring of 1918 she was eager to push ahead on those parts of the NAC's recommendations to the Council of National Defense that could not be grafted onto the Division of Immigrant Education's work. As she complained to Commissioner of Education P. P. Claxton, "notwithstanding the many plans outlined, the work actually in hand of the Division is on the subjects of teaching English and civics and reducing illiteracy, and getting the support of various agencies for this work." What was needed, she argued, was a new agency, nominally under the Bureau of Eudcation, but staffed, financed, and directed by the NAC. The need, she wrote, was urgent:

> I am deeply concerned by the realization that no existing
> Government agency is effectively reaching the non-English-
> speaking groups and that the most insidious forms of
> propaganda are making headway unchecked among them.

There are literally thousands of foreign-language organizations in the United States fighting among themselves for
independent and united native countries or to preserve
their racial solidarity here. On the other hand, there are but
few such organizations whose first interest is Americanization or to help America win the war. Is there not some way
that this can be done by increasing the scope of the work
you have already started?

It seems to me that the time is just right for the Department of the Interior to take this whole situation in hand
and make a big contribution to war work, because we
cannot succeed with armies and munitions unless we get
united support behind them.

The "big contribution" involved a massive effort to co-opt the foreign-
language organizations in the country. Some of Kellor's plans included
the creation of "loyal" ethnic associations, the recruitment of "racial"
leaders, the supplying of patriotic copy to the foreign-language press,
and the establishment of a nationwide "information" network consisting of "correspondents" in "schools, industries, churches . . . and other
local organizations that now directly and easily reach the foreign-language
groups." The surveillance of aliens, in other words, was still on the NAC
agenda. Such a large effort would ultimately require congressional fund-
ing; Kellor suggested an initial appropriation of $500,000. She, however,
had no desire to wait for Congress to act. "The question of funds should
not stand in the way of this immediate war work, and I think they can
be provided until such time as the Government can finance it wholly, if
a satisfactory plan of administration can be adopted."[35]
    "A satisfactory plan of administration" was worked out within a few
weeks. It involved the wholesale appointment of the NAC's staff as "special
collaborators" in the Bureau of Education at a salary of $1 a year. Kellor
became the "special advisor" to the commissioner, with direct supervision
over the new agency, which was called the War Work Extension. Tech-
nically, all policies of the extension were to be determined by the commissioner of education under the direction of the secretary of the interior,
but all were also to be, "before their adoption, . . . discussed with duly
authorized representatives of the National Americanization Committee."[36]

In practice, all policy initiatives came from Kellor. The NAC paid the
piper; it also called the tune.

There is no way of telling how large the extension might have become
had the war not ended a mere six months after its creation and had Congress not decided to prohibit the use of private moneys by public agencies. Certainly Kellor's plans were grandiose enough, and certainly she
had more than enough persistence and ingenuity. She had a secure base
of operations within the Bureau of Education; she had powerful business
support; she had already demonstrated the superfluity of congressional
action; and she had maneuvered her way around the opposition of the
Council of National Defense. She even managed to work out an "understanding" with a potentially dangerous bureaucratic rival, George Creel,
whose Committee on Public Information's mandate extended to many
of the areas she had marked out for the extension. These areas of overlap
can be most easily seen by comparing Kellor's description of the extension's work with Creel's account of his agency. Kellor claimed that the
purposes of the extension were:

> As a war emergency [,] through the cooperation of loyal
> leaders of racial groups and otherwise [,] to win the full
> loyalty of all classes of our foreign-born population by
> instruction through the foreign language press and otherwise
> in regard to the history and resources of the country, the
> principles of democracy, our manners and customs and our
> social, civic, economic and political ideals, and to give instruc-
> tion in regard to the causes of the war, its aims and purposes,
> the methods of prosecuting it and the relation of the foreign-
> born population thereto.[37]

The Creel committee clearly tried to monopolize federal publicity and
propaganda; and its Division of Work with the Foreign Born inundated the
foreign-language press with patriotic copy. Creel estimated that some
600 of these papers, with a combined circulation of over 5 million,
"turned over their news and advertising columns" to his committee. The
Creel committee also recruited "racial" leaders and used them to establish
"loyal" ethnic associations such as the "American Friends of German
Democracy."[38]

It is not at all surprising that the two agencies should have embarked on such similar programs, since Kellor had drawn up her plans for the extension while supervising a study of ethnic organizations undertaken by the NAC for the Creel committee.[39] Although Creel later tried to disclaim any connection with those he called the "professional Americanizers,"[40] a category that surely included Kellor and the NAC, the programs of both his committee's Division of Work with the Foreign Born and the War Work Extension grew out of Kellor's study. The central focus, as befitted any NAC-inspired project, was on America's "serious industrial situation." Industrial "preparedness" gave way, with the outbreak of war, to industrial "Americanization"; but the content of the scheme changed little. It still combined, that is, scientific management techniques with cultural hegemony. "Industrial Americanization," wrote Kellor, "holds the greatest hope for the prevention of labor troubles, for the stabilizing of the labor market, for increased production through securing the cooperation of foreign-language groups, for enabling our industries to stand the strain of the economic changes of the war."[41]

Kellor claimed that "Mr. Creel authorizes me to say that this program will have his full cooperation . . . so much is he convinced of the immediate necessity of the undertaking of this work on a broad scale that upon my request and with the Secretary's [that is, Franklin K. Lane's] approval, he will go personally to the President and urge that an appropriation be made from this general fund for the work in your [P. P. Claxton's, the Bureau of Education] Bureau." And when Claxton spoke with Creel on the subject, he was able to report to Lane that Creel thought "Miss Kellor is admirably fitted for this work. . . ."[42]

Creel and Kellor continued to cooperate for the duration of the war. Once her extension and his committee's Division of Work with the Foreign Born were both launched, there was considerable danger of overlap, not to mention competition. To forestall this, the Creel committee, the Bureau of Education, and the Council of National Defense entered into a formal "understanding," which provided for weekly meetings to coordinate their efforts. It also recognized the leading role in Americanization to be played by the extension providing a full description of its activities while describing the Creel committee and the Council simply as "also interested in certain phases of this work. . . ."[43]

Whether this agreement would have held up over the course of a longer war is a moot point. Creel had great ambitions for his committee, and it may be he would have tired of playing second fiddle. Certainly it did not take him long, once the war was over, to try to disassociate himself from the "understanding." There is no mention of it, for example, in his *How We Advertised America.* He did mention Kellor's study of ethnic associations, but omitted both her name and her connections with the NAC. And he claimed that his agency "steered clear of the accepted forms of 'Americanization'. . . ."[44]

It was not so much the Armistice as the congressional ban on the use of private funds by public agencies that led to the demise of the War Work Extension. By the end of 1918, NAC chairman Frank Trumbull could report that fourteen of the original twenty-one recommendations his organization had made to the Council of National Defense had been wholly or partially implemented.[45] He did not bother to mention that the council had once rejected all of them. Businessmen in the NAC had reason to bemoan the loss of their connection with the Bureau of Education, especially because the extension had built up a network of "hundreds" of leaders of foreign-language groups who were cooperating with its work.[46] Peace had not, in the eyes of the NAC, in any way lessened the urgency of Americanization.

True, the dangers of German propaganda, industrial espionage, and sedition had passed; but the Bolshevik revolution in Russia and the gathering signs of labor militancy in the United States seemed to pose still greater dangers. Kellor warned that the postwar immigrant would be "a new kind of workman who brings with him the Bolshevist theory of 'working slowly on the job,' " and she wondered:

> who can foresee what it will cost American business to re-
> ceive a million immigrants a year, teach them American
> methods, American technical skill, American ideals, the
> English language; and then have half of them, or more, re-
> turn to their native land in an unfriendly and unsympathetic
> attitude towards American business and towards the country,
> and with the bulk of their savings from American wages in
> their pockets.

Yet such immigrants were vital to the health of American capitalism. As Kellor put it, "the United States is now bent upon increasing production and lowering its cost, upon an open shop contest, and to further this it wants immigrant manpower." The newcomers were also needed as "consumers to take up the cheaper lines of goods to prevent waste, and thus lower the cost of living."[47]

So the need for Americanization was, if anything, even greater than before, and the NAC was not about to abandon the headway it had made as the War Work Extension. Its first step, in keeping with its strategy of co-opting "racial" leaders, was to reorganize itself in March 1919 as the Inter-Racial Council.[48] Kellor was vice-chairman. Next the council purchased the American Association of Foreign Language Newspapers. The association had been owned and managed by Louis N. Hammerling, who, although he had cooperated actively with the Creel Committee, had come under attack in the English-language press for accepting "neutrality" advertisements against the shipment of munitions prior to the American entry into the war.[49] The association supplied news stories and advertising to the foreign-language press, and the Inter-Racial Council intended to use it as part of its campaign against labor radicalism. With her customary candor, Kellor told the National Association of Manufacturers (NAM) that "we can make" the foreign-language papers "pro-American if we go about it in the right way." The "right way" was for the NAM to use the advertising facilities of her association as "a means of controlling the foreign-language press and shaping its influence along the lines of a better Americanism and in opposition to Bolshevism." The NAM endorsed her proposal; and because the Inter-Racial Council continued the NAC practice of financing the Immigration Committee of the U.S. Chamber of Commerce, Kellor's position as spokesperson for welfare capitalism became stronger than ever.[50]

In view of all this success, why was the Inter-Racial Council defunct by 1921? Businessmen, faced with warnings like Kellor's of the "new kind" of radicalized immigrant and faced with the economic downturn of 1920-21, turned to a simpler and less expensive form of relief than Americanization—restriction.[51] Kellor's elaborate schemes of education, propaganda, and co-option made sense to her backers only as long as cheap immigrant manpower seemed necessary. By 1921 many businessmen had come to doubt that it was. Congress, which had consistently refused to fund federal Americanization programs, reached the same conclusion by 1919. The report of the Committee on Immigration and Naturalization singled out three overriding reasons for restriction. One

was the rising rate of unemployment caused by military demobilization.
A second was the need to offer the recently discharged soldier first opportunity in obtaining a job. And the third was the belief that aliens were
entering the United States faster than they could possibly be Americanized.
The committee reasoned that the best way of keeping Bolsheviks out was
to keep everyone out.[52]

Kellor's success, then, was temporary at best. She accomplished what
she did, and it was considerably more than any other expert accomplished,
by promoting her ideas as necessary to the interests of her supporters. In
fact, she made those interests her own. Americanization became "the
systematic integration of the immigrant into American economic life."[53]
As such, Americanization had to meet the same test all business trans-
actions must: Did it pay? By 1921 businessmen began to doubt that it did.

Kellor's extensive connections with the Americanization work of the
Bureau of Education did not bode well for Dewey's hope that public
school teachers could somehow prevent the fostering of "an inclusive
nationalism" that appealed "to our fears, our suspicions, our jealousies,
and our latent hatreds." In fact, Dewey's formulation of inclusive nationalism could scarcely be improved upon as a description of the bureau's
approach to Americanization. It is not clear how much influence the
bureau actually exercised over classroom teaching. The bureau never tried
to measure its own effectiveness, and its contacts with local school officials seem to have been mainly through circular letters. How many of
these were read will never be known. Yet, a survey of local conditions
indicates surprisingly little diversity between federal and local approaches
to Americanization.

Although public school teachers may well have been, as Dewey claimed,
"the consecrated servants of democratic ideas," defining those ideas was
a political rather than a philosophical process. His hopes, therefore, rested
less upon teachers' ideals than upon how school board members, superintendents, principals, and other school officials chose to interpret American
ideals. Virtually all of them subscribed to David Rosenstein's dictum that
"education . . . is the only sure, unfailing weapon in this struggle" for
Americanization. And most would also have agreed with J. George Becht,
of the Pennsylvania Board of Education, that there was "no branch of
study that will not lend itself to training for civic righteousness and civic
efficiency."[54] On the other hand, few school systems prior to 1917 even
had programs to teach the English language to immigrants, to say noth-

ing about American ways. In fact, the New York State Department of Education inaugurated the first statewide program of any kind in 1916.[55] The school programs were conceived of and carried out as "war measures."

This alone would have been sufficient to crush the hopes of Dewey or those of immigrants like Lewis Rockow that "Americanism . . . should not be considered by any one of our citizens as the catch-word by which one racial group covers its attempt to dominate the other racial factors." Americanism covered that much and more. Even before the United States entered the war, the Los Angeles school board forbade "criticism of the President of the United States or Congress by teachers in the Los Angeles public schools." Howard K. Beale reported cases of teachers ordered to limit their classroom presentations to only those materials in their textbooks. One teacher in Maine was dismissed for taking driving lessons from an unnaturalized German immigrant.[56]

In New York City, which had the largest foreign-born population in the country, John L. Tildsley, associate superintendent of schools, spearheaded the drive for conformity. He charged that in city high schools, "where the pupils are largely foreign born or of foreign-born parents, it cannot be denied that Socialistic views are in the ascendency." He blamed "the attitude of some of the teachers" because "being themselves pacifists, internationalists or even Socialists, they only mildly rebuke pupils who express unpatriotic sentiments." For himself, Tildsley differed "absolutely" with "a lot of these teachers" who believed "that by giving absolute freedom of discussion to children you enable them to reach proper conclusions." And he allowed no doubts about what the "proper" conclusions were to be. Because "public school teachers are state servants," they had "obligations to the state higher than those of ordinary citizens." It was "their business to support organized institutions, not to oppose them." It was the teachers' duty to teach that whatever was, was right. Or, as Tildsley put it while interrogating teachers at De Witt Clinton High School: "Should not children leave high school with the idea that whatever institutions have survived the test of time are more probably right than those that have not?" The superintendent's besetting fear was that students would think for themselves. "What would you do," he demanded of Clinton teachers, "to curb the individualistic tendencies of our boys— Russian Jews?" Not all of the answers, apparently, were acceptable, because three teachers were dismissed and six more transferred.[57]

New York City teachers learned their lesson. A. Franklin Ross, of

Stuyvesant High School, another school with large numbers of first- and second-generation Americans, wrote that "the spirit of America . . . can be clearly defined and taught with brilliant results." His definition stressed the "willingness to sacrifice all that one has of material goods or of life itself, if need be, to preserve the state." Meanwhile, the mayor's Committee on National Defense, calling for "One City, One Loyalty, One People," planned to make over the city's evening schools for foreigners.[58]

Teachers elsewhere learned as well. Peterson and Fite estimate that there were many episodes similar to those in New York of which no records remain because the accused received no hearing. And Howard K. Beale concludes that in "thousands of cases" teachers were so cowed by administrative pressures "that they ceased, for the duration of the War, to have views of their own."[59]

All of these cases can be viewed as the regrettable excesses of a too intense patriotism, a patriotism that Dewey warned against and that teachers were powerless to influence. But the De Witt Clinton episode clearly demonstrates that patriotism had its ulterior uses as well. It may not have been merely coincidental that all of the dismissed teachers, and four of the six transferred, were Jews. Nor may it have been coincidental that all nine had been active in trying to set up a Teachers' Council to influence school policy and were members of the Teacher's Union.[60] This was a pattern that persisted, in New York City at least, into the postwar era. At that time, Superintendent of Schools William L. Ettinger was leading the crusade. One of his more celebrated victims, Benjamin Glassberg, charged "because I am a Jew, a Socialist and a member of the Teacher's Union I have been dismissed."[61]

Not only could school officials use Americanization as a bludgeon against those who challenged their authority, they could also inculcate a general economic and political conservatism in its name. As early as 1915, for example, Lew M. Dougan, principal of the Shaw School in St. Louis, suggested to a meeting of superintendents at the National Education Association convention that "we shall do well to consider carefully whether it is not better to teach these men [northern Italians and Sicilians] to live decently and happily in the station they now occupy than to push them upward and get another shipload to take their places." Two years later, Commissioner of Education Claxton summoned an "America First" conference of school authorities to meet jointly with the U.S. Chamber of Commerce. The goal was to bring "into practical relation employers and educators."[62]

Nationwide, the schools took a hard line. State after state required that all instruction, public or private, be in English so that, in the words of Chicago School Board member Max Loeb, immigrants could be "subject to the influence of the daily English newspaper—the one great common unifying factor." Several states also passed loyalty laws to govern teachers. Iowa even prohibited the use of all foreign languages in public. Telephone conversations and religious services also fell under the ban.[63]

As the gale of repression mounted, a third group of experts, the settlement workers, sought to channel popular pressure for Americanization into support for their own programs. Settlement workers provide excellent cases for the argument that experts viewed Americanization as a professional opportunity and presented their expertise as indispensable in the campaign for "100 percent Americanism." The settlement workers had made a heavy rhetorical commitment to protecting their immigrant neighbors. If any group of experts could have been expected to resist the rush to conformity, it would have been these. And, in fact, Mary K. Simkhovitch, president of the National Federation of Settlements (NFS) in 1917, called on the member houses to "protect from inconsiderateness or insult Americans of German or Austrian descent." "Now," she urged, "is the very time to love our neighbors as ourselves."[64] On the whole, however, these experts were neither willing nor able to afford immigrants much protection.

Their general approach was to insist that the laudable goal of Americanization could be best achieved through their own special methods. Graham Taylor, for example, president of the NFS in 1918, criticized the enforced use of English in Iowa on the grounds that "the methods of suppression" have "failed always and everywhere." He did not dispute that "required schooling in the English language and in preparation for citizenship is indeed the demand and the response of the hour. . . ." All he wished was that "in this just requirement" compulsion be "offset" by persuasion.[65] This was much the same strategy Dewey had urged upon teachers, namely, to ennoble war-inspired nationalism by emphasizing its positive side. So Taylor and NFS secretary Robert A. Woods greeted, in 1918, as a token "of the greater America that is to be" the "new national consciousness, embracing all races, classes and conditions among us in one great community of interests."[66] There is no denying that immigrants would have had it easier under this policy of persuasion; but like the public school teachers, the settlement workers found they could not compete successfully with the advocates of coercion. It was the National

Americanization Committee that won public and business support. Instead of presenting a real, if much smaller, alternative to the NAC, settlements tended to provide a pallid and euphemistic shadow of it.

Kingsley House in Pittsburgh was one of the many settlements that discovered in 1917 that " 'Americanization' better expresses" its "citizen making" purpose. The United Neighborhood Houses (UNH), an association of New York City settlements, also boarded the patriotic bandwagon with a financial appeal featuring testimonials from Charles Evans Hughes and others attesting to their worth "as Americanizing agencies and stabilizing influences in these critical times [1919] of unrest."[67] But while settlement leaders hoped that "those who sincerely desire Americanization" would be "the very ones to be staunch supporters of the settlements at this time," it was not to be. The NAC's survey of organizations working with the foreign-born did concede that settlement houses had "the welfare of America at heart" (Kellor was, after all, a former settlement worker). Its main conclusion, however, was that they proceeded "in a disorganized and aimless way."[68]

A Carnegie Corporation committee "to study the agencies and processes that affect the fusion of native and foreign-born Americans" reached similar conclusions even though the chief of its investigation, Allen T. Burns, was himself a former settlement worker.[69] This criticism from a quarter that might have been expected to form a more generous estimate of their activities raised serious problems for the settlements. This was especially so for the NFS, which was seeking Carnegie funds for itself. The NFS's contact with the corporation was Charles L. Taylor, the former president of Kingsley Associations. His advice, relayed to Woods by Kingsley head worker Charles C. Cooper, was for the NFS to ignore "the criticisms of the Americanization study." The corporation "would decline to make any contribution to the settlement movement, if the same could be construed as condemning their own published reports." Cooper's advice was to "make our appeal on more general and broad lines, as educational institutions, especially necessary in this period for their stabilizing influences in foreign and in some cases, unfriendly neighborhoods." With "our houses . . . nearly all to-day gravely embarassed [sic] for funds," Woods agreed that, for the purposes of soliciting Carnegie money, "the settlement is distinctively educational. . . ."[70]

To judge from the programs of the UNH there was a good deal of truth to the criticisms. It was not until the end of 1920, when the UNH came under fire from the New York State Joint Legislative Investigating Committee as a breeding ground of anarchy and sedition,[71] that it even drew up a formal Americanization program. It had, on the other hand, been raising money as an Americanizing agency for some time previously. The program it finally adopted embodied the settlements' familiar contention that the state could catch more flies with honey. This was a *pro forma* position. The UNH felt "no measure affecting the foreign-born population should be finally adopted [by New York State] without consultation with the local leaders of the foreign-born groups affected." For "their advice will result in changing the form of a measure without affecting its intention." The UNH, that is, like the NAC and the Creel committee, believed in co-option. This was all the "protection" the UNH wanted to offer the immigrant. For the rest it was eager to transform itself into an active agent of the state. Since "Americanization is an educational process," the UNH urged the state Department of Education to subsidize settlement houses so that they could "secure trained and fit instructors capable of organizing and conducting groups in English, civics, literature and debating and public speaking." In this connection "a special system of instruction should be devised by which American ideals and customs should be taught in connection with classes in English." And, as if this were not enough of a duplication of the NAC program, "pamphlets should be prepared meeting Anti-American propaganda and given free circulation through all available agencies."[72]

The contrast between this militant rhetoric and the actual Americanization programs of the city's settlements is stark. The College Settlement, for example, did "little Americanization work." Its main effort, it reported to the UNH, was its camp at Mount Ivy, where it was "fighting [the] natural Jewish aversion to [the] out of door life." The Hudson Guild reported it had "no need of [a] definite program" because it was located in an Irish neighborhood. The fact is that most settlements could only point to clubs or societies like the East Side House Loyalty Club for examples of their Americanization activities. The East Side House Loyalty Club was for foreign-born mothers who marched into a meeting room, saluted the flag, sang club and other songs, and conducted meetings "in very broken English." "Following the meeting is a program of games which had been suggested by the Social Committee and accepted in the business meeting. Refreshments are served at about twenty minutes before ten and followed by dancing until a few minutes after ten."[73]

In February 1921 the UNH finally got around to trying to coordinate
its Americanization programs, such as they were. The chairman of its
Americanization Committee, Dr. Henry Fleishman, of the Educational
Alliance, told a series of meetings that for years "settlements had waited
for the immigrant to come to them" and that "the time had now come
for the Settlements to go to the immigrant." He proposed dividing the
city into districts, with each house serving as a center for one district.
Lists of new immigrants could then be "divided amongst all [the] districts and sent to the different settlements." Tentative plans were drawn
up to put this plan into effect in the fall of 1921, but the federal policy
of restriction made them academic.[74]

Neither its bristling rhetoric nor its innocuous programs sufficed to
protect the UNH from legislative harassment, and neither permitted the
settlements to play much of a role in Americanization. Kellor's assess-
ment was correct. They had the best interests of America at heart; that
is, they defined those interests as she did; but they proceeded "in a disorganized and aimless way."

By the mid-1920s, the UNH had retreated from most of the positions
it had staked out for itself as an Americanizing agent and began to ac-
knowledge what it had always been doing, working with immigrants.
No longer preoccupied with demonstrating that they could scientifically
transform an alien into a "100 percent American," settlement workers
took up the difficult questions of whether it was better to work with
children or adults, whether settlement clubs should be organized along
racial or international lines, whether workers should build upon or disregard their clients' religious commitments. All were crucial issues if the
settlements were to foster assimilation. None, however, had been resolved
to the UNH's satisfaction. Individual settlements, that is, continued to
operate on a trial-and-error basis, doing whatever seemed to work best in
their particular neighborhoods. A committee looking into these questions
acknowledged that the catch-as-catch-can reality of settlement work with
immigrants indicated that more than thirty years of experience with the
foreign-born had yielded no "scientific" answers and consoled itself with
the hope that an increased awareness of the difficulties would "at least
provoke further and more detailed study. . . ."[75]

If the UNH had no hard and fast answers to the questions it was facing,
at least it had asked them and had admitted its own ignorance. This
honesty marked a return to sanity. The settlements had no foolproof

formulas for assimilation; but they did, by 1925, once again have mastery of their souls.

With the settlements' belated return to normalcy, there were only a few experts left to carry on the campaign for scientific Americanization. The most interesting were those associated with the Foreign Language Information Service (FLIS). They were social experts, journalists, and foreign-born intellectuals; and they defined their "job of understanding," as the title of one of their pamphlets has it, as being: "To interpret America to the Immigrant and the Immigrant to America to the end that the Immigrant may adjust himself to his new environment and that a mutual understanding and common purpose may be the heritage of all our people."[76] They are interesting because if the career of Kellor illustrates the price, measured in terms of intellectual integrity, an expert might pay for institutional support, the history of FLIS, once its umbilical cord to the wartime Committee on Public Information was cut, indicates that the lack of such support could exact an equal cost.

FLIS was a war orphan, and it spent its early years shuttling from one foster home to another. Like many another orphan, it suffered from the feeling of being unwanted. FLIS was eager to convince each prospective foster parent that, if adopted, it would fit into its new home. There was little chance, under these circumstances, that FLIS would develop any independent approach to Americanization; and, in fact, it did not. Instead, it tended to take its definition of the America it interpreted for the immigrant from whatever institutions gave it support.

The service began as the Division of Work with the Foreign Born in Creel's Committee on Public Information. The original inspiration for the division was Kellor's report to Creel on the loyalty of foreign-language organizations in the United States. We have already noted some of the resulting parallels between the division's activities and those of Kellor's own War Work Extension. Both Creel and division director Josephine Roche were quick, once the war was over, to condemn Kellor's brand of Americanization. Roche wrote of the "abuses which took place under its name" that made Americanization "an intolerable expression to the foreign born." As she put it in a report incorporated into Creel's *How We Advertised America:*

     . . . the ignorance of many native-born Americans about European peoples and their contemptuous attitude toward

persons with different customs from their own are just as
serious obstacles to assimilation and unity as the tendency
of some immigrants to cling to Old World ways; understanding must come on our part of the heritage of these newcomers, their suffering and struggles in Europe and the
contributions they bring us if we will only receive them.[77]

Such a call for understanding seems a far cry from Kellor's formulation
of assimilation as the "systematic integration" of the alien into the economy. Yet the activities of the division paralleled rather than challenged
those of Kellor's group. Starting from the NAC-supplied survey of "safe"
ethnic leaders, the division set up some fourteen associations such as the
American-Hungarian Loyalty League and the American Friends of German
Democracy. Roche described this as "a thoroughly democratic plan," but
it was actually thoroughly manipulative. The associations allowed the
government to display the loyalty of carefully selected immigrants in
carefully stage-managed settings. The most spectacular was arranged for
July 4, 1918 (under the terms of his understanding with the War Work
Extension, Creel got the Fourth of July whereas Kellor had to make do
with Flag Day). The idea, said Creel, was to have "Americans of foreign
birth and descent . . . manifest their loyalty." Through its ethnic contacts,
the division "put the idea up" to thirty-three language groups who agreed
to send a CPI-drafted petition to President Wilson. All went as planned.
On the great day itself representatives of the thirty-three sailed up the
Potomac on the presidential yacht to Mount Vernon, there to lay wreaths
on Washington's tomb and listen to a Wilson discourse on the proposed
League of Nations.[78]
The Fourth saw similar pageants in every major city, and each was
carefully planned by the division. A frantic telegram from division official
Will Irwin to the chairman of the Wisconsin State Council of Defense
captures the tenor of their planning:

Understand proposed mix all races up in procession at
Milwaukee celebration stop Purposes of the celebration cannot be fully carried out unless people march in racial groups
as they are doing in other large cities stop If this plan is
departed from in Milwaukee which is considered such a great
German stronghold it will be thought that Germans were
trying to evade proper representation in parade.[79]

Irwin's point is clear. How can you show off your loyal Germans if they
disappear into the general population?

The Fourth was good public relations, and that is what the Creel committee really meant by mutual understanding. Its major efforts were devoted to an extensive propaganda campaign among immigrants. The
division translated pamphlets and broadsides into nineteen languages.
Special material for foreign-language groups "sternly" revealed "the
methods and principles of Germany" and emphasized the "ideals of
America."[80] How well did all of this comport with the division's claim
to appreciate the "heritages" of America's foreign-born? Obviously,
appreciation disappeared in the insistence on conformity.

Witness the division's response, in its German Democracy *Bulletin,*
to a minor postwar incident. A group of German-Americans were enjoy-
ing an evening of song in the Far Rockaway section of New York City
when some of their native-born neighbors, who objected to the use of
the German language, summoned the police. The singers stood on their
constitutional right to sing whatever they wished, but they did agree, for
the future, to stick to English-language songs. One might expect the
division, given its ringing language about interpreting immigrants to
America, to have defended the singers. It might, for example, have defended their right to free speech or extolled the musical contributions
of Germans to American culture. The division, however, saw the matter
differently. In its view, the singers were clearly in the wrong. It was "not
primarily the language which is objectionable." Nor could it be because
the division was committed to the necessity of ethnic groups retaining
their own languages for the foreseeable future. Rather, it was that in
"many songs . . . something German is glorified—German land, the 'German Rhine,' the 'German heart,' 'German fidelity' " and so forth. Such
a song "arouses a sentimental often extravagant love for the days of one's
youth, what one loved in the past, what one left behind." Memories
were dangerous. They led to "a certain amount of homesickness and whoever is homesick for another country is lost for America." The proper
solution to the menace of homesickness was not English translations of
German songs. They would still be about the Rhine or the German heart
after all. No, the solution was German translations of English-language
songs, something the American Friends of German Democracy had taken
it upon themselves to provide. What the newcomer could keep was his
language—once it had been purged of Old-World sentiments. For the rest
of his heritage, "influence must be brought to bear upon the individual

who is to be Americanized in *every* thing that concerns his mind and his heart."[81]

The incident itself was a trivial one. But it is just for that reason that it is so revealing. It shows the true "100 percent Americanism" mentality at work. In such a perspective, no incident was minor. As Theodore Roosevelt had said in 1916, those who were "pro-anything else at all" could not be true Americans. In the same way, the "letter of the law" could not stand up to "the right of America to a homogeneous nation." That "right" was "above everything else." In every case, no matter how minor, "that must decide."[82]

Between the division's rhetorical commitment to understanding and tolerating ethnic diversity and its day-to-day work with immigrants there loomed an ever-widening chasm. This was not because Roche and her cohorts were insincere or hypocritical in their allegiance to mutual understanding and democracy. It was just that those objectives could not withstand prolonged exposure to an organization dedicated to bringing patriotism to a "white hot" level.

As we shall see in the next chapter, the Wilson administration responded to the armistice with a rapid and wholesale demobilization despite the strenuous protests of many experts that some of the wartime programs they had been associated with would prove equally necessary in peacetime. Hence it was that the Creel committee was disbanded in May 1919 even though, in those days of the Red Scare, concern for immigrant loyalty was running higher than ever. Unlike most experts, however, the staff of the Division of Work with the Foreign Born managed to keep their agency afloat. First they received a "special emergency" grant from the Carnegie Corporation. Then, on August 1, 1919, the division became the Foreign Language Information Service of the War Camp Community Services (WCCS). That arrangement lasted only to the end of the year because the WCCS found itself hard-pressed to raise money once the war was over and had to cut back its operations. As 1919 drew to a close, the FLIS, as it was now called, faced extinction. Only the willingness of its staff to work without compensation allowed it to survive until February 1920 when the American Red Cross came to its rescue. This arrangement too proved short-lived as even the Red Cross had to tighten its belt in the postwar period; and in mid-1921 the service became an independent agency, largely financed by foundations.[83]

On this basis FLIS survived, even if it did not precisely prosper, and was able to continue to practice its own brand of scientific assimilation. But was it truly FLIS's own? FLIS faced more than budget cuts as it searched for a stable financial base. It faced accommodating the interests of its potential backers, and that proved to be a more severe constraint on its program than lack of money.

Late in 1919, after it had become clear that the WCCS would discontinue its support and before the Red Cross agreed to step into the breach, FLIS's staff were desperately looking for a sponsoring agency. Just how desperate they were may be gathered from the fact that they tried to persuade Attorney General A. Mitchell Palmer to make FLIS a part of the Department of Justice. Palmer's demagogic red baiting was already fully apparent as was his belief that the "immigrant problem" was more quickly solved with prison sentences and deportations than by mutual understanding. Indeed, it would have been difficult to find a public official who believed less in understanding. Still his Justice Department was the government agency most actively involved with immigrants in 1919, and it was to Palmer that FLIS turned. Its American Press Bureau manager, Edward Hale Bierstadt, wrote to the attorney general requesting an interview. "I should like," Bierstadt wrote, "to lay before you some data respecting the present situation of the foreign born in America. I believe that you will find this material to be of interest, and, I trust, of service also."[84]

Palmer was too busy, perhaps planning the nationwide raids his department staged on New Year's Day, to see Bierstadt; but he did arrange an interview for him with his secretary, Robert T. Scott. This meeting was followed by a long letter, from Bierstadt to Scott, detailing FLIS's understanding of the alien situation and its recommendations for government action. The letter nicely illustrates the service's dilemma. FLIS needed a home, and Justice could provide one. But the hardliners in the department favored repression over understanding in dealing with immigrants. And the hardliners, headed by the attorney general himself, were in charge. How was FLIS to win Palmer's support when it thought his policies thoroughly wrongheaded?

To its credit, FLIS chose candor: "We realize . . . we are not placing ourselves in a friendly light. . . . It is only that we believe that the interests of this country are far more important than our own."[85] So saying, Bierstadt launched into a searing critique of the Red Scare and of Justice's role in it.

First of all he defended the loyalty of the foreign-language press (which, of course, was FLIS's bread and butter). "Our facts and figures do not at all agree with the list of the Attorney General [of seditious publications], and we are definitely of the opinion that Mr. Palmer has been misinformed." Moreover, Bierstadt maintained that Palmer's strong-arm tactics would prove less effective than FLIS's more subtle approach. "The small section of the frankly seditious press can best be hamstrung, not by dealing with it too openly and too severely, but by so strengthening the really constructive press that the seditious element will be snowed under." Echoing the arguments of Dewey and the settlement workers, Bierstadt held that "to chop off the head of the press suddenly, to suppress it violently would be to turn certain other elements, now semi-conservative at least, frankly toward radicalism."[86]

As this passage makes clear, FLIS's objections were over tactics, not goals. It had no quarrel with the suppression of radicalism, but it did object to the means. Palmer's coercive policies, Bierstadt argued, would actually further radicalize the foreign-born:

> We are also strongly of the opinion that the conduct of the raids upon such places as the Russian People's House in this city [New York] has been such as to terrorize and drive to the very border of panic many perfectly innocent people. . . . The effect of this on our foreign-born population is disastrous to a degree. They argue, and with some reason, that they are being treated no better than they used to be under the old tyrannical regime in their own country. Their lives and their property are in danger. Why not turn anarchist? They have nothing more to lose.[87]

The lesson for Justice, said Bierstadt, was that "the Government must not only deal with that portion of the foreign born which is considered to be dangerous, but it must support openly that far larger and stronger portion which is frankly loyal, lest this portion grow less." For that, it goes without saying, the department should turn to FLIS, which enjoyed the trust of the loyal foreign-language press. Otherwise sizable numbers of immigrants "will be driven forthwith into Bolshevism."[88]

Justice, by preferring repression to persuasion, was playing into the hands of a sinister conspiracy:

We are of the opinion that the foreign born . . . are being
used as a scape-goat by both organized capital and organized
labor. Public opinion is such, and has been deliberately made
such, that the alien is the most obvious and convenient element to blame for agitation in general. He is being used to
cloak the misdeeds of others. The conduct of the steel strike
by the owners was disgraceful in the extreme. . . . We are of
the opinion that the effort to discredit the alien is organized;
that literature, and even bombs [,] have been "planted"
before raids in the attempt to focus the mind of the general
public on a false issue. The proverbial red herring is being
dragged accross [sic] the trail.

We are further of the opinion that there is a small but distinct group of organized capital in this country today which
would ask for nothing better than an armed outbreak on the
part of some portion of labor.[89]

This was strong language, but not one word of it ever appeared in any
of the tens of thousands of press releases the service sent out to the
foreign- and English-language press. In fact, when the head of FLIS's
Danish Bureau sent out a release praising Louis F. Post, the assistant
secretary of labor, for reversing many of Justice's deportation orders,
Bierstadt replied to complaints from the Bureau of Investigation: "It
is so far from our policy to permit anything of this kind, that I could
hardly believe it; but having ascertained the truth, I thrashed the matter
out with him [the Danish Bureau chief] fully, and I assure you that there
is no possibility of its occurring again." Bierstadt himself had, in his letter
to Scott, stated "flatly that of the (approximately) 150 Russians de-
ported today, not more than 20 can be considered as really dangerous."
The others "could not well be considered seriously as either conspirators
or even agitators." The Justice Department's attitude "is a vastly mistaken one." All of this Bierstadt said himself, in FLIS's name, in a private
letter. But when the chief of the Danish section wrote "During the last
year [1919] hundreds of cases have appeared in which innocent persons
have been arrested on suspicion of their being anarchists . . . ," Bierstadt
rebuked him for "gross carelessness." The reason was that "no matter
what his personal feelings were, he had no right to express them officially,
as a member of this organization."[90]

FLIS's policy was to take no sides, in public, on controversial questions. The reason for this, the service maintained, was to preserve its "impartiality." But what did this amount to under these circumstances? Living from hand to mouth, FLIS always had to make sure that not even the slightest hint of suspicion had become attached to its work. For that reason, it would release no material even remotely critical of the government or important American institutions.

This policy was fully discussed at a joint meeting of its staff and board of trustees. Board chairman Allen T. Burns, who had previously headed the Carnegie Corporation's Americanization studies, asked if "Federal government material [over two-thirds of all FLIS releases came from federal sources] furnish a sufficient basis for the most effective press work—and to what extent, if any, [it] should . . . be supplemented." The danger of going outside of the government for material, he added, was that it might prove to be "propaganda." The chairman of FLIS's Editorial Committee agreed that "Government material is [the] best that can be used on [the] one hand for it reassures a number of our supporters who regard the foreign born as potential anarchists, or regards them with suspicion." Unfortunately, "from the journalistic point of view," "Government material is not so good." Therefore, the service was supplementing federal releases with "utilitarian and interpretative subjects." These were proving far more popular with the foreign-language press. "Yet," said Burns, "how could we quiet in the minds of our friends the question which might arise as to whether this material was as harmless as government material?" After all, "if we call it interpretative, they could question whose interpretation it was." Here is the core of FLIS's problem. It was organized to "interpret" America to the immigrant. "Whose interpretation" was precisely the question. The major part of the answer was "the government's." For the rest, one staffer offered "we might say it is from the encyclopedia." Read Lewis, who succeeded Roche as FLIS director, added "we have always said 'government and other authoritative sources.' " And still another staff member said "from school textbooks— We want to give [the immigrant] some knowledge of what [every] American boy acquires in school." Said Burns, "very good indeed. We use geographies and histories in schools and these certainly have the sanction of the government—[it] is good material and yet unquestionable as [a] source."[91]

FLIS would publish no material that its supporters might question. It would and did publish what it thought might please them. One example is a 1926 series of articles on American business firms. Its "primary purpose," wrote Lewis, was to acquaint immigrants with "the activities and significance of the great firms whose names are household words in America," but it "would also furnish the opportunity of acquainting the concerns described with the work of the F.L.I.S." and thereby lay "the basis for a subsequent financial appeal." Lewis recognized that "in the possible combination of these two things there are dangers of misunderstanding."[92] But he also knew how badly FLIS needed the money. The service had clearly come a long way from its 1919 view that a business conspiracy was responsible for the Red Scare.

Fears that the merest tinge of radicalism in its publications would drive away FLIS's supporters were derived from more than the conformist atmosphere of the day. Twice in its early years the service had had to defend itself against precisely this charge and so could cite its own experience on the necessity of being as above suspicion as Caesar's wife.

The first episode occurred during FLIS's association with the American Red Cross and involved the chief of its Ukrainian section, Nicholas Ceglinsky. Someone had apparently informed J. S. Ellsworth, chairman of the board of directors of the New York County Red Cross, that Ceglinsky was a Bolshevik sympathizer. A check with the Department of Justice, which turned over its raw (uncorroborated) files to the Red Cross, produced further charges. Ceglinsky had allegedly entered the country illegally and under an assumed name; he was a close associate of another alleged Bolshevik, Miroslav Sichinsky, who had supposedly "shot and killed Count Andrew Potocki," the Austrian governor of Galicia. Both were also charged with attacking "in their writings, the government, the President, Secretary [of State Robert] Lansing, and the issuance of Liberty Loan Bonds." Roche leaped to Ceglinsky's defense saying that "no one has done more effective work against the extremist movement than he." The charges, she claimed, came from "a small group" of Ukrainians whose efforts to exploit their fellow countrymen Ceglinsky had exposed. His position with FLIS was saved "because of his effective work against radical propaganda" and because of his extensive contacts in the Department of State and the Bureaus of Immigration and Naturalization.[93] But the lesson of the episode was not lost on FLIS.

Not four years later the service found itself in a similar situation. Now an independent agency, it received much of its support from the Laura Spelman Rockefeller Memorial Fund. And one of the fund's trustees received a "tip" that the service was "engaged in propaganda work." The foundation ordered an investigation of the service by two outside experts. Their report completely exonerated the agency,[94] as well it should have, because, as we have seen, FLIS carefully toed the patriotic mark.

Keeping up to the mark ensured FLIS's survival; it also defined the "America" it interpreted to immigrants. No meaningful independence of judgment was possible as long as the service limited itself to translating government materials. Some of these, for example information about tax laws, of course were helpful to immigrants. Some were innocuous. "Geographical Comparisons Between America and Europe" was both interesting and harmless. But some furthered policies that FLIS privately opposed. The service, that is, was easily co-opted in its early years. One case involved Secretary of Labor James J. Davis's scheme to register all aliens in the United States. Another was FLIS's cooperation with the Americanization work of the Bureau of Naturalization.

Davis, himself an immigrant from Wales, promoted registration as a virtual panacea. Fees would finance English and civics classes for aliens, and the registration card would identify each legal entrant to the country and thus help authorities apprehend those here illegally. Further, although Davis strongly denied that registration would involve anything like surveillance, it would, he claimed, allow the government to identify newcomers who had radical sympathies.[95] The foreign-language groups were understandably hostile to the plan. Many identified it with Old-World police state methods, and all objected to being singled out for special supervision.[96] And FLIS, when it finally took a stand on the issue in 1930, was equally opposed. Registration, its board resolved, was "unsound in principle, contrary to American ideals and traditions of personal liberty and would create abuses and problems more fundamental than any evil it might aim to cure. . . ."[97] But FLIS did not take this stand until almost a decade after Davis had proposed his scheme, and in 1921 it had begun a regular program of cooperation with the Department of Labor that involved promoting registration. The service reported to Davis on editorial reaction in the foreign-language press and translated and released material supporting his scheme.[98] "Impartiality" of this sort constituted an implicit endorsement.

FLIS also cooperated with the Bureau of Naturalization, supplying it with the names and addresses of foreign-language organizations interested in citizenship training. Yet, in its application for grant money from the Commonwealth Fund, the service described the bureau as overstepping the bounds of its authority in undertaking this kind of work and echoed the "adverse comment" made by educational authorities of the bureau's "educational methods."[99] The point is not that FLIS personnel were deceitful or opportunistic. The service depended on government agencies for its materials, and so it routinely cooperated with them. Both of these examples are of just such routine work. And that is the point. Co-optation involved no moral corruption. It was built right into the way FLIS operated.

Kellor identified from the outset with her business supporters. Her Inter-Racial Council openly avowed its intent to "guarantee certain standards in the editorial, news, and advertising columns" of the foreign-language press. It would "undertake to sell Americanism to the foreign-language press by giving it American advertising, promoting American living and standards, thereby enabling it to interpret America more fully than is now possible with sources of income and contacts so largely foreign." FLIS spoke far more softly. As its director, Read Lewis, said in a fund-raising letter:

> Working through the press . . . the Service is trying to do in
> a very practical way a sensitive and delicate thing; by means
> of accurate information and sympathetic understanding,
> to work out among the many different elements in our pop-
> ulation a more tolerant and effective unity, to replace prej-
> udice and suspicion with a sense of the common humanity
> shared alike by native and foreign born.[100]

But FLIS also sought to maintain "certain standards" of Americanism that gave its releases a fundamentally conservative, pro-business cast. It did so because to have done anything else would have frightened away its government contacts.

Once this has been established, it is important to credit FLIS with two substantial achievements. One is that it carefully avoided what Lewis stigmatized as appeals "to ignorance or fear." Had the service joined in the popular nativism of the day, "we might have rallied support more quickly, but we should have denied the very forces of intelligence and good will on which any solution of this interracial problem must be worked out."[101] The service did uphold standards of decency and tolerance in a period in which they were sorely needed.

The service also, beginning with its association with the War Camp Community Services in 1919, responded to tens of thousands of requests for information and aid from individual immigrants. Sometimes this involved getting refunds for aliens who had overpaid their taxes. Sometimes it meant locating missing relatives and friends. Sometimes it extended to gathering evidence for newcomers mistakenly accused of radical activities. In all cases FLIS was willing to help, and many an immigrant had reason to be grateful.[102]

All four of our case studies point to the same moral. Experts, given a choice of scientific orientations to the assimilation question, tended to select what we have called "cultural hegemony." This was, quite simply, the position that maximized the importance of their services. The others did not. Racialism asserted the rule of heredity; the economic orientation accented the impact of "low standard" immigrants on the labor market. Both led to restriction, a solution that did not require expertise to be implemented.

Cultural pluralism also asserted the superfluity of the experts. Even those few experts who espoused pluralism found this aspect of it unacceptable. Take, for example, the views of Julius Drachsler, a professor of government and sociology at the City College of New York. He argued that two factors were "irresistibly making for the amalgamation of the European peoples in this country." One was psychological; namely, "the keen desire, the almost pathetic willingness" of most immigrants "to fit as quickly and as inconspicuously as possible, into the general life about them." The other factor was biological, the "steadily increasing rate of intermarriage, breaking down within the span of one generation the solidarity of the group." Had the war not "crystallized the vague uneasiness . . . about the alien, into a neurotic dread of him, it is an open question, to my mind, whether these psychologic and biologic forces would not normally, naturally have fused, sooner or later, the great variety of groups making up the American population." Drachsler, however, did not call upon experts to leave well enough alone. His objection to the "laissez-faire policy" was that it lacked "that element of deliberateness which is the chief earmark of a social policy."[103] One could not ask for a clearer statement of the expert's creed: A consciously designed and managed policy was preferable to one of laissez faire no matter how well the latter worked.

Most experts, unlike Drachsler, were not products of immigrant neighborhoods and had little appreciation of the forces working "normally, naturally" for assimilation. Instead they shared the "vague uneasiness" of other native Americans about the immigrant. And the war "crystallized" these feelings into the "neurotic dread" Drachsler criticized. These experts assumed that assimilation would entail conformity to middle-class Protestant values. Cultural hegemony expressed their uneasiness and/or dread, their ethnocentrism, and their professional ambitions.

Hegemonists had little success in winning support until the war, and then they sought to make the most of the opportunities it seemed to afford. Their bids for support rested on the argument that the menace of the alien saboteur or subversive could be best met by broadly based educational programs directed at the entire alien population. Their argument adopted the exaggerated accounts of the immigrant peril that fueled the hysteria of the war and postwar years; their solutions, however, were curiously complex and roundabout. Espionage and sedition laws, the restriction of immigration—these were not enough said the experts. Vast schemes of uplift were also necessary.

Obviously the complex question of ethnic diversity could not be met by the wholesale imprisonment or deportation of aliens accused of disloyalty. But ethnic diversity was not the issue after 1916. The antihyphen crusade, in which many experts participated, had radically simplified matters. The issue had become "100 percent Americanism." Immigrants were to be pro-American "first, last, and all the time" and not "pro-anything else at all." For that the instruments of coercion were admirably suited. What use, after all, were English classes in catching spies? Would civics lessons curb labor militancy? Experts lost their credibility once the issues were so starkly posed. The best way of keeping Bolsheviks out of the country was to keep everyone out. The best way to deal with the disloyal already here was to send them back to where they came from. Restriction and repression, not Americanization, prevailed.

Furthermore, as we have seen, experts had to bid for power in institutional settings they did not control. These four cases yield four distinct strategies dictated by the particular circumstances each group faced.

Frances Kellor exercised the most influence of the four but only by making herself the spokeswoman for the welfare capitalists who funded, and set the policy of, the NAC. Some schoolteachers also chose to identify with the views of those in positions of power. Others chose resistance and were quickly crushed. Most, however, chose silence. They ceased, as Howard Beale wrote, to have opinions of their own. Settlement workers chose a third path. They appropriated the label "Americanization" for their ongoing programs. This, they hoped, would lead to increased contributions. Finally, we have seen the Foreign Language Information Service try to combine brave words about toleration and mutual understanding with reassurances to government, foundations, and other supporters that its work was entirely "safe."

Of the four strategies, Kellor's clearly worked best. She was able, at least for a time, to develop a strong base of support and use it to maneuver at the highest levels of government and finance. She could do so, however, only within the constraints of welfare capitalism; and her support evaporated when businessmen came to doubt the profitability of Americanization. Schoolteachers and settlement workers did considerably worse. The former could hope only to ride out the storm. The latter managed to raise some money; but as we shall see in Chapter 7, their militant rhetoric did not save them from crusading nativists in the New York legislature. FLIS spent its early years proving the impotence of impartiality. Like the settlements, however, FLIS did manage to survive and to help some individual immigrants; that, at least, was something.

All in all, experts had little impact on the nation's immigrant policies. They did not occupy the "command posts" of power; and they could influence those who did only by persuading them that expert schemes would promote *their* interests. This was a dubious proposition; and even Kellor, the most persuasive of them all, had to admit defeat. Before that happened, she admitted something else. "There is," she wrote, "no science of race assimilation."[104] She was in a position to know, and the evidence supports her judgment. The settlements had had the longest continuous experience in working with immigrants; and they, as we have seen, conceded her point once the war era's hysteria quieted down. FLIS demurred, but its own view of its Americanizing role was belied by its concern with how its work appeared to outsiders. This even extended to so central a question as whether immigrants ought to be pushed to learn English. Early in 1924, FLIS director Lewis "asked everyone to be thinking how

the FLIS could do more to promote the knowledge of English among
the foreign language groups." Why should a foreign-language service promote the use of English?

> He [Lewis] said that native born Americans always feel that
> we ought to encourage the use of English in the place of
> foreign languages, and that our work would be in [a] much
> stronger and more strategic position if at the same time we
> were giving out information in the immigrant's own language
> we were also promoting his knowledge of English.[105]

Kellor's judgment rings true. There was no science of race assimilation,
no genuine body of knowledge for experts to draw upon. There was, in
fact, no genuine expertise in this field. There were only "experts."

NOTES

1. Henry W. Jessup, J. D., "The New Flood Tide of Immigration:
A Policy and a Program," *Annals of the American Academy of Political
and Social Science* 93 (1921): 213.

2. Ibid.

3. H. R. 14196, sect. 1a, par. 2, 66th Cong., 2nd sess. The measure
was introduced by the Hon. Benjamin F. Welty, May 22, 1920.

4. Jessup, "The New Flood Tide of Immigration," pp. 217, 212,
215, 216, 215, 217-18. See also "For a Constructive Law on Immigration,"
Survey 39 (February 23, 1918): 575.

5. See Allen F. Davis, *Spearheads for Reform: The Social Settlements and the Progressive Movement, 1890-1914* (New York: Oxford
University Press, 1967), chap. 10, "The Progressive Crusade."

6. "Effect of the President's Plea for Preparedness," *Literary Digest*
52 (February 12, 1916): 361; "Roosevelt or Hughes?" *Literary Digest*
52 (April 15, 1916): 1043.

7. "Colonel Roosevelt's New Crusade," *Literary Digest* 52 (June 3,
1916): 1618. Among the newspapers sampled were: in Boston, the *Trans-
cript* (Rep.), *Journal* (Ind.), and *Advertiser* (Ind.); in New York, *Times*
(Ind.) and *Sun* (Ind.); in Syracuse, the *Herald* (Ind.); in Philadelphia, the
Public Ledger (Ind.); in Baltimore, the *News* (Ind.); in Washington, the
Times (Ind.); in Detroit, the *Free Press* (Ind.); and in Chicago, the *Herald*
(Ind.) and *Daily News* (Ind.).

8. "Democratic Campaign Issues," *Literary Digest* 52 (July 1, 1916):

4. The St. Louis *Post-Dispatch* (Dem.) called this "the most important plank in any platform." The *New York Times* (Ind.) editorialized "that is the very backbone of Americanism."

9. "Progressive Leaven in the Republican Lump," *Literary Digest* 52 (September 30, 1916): 819; "Mr. Hughes and the Hyphen," *Literary Digest* 52 (September 16, 1916): 658. Hughes telegraphed his hearty congratulations to Roosevelt for this speech.

10. "The President and the Hyphen," *Literary Digest* 52 (October 14, 1916): 935. The New York *Tribune* (Rep.) quoted one Democratic national committeeman as saying: "We are going to make the hyphen the big talking point of the campaign. There isn't any other issue."

11. Grace Abbott, "The Democracy of Internationalism," *Survey* 36 (August 5, 1916): 479, 480; Israel Friedlaender, "The Americanization of the Jewish Immigrant," *Survey* 38 (May 5, 1917): 107; and Edward A. Steiner, "The Face of the Nation," *Survey* 37 (November 4, 1916): 127.

12. See Chapter 6.

13. John Dewey, "Nationalizing Education," *National Education Association Addresses and Proceedings* (1916), pp. 183, 184-85, 185, 183, 184, 188-89. For a similar distinction, see "Americanism," *New Republic* 8 (June 3, 1916): 105-06.

14. John Dewey, "Force, Violence, and Law," *New Republic* (January 22, 1916), and "Force and Coercion," *International Journal of Ethics* (April 1916). Both are reprinted in Joseph Ratner, ed., *Characters and Events* (New York, 1929), 2: 636-41, 782-89. See also Morton White, *Social Thought in America: The Revolt Against Formalism* (Boston: Beacon Press, 1957), chap. 11, "Destructive Intelligence," and Alan Cywor, "John Dewey in World War I: Patriotism and International Progressivism," *American Quarterly* 21 (Fall 1969).

15. In both situations it was Randolph Bourne who provided the most cogent critiques of Dewey. See Randolph Bourne, "The War and the Intellectuals," and "Trans-national America," in Carl Resek, ed., *War and the Intellectuals: Collected Essays, 1915-1919* (New York: Harper & Row, 1964), pp. 3-14, 107-23.

16. Quoted in Edward Hartmann, *The Movement to Americanize the Immigrant* (New York, 1948), p. 38.

17. For membership, see ibid., p. 56.

18. Ibid., pp. 70, 72.

19. See Frank Trumbull (committee chairman) to P. P. Claxton (commissioner of education), Apirl 1, 1919, in Bureau of Education Papers, R.G. 12, Box 106. Between April 1, 1914, and the end of fiscal 1919, the bureau received $85,247.80, which constituted its *entire* budget for Americanization work.

20. H. H. Wheaton, "The United States Bureau of Education and the Immigrant," *Annals of the American Academy of Political and Social Science* 67 (September 1916): 279.

21. Hartmann, *The Movement to Americanize the Immigrant,* pp. 108-12. See also "Spread of Americanization Day Plans," *Survey* 34 (June 19, 1915): 261; "Americanization Day," *The Outlook* 110 (June 30, 1915): 485; and "Americanization Day in 150 Communities," *Survey* 34 (July 31, 1915): 390.

22. According to the chairman of all three, the NAC "largely financed the work of the Immigration Committee of the Chamber of Commerce of the U.S.A. . . ." Trumbull to Claxton, April 1, 1919.

23. See Bureau of Naturalization Papers, R.G. 85, File No. 27671/ 1832.

24. Frances Kellor, "Americanization: A Conservation Policy for Industry," *Annals of the American Academy of Political and Social Science* 65 (May 1916): 240, 241-42.

25. Frances Kellor, "How to Americanize a City: The Assimilation of the Immigrant Is a Problem in Which Every Civic Agency Is Directly or Indirectly Concerned," *American City* 14 (February 1916): 165.

26. See John Higham, *Strangers in the Land: Patterns of American Nativism, 1865-1924* (New York: Atheneum, 1963), pp. 248-49. See also James Weinstein, *The Corporate Ideal in the Liberal State, 1900-1918* (Boston: Beacon Press, 1968).

27. W. E. Gifford [director, Council of National Defense] to P. P. Claxton, January 24, 1918; "Memorandum on the Alien Situation in the United States," n.d., 1; both in R.G. 12, Box 106.

28. Committee for Immigrants in America, *Memorandum to the Advisory Commission of the Council of National Defense Concerning a War Policy for Aliens,* October 31, 1917, p. 5; quoted in Hartmann, *The Movement to Americanize the Immigrant,* pp. 169, 170.

29. "To Make Us Spy-Proff and Bomb-Proof," *Literary Digest* 54 (March 10, 1917): 610.

30. Committee for Immigrants in America, *Memorandum . . . Concerning a War Policy for Aliens,* pp. 15, 38; quoted in Hartmann *The Movement to Americanize the Immigrant,* pp. 170, 171, 171-72.

31. "Memorandum on the Alien Situation," p. 5; Gifford to Claxton, January 24, 1918.

32. "Memorandum on the Alien Situation," p. 2. Hartmann incorrectly claims the council endorsed the NAC program (*The Movement to Americanize the Immigrant,* pp. 188-89). Henry M. Robinson [assistant chief, State Councils Section, Council of National Defense] to P. P. Claxton, February 12, 1918, in R.G. 12, Box 106. For the parallels be-

tween the NAC and Bureau of Education proposals, compare "Memorandum to the Advisory Commission" and Council of National Defense, Bulletin No. 86, *Americanization of Aliens,* February 12, 1918, in R. G. 12, Box 106.

33. George Creel, *How We Advertised America* (New York, 1920), pp. 180-81.

34. Between October 1, 1916, and September 30, 1917, the NAC raised $41,399; between October 1, 1917, and March 31, 1918, it raised another $24,757.50. See "Contributions Received . . ." in R.G. 12, Box 106. Out of this, the NAC funded the New Jersey Bureau of Immigration, the Immigration Committee of the Chamber of Commerce, the Division of Immigrant Education, and its own work.

35. Kellor to Claxton, April 10, 1918; Kellor to Claxton, n.d. (c. April 10, 1918). Both letters were enclosed in a series of "documents" (and labeled "A" and "C" respectively) that were sent by Claxton to Secretary Lane. See Claxton to Lane, April 16, 1918, in R.G. 12, Box 106.

36. "Memorandum of Understanding Between the Secretary of the Interior and the National Americanization Committee for the Extension of the Work of the Division of Immigrant Education in the Bureau of Education," R.G. 12, Box 106.

37. Administrative Chart and Budget, War Work Extension/Division of Immigrant Education, May 3, 1918, marked "Final Draft, OK" and signed by Frances Kellor, in R.G. 12, Box 106.

38. Creel, *How We Advertised America,* pp. 187-92, 162.

39. Trumbull to Claxton, April 1, 1919; Howard C. Hill, "The Americanization Movement," *American Journal of Sociology* 24 no. 6 (May 1919): 614-16; James R. Mock and Cedric Lawson, *Words That Won the War: The Story of the Committee on Public Information, 1917-1919* (Princeton, N.J., 1939), 216-29.

40. Creel, *How We Advertised America,* p. 184.

41. Copy of report made by Frances Kellor to the Committee on Public Information, April 1, 1918, p. 9, document "G" in Claxton to Lane, April 16, 1918.

42. Kellor "Memorandum on Ways and Means," April 10, 1918, document "B," Claxton to Lane, April 16, 1918.

43. "Memorandum of Understanding Between the Commissioner of Education, the Chairman of the Committee on Public Information, and the Chief of the States Councils Section of the Council of National Defense," May 16, 1918, in R.G. 12, Box 106.

44. Creel, *How We Advertised America,* p. 184.

45. "Summary Report of the National Americanization Committee Confirming in Particular Its Relation to the United States Bureau of Education, Recommendations Made to the Council of National Defense, October 17, 1917, and Action Taken Thereon," enclosed in Trumbull to Claxton, December 5, 1918, in R.G. 12, Box 106.

46. Trumbull to Claxton, December 5, 1918.

47. Frances Kellor, "Immigration and the Future," *Annals of the American Academy of Political and Social Science* 93 (January 1921): 205, 206-7, 203.

48. Frank Trumbull to P. P. Claxton, April 1, 1919, in R. G. 12, Box 106. This letter was a kind of final "résumé" of the work of the NAC. ". . . as The Inter-racial Council was organized by members of the National Americanization Committee . . . it was voted to invite that organization to take over all of the work (not covered by the Department of the Interior) previously performed by the National Americanization Committee and the Committee for Immigrants in America—and I am glad to report that the invitation was promptly accepted." For a list of the members of the new organization, see Hartmann, *The Movement to Americanize The Immigrant,* pp. 220-221 n.

49. *Survey* 41 (March 22, 1919): 909.

50. Frances Kellor, "Address of Miss Frances A. Kellor," *Proceedings* of the 24th Annual Convention of the National Association of Manufacturers of the United States (1919), pp. 361-68, 367-68; *Proceedings* of the 25th Annual Convention . . . (1920), p. 297; Robert E. Park, *The Immigrant Press and Its Control* (New York, 1922), pp. 451-57.

51. Hartmann, *The Movement to Americanize the Immigrant,* p. 265.

52. Cited in "Closing the Door to Bolshevism and Anarchy," in Edwin Wildman, ed., *Reconstructing America: Our Next Big Job* (Boston, 1919), pp. 253-59.

53. Kellor, "Immigration and the Future," p. 210.

54. David Rosenstein, "A Crucial Issue in Wartime Education—Americanization," *School and Society* 7 (June 1, 1918): 631. (This was originally a paper presented at the National Conference on Americanization called by Interior Secretary Lane on April 3, 1918.) See also J. George Becht, "The Public School and the New American Spirit," *School and Society* 3 (April 29, 1916): 616. (This was originally an address before the National Superintendent Convention, February 23, 1916.)

55. Hill, "The Americanization Movement," noted that as late as 1919 "many large schools in American cities have been spending more for teach-

ing German to American children than for teaching English and civics to aliens" (p. 612). "New York State and the Americanization Problem," *School and Society* 3 (May 27, 1916): 776.

56. Lewis Rockow, "Americanization and the Pillar of Democracy," *Education* 37 (November 1916): 174; Los Angeles *Times,* April 3, 1917, quoted in H. C. Petersen and Gilbert Fite, *Opponents of War* (Seattle, Wash.: University of Washington Press, 1957), p. 111; Howard K. Beale, *Are American Teachers Free?* (New York, 1936), p. 22; Petersen and Fite, *Opponents of War,* p. 111; see also pp. 102-12 for a number of similar cases including the notorious dismissals at Columbia University.

57. Winthrop D. Lane, "Teaching Respect for Authority," *Survey* 39 (December 1, 1917): 250.

58. A. Franklin Ross, "American Ideals: How to Teach Them," *Educational Review* 56 (December 1918): 400, 399; "To Make New York an American City," *Survey* 38 (September 15, 1917): 527-28.

59. Petersen and Fite, *Opponents of War,* p. 112; Beale, *Are American Teachers Free?* p. 37.

60. "New York School House Cleaning," *Literary Digest* 56 (January 5, 1918): 26; Winthrop D. Lane, "Giving the Teachers a Voice," *Survey* 39 (December 8, 1917): 280.

61. Quoted in Robert K. Murray, *Red Scare: A Study in National Hysteria, 1919-1920* (New York: McGraw-Hill 1964), p. 171. See also Chapter 7.

62. Lew M. Dougan, "The Education of Adult Immigrants," National Education Association, *Addresses and Proceedings* (1915), p. 441; "America First Conference," *School and Society* 5 (January 27, 1917): 106.

63. A summary of this legislation can be found in "Legislative Notes & Reviews," Harry Rider, "Americanization," *American Political Science Review* 14 (February 1920): 110-15; see also Chapter 7 for an account of the "Lusk laws" in New York. Max Loeb, "Compulsory English for Foreign-Born," *Survey* 40 (July 13, 1918): 426; Graham Taylor, "Enforcing English by Proclamation," *Survey* 40 (July 6, 1918): 394-95.

64. "Neighbors [an Open Letter], to the Settlements of the United States from Mary K. Simkhovitch," *Survey* 38 (February 17, 1917): 581.

65. Taylor, "Enforcing English by Proclamation," p. 395.

66. Graham Taylor and Robert A. Woods, "The War-Time Outlook of Social Settlements," reprinted in the *Survey* 40 (August 31, 1918): 617.

67. Report of Charles L. Taylor, President, *The Kingsley Association*

Year Book (Pittsburgh, 1917), 31 in NFS Papers, Folder: 510; "An Appeal for Settlements," in United Neighborhood Houses Papers, Folder: 461.

68. Mary K. Simkhovitch, "A Settlement War Program," *Survey* 38 (May 5, 1917): 111; Hill, "The Americanization Movement," p. 615.

69. "To Study the Immigrant on a Large Scale," *Survey* 40 (April 27, 1918): 96. An advisory committee of Theodore Roosevelt, Professor John Graham Brooks, of Harvard, and John M. Glenn, director of the Russell Sage Foundation, supervised this study. For its staff, see "Further Plans for the Study of Americanization," *Survey* 40 (July 13, 1918): 431.

70. Charles C. Cooper to Robert A. Woods, August 9, 1921; Woods to Cooper, October 11, 1921. Both in NFS Papers, Folder: 120.

71. See Chapter 7.

72. Committee of United Neighborhood Houses to Joint Legislative Investigating Committee, Attention of Archibald E. Stevenson, Esq., Prince George Hotel, New York City, December 30, 1920. In UNH Papers, Scrapbook 3-3, Legal Folder: 13. The letter was subsequently published as a pamphlet, *The Americanization Program of the United Neighborhood Houses of New York.*

73. Unsigned, undated (c. 1921) memorandum in UNH Papers, Scrapbook 3-14, Legal Folder: 13; Synopsis of a report of East Side House Loyalty Club given by Miss Helen Hart at meeting of Mothers' Clubs Leaders, January 16, 1925, in UNH Papers, Scrapbook: 6-73, Legal Folder: 23.

74. Association Meeting *Minutes,* February 8, 1921, Scrapbook: 1-19A; Executive Committee Meeting *Minutes,* February 9, 1921, Scrapbook: 1-20; Headworkers and Presidents of Boards Meeting *Minutes,* February 16, 1921, Scrapbook: 1-21; Executive Committee Meeting *Minutes,* March 2, 1921, Scrapbook: 1-21; and Annual Meeting *Minutes,* May 10, 1921, Scrapbook: 1-25. All in UNH Papers, Legal Folder: 9.

75. "Tentative Report [of the] Joint Committee on Work with Adult Immigrants," United Neighborhood Houses, The Committee on Immigrant Education [1925] in American Council of Nationality Services Papers, "Americanization—Assimilation," Shipment 2, Box 1 (hereinafter cited as ACNS Papers).

76. Foreign Language Information Service, *A Job of Understanding* (New York, 1924), p. 2.

77. Josephine Roche, *Report on the Division of Work with the Foreign Born of the U.S. Committee on Public Information,* p. 46 in Josephine Roche Papers, FLIS materials; Roche, "For Submission to the Commonwealth Fund to interest them possibly in contributions and grants to the Foreign Language Information Service approximately 1919 or 1920"

(actually, c. 1923), p. 49 in Josephine Roche Papers, FLIS materials.

78. Roche, *Report on the Division of Work with the Foreign Born* . . . , pp. 2-3; "Memorandum of Understanding Between the Commissioner of Education . . . and the Chief of the States Councils Section of the Council of National Defense"; P. P. Claxton to Frances Kellor, June 6, 1918, in R.G. 12, Box 106; Creel, *How We Advertised America,* pp. 200-7; and "The New Independence Day," *Survey* 40 (July 13, 1918): 419-21.

79. Will Irwin to [Wheeler] Bloodgood, June 24, 1918, in Division of Work with the Foreign Born, Washington and New York Offices, Committee on Public Information Papers, Reel 31 (Hereinafter cited as CPI Papers).

80. Creel, *How We Advertised America,* pp. 113, 114.

81. "In Literature and Song: How can Americanization Be Furthered by the Stage?" *German Democracy Bulletin* 2, no. 3 (1919) p. 2. In CPI Papers, Reel 31. Italics added.

82. Ibid.

83. See "The Work of the Foreign Language Information Service" (May? 1921), in File 140.11 Civilian Relief, Dept. of—FLIS Creation, Function etc., 1917-21, American Red Cross papers. Xerox copy in ACNS Papers, Shipment 7, Box 7; Memo, April 19, 1921, [Jason S.] Joy to [W. Frank] Persons, ACNS Papers, Box 7; Daniel E. Weinberg, "The Foreign Language Information Service and the Foreign Born, 1918-1939: A Case Study of Cultural Assimilation Viewed as a Problem in Social Technology" (Ph.D. dissertation, University of Minnesota, 1973), pp. 22, 107-11.

84. Edward Hale Bierstadt to A. Mitchell Palmer, November 21, 1919, in ACNS Papers, Shipment 8, Box 10.

85. Edward Hale Bierstadt to Robert T. Scott, draft of letter sent December 24, 1919. In the final version this passage was changed to read: "We feel that we can best serve you by being perfectly candid as to this" (ACNS Papers, Shipment 8, Box 10).

86. Bierstadt to Scott, December 24, 1919.

87. Ibid.

88. Ibid.

89. Ibid.

90. John T. Creighton [chief, Bureau of Investigation] to Bierstadt, May 27, 1920; American Red Cross Foreign Language Information Service Danish Section, "The Foreign Born 'Anarchists,' " April 29, 1920; Bierstadt to Creighton, June 17, 1920; Bierstadt to Scott, December 24, 1919. All in ACNS, Shipment 8, Box 10.

91. *Minutes* of Joint Meeting of the Board and the Council, March 24, 1924, ACNS Papers, Shipment 6, Box 2.

92. [Read Lewis], "Policy of Releasing to Foreign Language Press Articles on Principal American Industrial Concerns," March 31, 1926, in FLIS, Foreign Language Press Division Reports, 1927-35 (2), ACNS Papers, Shipment 3, Box 9.

93. Memo, L. E. Stein [acting director general, Red Cross Department of Civilian Relief] to F. C. Munroe [general manager], December 17, 1920; Memo, C. M. Sale to Munroe, December 22, 1920; Munroe to J. S. Ellsworth, December 24, 1920; Josephine Roche to Lewis E. Stein, January 21, 1921; L. E. Stein to J. S. Ellsworth, January 31, 1921. All in File 140.12, Civilian Relief, Dept. of—FLIS, American Red Cross Papers, Xerox copy in ACNS Papers, Shipment 7, Box 7.

94. See *Minutes* of Council Meeting, February 8, 1924 in FLIS, Minutes of the Advisory Council, 1923-26, and *Minutes* of Joint Meeting of the Board and the Council, March 14, 1924. Both in ACNS Papers, Shipment 6, Box 2.

95. James J. Davis to Hon. [Senator] Samuel M. Shortridge [Rep., California], December 3, 1921, in National Archives, R.G. 174, File No. 163/127. Shortridge and Rep. Albert Johnson [Rep., Washington] sponsored the registration bill.

96. See news clippings in Alien Registration—Pro and Con (Articles) ACNS Papers, Shipment 2, Box 1.

97. "Registration of Aliens," resolution adopted by the Board of Trustees of the Foreign Language Information Service, March 5, 1930, FLIS Reports, ACNS Papers, Shipment 6, Box 3.

98. "Summary of the Work of the Foreign Language Service January 1 to June 30, 1922," in FLIS—Reports and Summaries of the Service's Work and Purposes, 1920-32, ACNS Papers, Shipment 6, Box 3.

99. *Minutes* of Council Meeting, October 2, 1923, in FLIS, Minutes of the Advisory Council, 1923-26, ACNS Papers, Shipment 6, Box 2; Josephine Roche, "For submission to the Commonwealth Fund to interest them possibly in contributions and grants to the Foreign Language Information Service, approximately 1919 or 1920" (actually, c. 1923), Josephine Roche papers, FLIS materials.

100. Inter-Racial Council, "Statement of Purpose," typescript copy in National Security League and Allied Organizations, n.d. (1921?), Americanization—Reports of Select Organizations, ACNS Papers, Shipment 2, Box 1; Read Lewis to members of FLIS Advisory Council, December 17, 1927, FLIS—Advisory Council Membership Suggestions, ACNS Papers, Shipment 6, Box 2.

101. Lewis to Advisory Council, December 17, 1927.

102. See Foreign Language Information Service, *A Job of Understanding,* pp. 9-12; "The Work of the Foreign Language Information Service," pp. 12-13. Between February 1920 and May 1921, the service handled some 14,852 cases—of which it settled 11,646. For the same period it also processed 12,438 requests for information.

103. "The Immigrant and the Realities of Assimilation," address given an FLIS—sponsored luncheon at the National Conference of Social Work, June 27, 1924, in FLIS Publicity, ACNS Papers, Shipment 6, Box 19.

104. Frances Kellor, "What Is Americanization?" *Yale Review,* n.s., 8 (1919): 282, 285.

105. *Minutes* of Council Meeting, January 28, 1924; FLIS, Minutes of the Advisory Council, 1923-26 in ACNS Papers, Shipment 6, Box 2.

chapter 6

The War as a Professional Opportunity: Mobilization and the Myth of Reconstruction, 1917-19

Repression and restriction proved more popular solutions to the immigrant "problem" than any of the experts' Americanization programs. The bureaucrats in the Wilson and Harding administrations, the politicians in Congress, and the businessmen in the National Americanization Committee, the Inter-Racial Council, and the Chamber of Commerce had their own ideas about the alien menace just as the Sage trustees had their own schemes for reforming industrial society. Because these latter groups monopolized the "positions of power," most experts redefined their Americanization schemes to cater to their interests. Frances Kellor, the expert most successful in gaining support, also went furthest toward making their interests her own.

These accommodations, however, succeeded only in eviscerating the experts' programs. Kellor's experience provides a convenient case in point. Her shrill antibolshevism overshadowed her proposals to "protect" and educate aliens at the same time that it made those programs appear to be ineffectual stopgaps. More than business control of the foreign-language press would be needed to meet the menace she described to the NAM. She did, at least, continue to oppose restriction. Other experts accepted even that in a vain effort to attach their ideas to the growing nativist sentiment. But as long as the immigrant was portrayed as a bearded, bomb-throwing radical, experts had no chance of influencing public policy.

Americanization offered experts, for a brief period, the illusion of power. They believed, for a while, that they could mobilize support by offering "scientific" versions of nativism. Wartime mobilization seemed to offer a similar opportunity, but it too proved to be more apparent than real. The well-known antiwar stands of a few prominent social experts like Jane Addams or Roger Baldwin have obscured the enthusiasm with which the great mass of social engineers enlisted in the war for democracy.[1] More representative, and more important in terms of the professional development of social engineering, were the views of Edward T. Devine, of the New York School of Social Work. As associate editor of the *Survey*, Devine clearly and enthusiastically promoted the war as a great professional opportunity. The *Survey*'s editor, Paul U. Kellogg, was a strong partisan of the opposing view; and so their magazine is a peculiarly important source for estimating the engineers' reactions to the war and its impact upon them. The *Survey*'s editors, however, felt constrained to treat some subjects gingerly, and so the material published must be read in the light of unpublished office correspondence. Kellogg described the magazine's general policy in these terms:

> We have both the advantages and disadvantages of being
> closely associated with those who are engaging actively in
> the wartime phases of social work and the social phases of
> war work. We have the advantages of relations of confidence
> with men and agencies, which gives us precise information,
> insight and perspective. We have the disadvantage of being so
> closely related as to make our handling of many matters
> delicate.[2]

Most delicate of all was the matter of whether the *Survey* should call for the United States to enter the war. Kellogg expressed the fear of some experts that ". . . the struggle has built up, in each of the Allied countries, a new Prussianism. . . ." He had in mind "an isolated nationalism which holds that force is the only method for maintaining a nation's rights, its security and development; that each nation is to be sole judge of its own cause and of its applications of force." According to Kellogg, "this [is] true not alone of Germany." ". . . even England, the home of civil liberties and the refuge of idealists of all Europe, has slipped back and back." What he found most troubling was that he found "it true of our own psychology in this national crisis."[3]

Yet this "isolated nationalism" inspired as well as discouraged. Devine saw in Great Britain not a new Prussianism but "such national unity, such exalted patriotism, such a fellowship of spirit" that witnessing it was "a thrilling experience." This enthusiasm for war was not as naïve as it might seem at first. Devine was not blind to the costs of war. He admitted that "what Europe is losing of political and civil liberty, of the capacity for seeing things in due proportion, of the power of forming rational judgements of men and measures, no one has yet even tried to tell."[4] He admitted, in other words, the force of Kellogg's argument; he supported the war with his eyes wide open. At the heart of that support was what C. Wright Mills would have called his professional ideology.[5] Devine claimed that it was "especially appropriate that social workers, who in their daily lives have to do with various aspects of social pathology, should realize that war is only an abnormal community convulsion." He saw, that is, the horrors of war as an opportunity for social workers because dealing with "abnormal community convulsions" was their particular province. War brings, Devine analogized, "tasks of relief, bigger and more difficult than others, but with a family resemblance. It destroys life and limb, but so do industrial accidents. It makes brothers hate one another another, just as unfair competition and inherited prejudices have always done." Completing this extraordinary parallel, he added, "it creates heroes, just as economic conflicts do, but it kills them in a remorseless tragedy only matched in the unrecognized, slowly moving tragedies of commerce and industry."[6] If Devine was naïve, it was not because he failed to see the darker side of war but because he too easily persuaded himself that the nation would turn to him and his fellow experts in the days ahead.

Kellogg tried to warn against this kind of easy optimism. "We can take a leaf out of the history of our domestic movements for social and industrial justice," he cautioned, "and ask ourselves whether the most active groups here in America who are espousing the war in the name of liberalism in Europe are those from which we expect leadership when democracy and privilege lock horns in municipality, state capital or Congress."[7] No such doubts haunted Devine. The professional opportunities he foresaw were too great to permit them. The war, he thought, would make the social expert indispensable. "Who else but social workers," he wrote, "have such a background of experience and such an acquaintance with human character under adversity as will enable them to understand the misery and to keep their poise in the sickening realities of war and its aftermath?" War held out the same promise as the Progressive campaign of 1912 when Jane Addams had seconded Roosevelt's nomination and a committee of the National Conference of Charities and Corrections had written the social welfare section of the platform. Social workers, Devine thought, would naturally "have a standing in the councils of those who would try to find a way out of the darkness."[8]

It was this matter of "a standing" in the national councils that Kellogg had questioned. He doubted that experts would be able to influence national policy or that mobilization measures would embody their proposals for a more scientific and equitable society. The war, he thought, would have the effect of "reaching and rending every community relationship in America, every settlement, neighborhood and tenement, every industrial town and crossroads, every phase of education and livelihood, every promise of youth and social advance. . . ." Devine remained convinced that a militant nationalism could be controlled in the interest of reform. "The war is something more than destruction and even in its destruction there is compensation." This was "a freedom from old prejudices and limitations . . . , a new liberty of thought. . . ." This freedom and liberty had, needless to say, nothing to do with the Bill of Rights. Patriotism might jeopardize "political and civil liberty," but it would also submerge class, ethnic, and religious divisions. "Men will be free hereafter to live larger and more beautiful lives than we knew before the war."[9]

This was the controversy as of mid-February 1917. As Kellogg wrote, "the columns of the Survey [sic] were up to that date open equally to those who held [views] pro and con, and thereafter closed equally for a period of three months, pending action at a full meeting of the board." Actually, it was not until the end of June that the Survey, in an editorial written by Devine, took a clear stand in favor of the war. Kellogg accepted the decision without any public protest, and took some solace in the fact that:

> to have held the Survey group together and to have carried
> conviction as to the fairness of its formula in a period when,
> as never before, public opinion has been rent and torn with

> conflicting opinion, has itself been no mean achievement
> and is an augury for the coherence and liberalism of the
> social movement of the future.[10]

The simple truth is that Devine's position, perhaps aided by the American entry into the war, became the *Survey*'s position as well. Kellogg wrote that "in the view of board and staff, the *Survey* has before it the opportunity of a generation. . . ."[11]

The "opportunity of a generation"—here in a single phrase is the key to understanding how experts viewed the war and their own role in it. To recognize that they saw the war as offering them an unparalleled opportunity is not to accuse them of opportunism. To say their viewpoint reflected their professional aspirations, that they, like Thorstin Veblen's farmers, cultivated "the main chance," is to say nothing worse about them than that they acted much as other organized interests did. The war promised a variety of opportunities to a wide array of groups. Moreover, social experts, like these other groups, did not see any antagonism between their interests and the nation's. Indeed, they felt the opposite was more nearly the case. They were specially fitted, as Devine wrote, to cope with the "abnormal . . . convulsion" of war. So their professional opportunity coincided, or so they convinced themselves, with their patriotic duty. As we shall see shortly, their patriotism ran deep.

This was equally true of that minority within the experts' ranks, represented by Kellogg, who resisted the call for American intervention. Nearly twenty years later, Kellogg attempted to explain why he and other experts in the American Union Against Militarism made their peace with the war. He isolated three reasons. One was that while they knew the war "to be provoked by rival capitalisms," the Russian Revolution "made it clearer cut that self-governing and subject peoples were pitted against autocracies." Another was "the haunting chance that with American inaction, victory might come to Prussian militarism and democracy in Western Europe go down." Finally, there was the suspicion "that Washington might know more of the situation than we could."[12]

Throughout this "period of tension: the Spring,"[13] social experts fell in with the pro-war line. As Kellogg's explanation suggests, those who were not pacifists were too riddled by doubts to continue their resistance, and the American Union Against Militarism "separated into the elements that composed it—some striving against the spread of militarism in wartime, some struggling against wartime suppression (the origin of the Civil Liberties Union) and some, a year later [1918], becoming the nucleus of what is now the Foreign Policy Association. . . ." Written in self-defense during a time when revisionist views of the war were very popular, Kellogg's account rings true. Mary Kingsbury Simkhovitch, 1917 president of the National Federation of Settlements, corroborated much of his version. She spoke, in an open letter in the New York *Evening Post,* in 1917, for the many experts who had questioned whether "the world's fate demanded positive and national action on our part" until "the Russian revolution, following the increased ruthlessness of Germany, resolved that doubt, and made it possible, and, yes, imperative, for many of us to hesitate no longer."[14]

A month earlier, on March 10, 1917, eighty-seven Boston social workers "with no love of war, but with a sense of the nation's duty" telegraphed their "unswerving support" to President Wilson for "immediate and forcible measures of defense." Two weeks later a similar group in Baltimore disavowed what they thought was the *Survey*'s "pacifism" and declared their support for a war policy.[15] Although social experts played little or no role in the agitation for intervention, most had come to believe, by early 1917, that intervention was necessary. And most had expressed their willingness to do their "bit" in the war effort. It was not such a long step from patriotic willingness to Devine's enthusiastic vision of mobilization as a unique opportunity for social engineering on a grand scale.

However much soul-searching intervention occasioned among experts, the leading social agencies almost automatically rallied 'round the flag. The Sage Foundation was typical. Even before the formal declaration of hostilities, foundation director John M. Glenn and the director of its Division of Statistics, Dr. Leonard P. Ayres, were in Washington conferring with Secretary of War Newton Baker, Director of the Council of National Defense Gifford, Oklahoma senator Robert L. Owen, and Ernest P. Bicknell, director of Civilian Relief of the American Red Cross, on ways in which the foundation might meet some of the needs of mobilization in the areas of statistics and recreation. The foundation immediately set to work and by April 30 Ayres, together with his staff from the Division of Statistics and that from the Division of Education, was working for the Council of National Defense. While the foundation kept four of these people on its own payroll, both divisions closed down for the next thirty months.

The staff of the foundation's Department of Recreation went to work for the Secretary of War as part of the Commission on Training Camp Activities. Even the director of the foundation's Department of Child Helping, Dr. Hastings H. Hart, went to work for the War Department drawing up "plans for the employment of inmates of jails as farm laborers and for other purposes." His associate, C. Spencer Richardson, joined the staff of the Bureau of Relief and Refugees of the Red Cross.[16]

The Red Cross moved into the field even before the Sage Foundation. By mid-March its acting chairman was already calling for "the undivided support of patriotic Americans everywhere." His appeal for 1 million new members was immediately endorsed by the Federal Council of Churches, which declared that "the 207,000 Protestant churches in the country could alone furnish this membership." "Every pastor," read the council's appeal, "should himself be a member of the Red Cross."[17]

One by one the other social agencies fell into step. At the end of March, Louisa Lee Schuyler introduced a resolution, unanimously adopted, at a meeting of the board of managers of the New York State Charities Aid Association offering the services of the association to the nation. On April 27, President Wilson gave official recognition to the YMCA "as a valuable adjunct and asset to the [military] service." In June, the National Federation of Settlements resolved "its loyal support of the government in the prosecution of the war to a successful issue. . . ." At about the same time, the National Conference on Social Work placed "on record on behalf of the great majority of its 4,300 members their intense loyalty and their purpose to support the President and the government of the United States in the prosecution of this war in the interests of liberty and democracy."[18] What would prove most significant about this outpouring of patriotism was not its near unanimity, but the agencies' willingness to abandon their peacetime activities while donating their staffs to the government. Whatever wartime gains the experts were to make, in other words, would be purchased at the price of discontinuing peacetime programs.

The war would put Devine's hopes (and Kellogg's fears) to the test. Meanwhile other experts came to share Devine's vision of the war as a unique opportunity to demonstrate the patriotic uses of expertise. Arthur P. Kellogg, reporting on the National Conference of Social Work, commented on the general feeling that "social workers . . . have a peculiar obligation and opportunity for service in wartime . . ." for "whether you

look on war as hell or as an instrument of democracy, its immediate fruits
are the fruits of calamity, and the fruits of calamity are the stuff with
which organized social work deals in the regular course of its daily work."
Organized social work in fact staked out an enormous claim for itself.
Conference president-elect Robert A. Woods predicted that "the agencies
represented by the conference must be relied upon to provide training
and leadership for all outside the military ranks who come forward to
re-enforce the army and sustain the fabric of the nation."[19]

The belief that, in the words of A. W. MacDougall of the Newark
Bureau of Charities, "this is, indeed, the day of those who have been
doing fundamental social work" rested upon two allied expectations.
One, as we have seen, was the notion that their experience in other social
calamities particularly fitted experts to lead the way in wartime. The
other was the widely held belief that reform could be made part of mobilization. Experts had presented their reforms as necessary to strengthen
the social fabric in a rhetoric rich in references to "the coming generation,"
"the family," and "the community." They had excoriated popular indifference as a major obstacle. By July 1917 Devine could proclaim that,
thanks to the war, that obstacle had been overcome. "Consciousness of
social problems, intelligent interest in them, and a genuine desire to do
something about them have never been so conspicuous as they are now.
Enthusiasm for social service is epidemic."[20]

Self-cast as the men of the hour, some experts apparently hoped they
could succeed in influencing policy simply by presenting whatever program they were interested in as essential to the war effort. So Dr. Alice
Hamilton's article on "The New Public Health," written before the declaration of war but published after it, was spruced up with an editorial note
that "war makes sanitation a common cause." Joining public health in
taking on "the sudden seriousness that tinges all activity today" were
"the prevention of tuberculosis," the promotion of "a better industrialism
and a sounder national economy." Such a list could be extended indefin-
itely. Henry Pratt Fairchild, for example, added the teaching of family
planning techniques.[21]

Anyone could play this simple game and many did. Unenlightened
employers, for example, pressed for the repeal of laws regulating women's
and children's work as a war-related emergency measure. This necessitated
a campaign by the American Association for Labor Legislation to shore
up these statutes. Mine owners in Arizona blamed their labor troubles on

IWW agitators allegedly in the pay of German agents. The difficulty was that what Devine had so sanguinely hailed as a general "intelligent interest" in social problems was really, he admitted three pages later, a "seething ferment" that "we accept . . . unquestioningly as evidence of tremendously vital forces, and we burn to add our own energies to these forces. It is all very exhilarating, stimulating, intoxicating." A sober Paul Kellogg commented, "we cannot expect to turn people's thoughts away from the war and its consequences."[22] The inevitable result was that experts found that every side of every issue was presented as essential to the war effort.

A more realistic look at the wartime excitement convinced Devine and other social engineers that their success would depend, as it had in peacetime, on winning over a much smaller public. "We shall be ready for whatever comes," Devine noted, ". . . if the country as a whole organizes through a network of quasi-official councils or committees of defense . . . ; and if the Red Cross is made the efficient and trusted agent of the whole population. . . ."[23] Within this "network" lay the real opportunity of the war for the experts. It consisted of the Red Cross, the YMCA, the War Camp Community Service, the various committees of the Council of National Defense and other "quasi-official" agencies. Their budgets were, by peacetime standards, astronomical; and influence in the war effort meant influence in these bodies. Thus experts encountered, on a far grander scale, the same organizational problems they had faced in the Russell Sage Foundation. They would find, that is, that "positions of power" in these agencies were filled by the same business and philanthropic elite they had been dealing with all along. They would continue to find that this elite had its own ideas about what needed to be done.

The Red Cross provides a clear case in point. President Wilson placed it on a wartime footing by calling a meeting of prominent businessmen for April 21, 1917. At this meeting he appointed the two bodies that were to run the Red Cross for the duration of the war. One was the War Council, chaired by former President Taft. Joining Taft were a half-dozen leading businessmen, including Illinois industrialist Edward N. Hurley, banker Charles D. Norton, philanthropist Grayson M. P. Murphy, Cornelius N. Bliss, Jr., and Eliot Wadsworth. Henry P. Davison, of J. P. Morgan and Company, connected the War Council, of which he was co-chairman, with the War Finance Committee, of which he was vice-chairman. The finance committee had a score of members, all businessmen. It was chaired by Sage trustee Cleveland Hoadley Dodge.[24] The *Survey* quoted one "official" as saying that the function of the finance committee was to raise money whereas the function of the War Council was to spend it. It further commented that the prominent role of Davison "is taken to mean that the financial and business machinery of the Morgan firm will be placed at the disposal of the Council to assist in the collection and disbursal of money."[25]

As was the case with the Sage Foundation, experts had no direct voice in the policy decisions of the Red Cross. Devine noted, in a very carefully worded critique, that "the control of policy and, therefore, the responsibility for the usefulness of the American Red Cross now rests upon . . . a body of financiers." This meant, he argued, that the War Council was "obviously at a disadvantage as a legislative and judicial body in not being in any broad sense representative." His solution was to make the Red Cross "democratic"; not, of course, in the sense of making the council elective, but in keeping "open" its "higher ranks" to "those who have shown preeminent fitness." At the least, Devine urged the council to seek out "expert advice."[26] Experts were preeminently fit, perhaps, but they still faced the necessity of gaining the ears and sympathies of powerful businessmen. In such a political situation, the limits of the Red Cross as an agency of domestic reform were quickly reached.

Not surprisingly those experts who moved into middle-echelon positions in the Red Cross were those who had already proved themselves to the eastern philanthropic establishment. Specifically, in the first year of the war, 75 percent of the major Red Cross appointments went to officials of the charity organization societies. A typical appointment was that of J. Byron Deacon as assistant director of civilian relief.[27] Deacon had first made his mark as financial secretary of the New York Charity Organization Society (COS), where he worked under W. Frank Persons, its general director. He then became secretary of the Pittsburgh Associated Charities and then, briefly, secretary of the Philadelphia Society for Organizing Charity before taking a leave of absence to organize the Home Service work of the Red Cross in Pennsylvania. Finally, his old boss, Persons, by then director of the Red Cross's Home Service section, brought him to Washington. He was succeeded in Philadelphia by Karl DeSchweinitz, a lecturer at the New York School of Philanthropy, run by the New York COS.

With such leadership and with such expert advice, the Red Cross moved smoothly along a predictable path. Its watchword was relief, not reform.

Paul Kellogg summarized its work abroad. "Its first duty is to serve the army of the United States. Its second duty is to serve the sick and wounded of the allied armies. Its third duty is to give such general assistance as it can to the French people." Kellogg was impressed. Red Cross work could "fire the vision" of the expert whether his motive was winning the war, "easing the suffering of the sick and wounded" or "conserving for the future, out of the wreckage of war, the human resources of France."[28] It was, in other words, the kind of work that allowed people like Kellogg to reconcile themselves to the war.

On the home front, the Red Cross concerned itself primarily with maintaining the morale of servicemen's families. Home Service, as it was called, made enormous drafts on the resources of social agencies. Persons, its director, commented that the Red Cross sought to enlist the services of "all in this country who are engaged and interested in social work." It is not possible to establish how close the Red Cross came to monopolizing social service, but the partial data that are available suggest that Home Service made substantial progress toward its goal. A survey taken by the Charity Organization Department of the Russell Sage Foundation in late 1917 shows that 151 charity organizations had 404 workers engaged in Home Service, of whom 181 were paid staff members. Another 202 staff workers were engaged in other Red Cross activities. Overall, out of 912 workers reported as involved in all forms of war service, two-thirds were working for the Red Cross.[29] The survey did not attempt to estimate what these numbers meant for the ongoing programs of agencies involved, but obviously they required a substantial cutback in services.

Red Cross work represented a triple drain on cooperating agencies. It drafted staff; it drafted money because many of these workers continued to be paid by their sponsoring organization; and it drafted resources. The pattern was established as early as April 1917 when the New York School of Philanthropy launched a ten-week training program for Home Service volunteers. Field work experience was supplied by the New York COS, the Association for Improving the Condition of the Poor, the Brooklyn Bureau of Charities, the State Charities Aid Association, and the United Hebrew Charities. In Chicago training was provided by the Chicago School of Civics and Philanthropy with the cooperation of that city's United Charities and the Chicago Federation of Settlements. By September, over 300 cities and towns had such programs under way; and Porter R. Lee, who directed the original course in New York, and Thomas

J. Riley, general secretary of the Brooklyn Bureau of Charities, were
named national directors of the Red Cross Institutes of Home Service.[30]

All of this machinery to boost the morale of men at the front by bringing cheer to their families back home may not have been what Devine
had in mind when he advanced the experts' particular fitness to lead the
way in wartime. Still experts grasped at what they saw as their opportunity.
Robert A. Woods, for example, congratulated his colleagues that "the
civilian service of the Red Cross is bringing to the front a group of remarkable leaders throughout the country who are lifting into the light of states-
manship the training and experience which they have had in the field of
charity organization."[31] The nature of the opportunity for experts was
in the process of being redefined. Experts had begun in the hope of influencing mobilization. As that hope faded, they came to regard the war
work they were doing as a demonstration of their general social usefulness, which they hoped to translate into influence in the shaping of
postwar "reconstruction" policy.

The price the experts paid for this opportunity came high. By June
1918 the Red Cross Home Service had 5,000 volunteers and 2,000 paid
workers organized in 5,000 chapters and was planning to expand its work
to reach every "melancholy" soldier overseas. Meanwhile, social agencies
at home faced a severe manpower shortage. Edith Shatto King, manager
of the National Social Workers' Exchange, estimated that the number
of trained workers was only a third of the available positions. "Moreover,"
she added, "the usual demand for trained workers is augmented by the
exodus of the most highly qualified men and women for service abroad."
Volunteers were flocking to the short Home Service training programs,
but only 500 people were enrolled in the regular two-year course in
social work across the country. Another measure of the price of opportunity is salaries. In many cases, according to the National Social Workers'
Exchange, "salaries fixed before the war have remained stationary."
Meanwhile, wartime inflation had produced a situation in which "visitors
and caseworkers in charity organizations receive less than competent
stenographers, while settlement and civic workers . . . are earning less than
men and women in the trades." All of this was so "despite the fact that
social work has become a recognized profession requiring special training."[32] The contrast with the Red Cross's $170 million budget for 1918
was obvious.

Joining the Red Cross in siphoning off the resources of the social agencies were the YMCA, the recreational programs of the War and Navy Departments, and the various committees of the Council of National Defense. The overall impact was devastating. Experts were drawn into work that, however useful, was peripheral to social change; at the same time, prewar programs were cut back or suspended for the duration. This happened because the experts had no say in setting policy. Furthermore, experts were more than willing to subordinate their plans for remaking society to the immediate needs of winning the war. Here again their chief spokesman was Edward T. Devine. The war made Devine the single most powerful figure in the profession of social work. In June 1917 the National Conference of Social Work asked the Council of National Defense to coordinate the work of its member agencies, thus turning over the direction of social expertise to the government. The council entrusted this task to its Committee on Labor, chaired by Samuel Gompers. He, in turn, delegated the job to the Committee on Publicity. The chairman of this committee was Devine. Devine also was a Columbia professor, director of the New York School of Philanthropy, general secretary of the New York COS, chief of the Red Cross Bureau of Refugees and Home Relief, chairman of the special section on social problems of the war of the National Conference of Social Work, and associate editor of the *Survey*.[33] He was the central connecting link between the war effort and those experts seeking a piece of the action.

His position made his opinions the orthodox view, and so they merit serious attention. "The starting point of all profitable discussion of social forces in wartime," he argued just two weeks before his appointment to the Committee on Publicity, was the recognition "that the nation at war has a prior claim on our services, intellectual and physical, on our possessions, on the institutions we have created, on the leadership and loyalty of which we are capable." Therefore, his idea of coordinating the work of social agencies was to divert their resources as systematically as possible to the military effort. In a passage entitled "The First Obligation," he urged that:

> young men of military age and normal physique who are
> social reformers by instinct and conviction will ordinarily
> find their best occupation at the present time in military

service. . . . there rather than in relief work, or in other
civilian occupations, should social workers and students of
social problems take their place.

National associations for publicity and research would find their "unique
opportunity" lay "not so much [in] carrying out wartime 'programs' in
their corporate capacity, but rather [in] lending their officials to government or to quasi-governmental agencies—usually at no expense to the
borrower. . . ."[34]

Just as he had advocated intervention while acknowledging the dangers
it posed, so too Devine recognized some of the risks his style of coordina-
tion entailed. "Social work," he acknowledged, "is endangered in the war
in various ways." Strapped for funds, "it must take second place to war
taxes, to such immense bond issues as the liberty loan, and to the demands
of war philanthropy." In addition, "it is threatened by the withdrawal of
workers for military duty and for emergency civilian relief." Nonetheless,
"there is no reason for undue alarm." His confidence reflected his priorities:
"the first task is to win the war" while "the second is to preserve what is
good in the nation." Unfortunately Devine did not recognize the risk that
he and his fellow experts might mistake activity in the war effort for influence. This is, in fact, what happened. While uttering hopeful words
about the special fitness of social workers to deal with the convulsions
of war, Devine preached—and practiced—a kind of blind loyalty to the
state that negated them. He claimed "the great social forces of the war"
to be

faith in the righteousness and justice of the national purpose;
reliance on the moral support of the whole body of the people; voluntary suppression of captious criticism; and stregnu-
ous [sic] unified support through all legitimate channels of
those who in the fighting forces or in the government are
carrying the burden of responsibility.

The "conspicuous part" of the "official and voluntary social agencies, educational and philanthropic institutions" was to aid "in securing this unity
of action and unanimity of support."[35]

"Unity of action" and "unanimity of support" were ringing phrases,
but their meanings were supplied by the financiers at the Red Cross and

the officials at the War and Navy Departments rather than by experts. The division directors of civilian relief of the Red Cross, meeting in July 1918, for example, recognized "that Home Service has the best opportunity that the country has ever presented for the widespread, practical teaching of the aims and ideals of social service." Nonetheless, "there was little disposition to encourage the extension of Home Service in any new direction or to widen its scope in any way not strictly necessitated by the needs of the families of soldiers and sailors."[36] This decision that, despite the fervent pleas of experts, mobilization would not be a means of general social reform was made again and again by official and quasi-official bodies.

We have already seen the high price the social professions paid for their commitment to boosting military morale through Home Service work. Maintaining military morals was to prove almost as expensive. This crusade seems to have been a favorite of Secretary of War Newton D. Baker. In May 1917 he appointed a Commission on Training Camp Activities under the chairmanship of Raymond B. Fosdick, of the Rockefeller Foundation, who had recently studied the incidence of venereal disease among General Pershing's troops on the Mexican border. Two months later, Secretary of the Navy Josephus Daniels announced a similar commission, also chaired by Fosdick, for naval and marine training camps. As President Wilson wrote:

> The Federal Government has pledged its word that as far as care and vigilance can accomplish the result, the men committed to its charge will be returned to the homes and communities that so generously gave them with no scars except those won in honorable conflict. The career to which we are calling our young men must be made an asset to them, not only in strengthened and more virile bodies as a result of physical training, not only in minds deepened and enriched by participation in a great, heroic enterprise, but in the enhanced spiritual values which come from a full life lived well and wholesomely.[37]

Wilson's rhetoric is characteristically abstract. In concrete terms, the commissions' initial steps to redeem this pledge were, first, the creation of a zone around each camp where no liquor could be sold and, second, the

pressuring of local city fathers to shut down the red-light districts in
their communities on penalty of having the entire city declared off limits.
As the official history of the commissions noted, "our War and Navy
Departments . . . have taken the position that alcohol and the prostitute
must be kept absolutely away from the soldier. . . ."[38]

Having boarded up the saloon and closed down the bordello and thus
made the city safe for the soldier, the commissions, through a joint Committee on Protective Work for Girls, turned, in the words of a *Survey*
writer, to the "task of protecting girls from the excitement and thought-
lessness produced by the emotions of war playing upon the emotions of
sex." Led by Maude E. Miner, secretary of the New York Probation and
Protective Association, and including Mrs. John D. Rockefeller, Jr.,
among its members, the committee recruited social case workers, probation officers, and "women trained in social service" to staff its protective
bureaus. This campaign too was a great success, and soon young couples
all over the country were being accosted and protected from their own
emotions.[39] If ever an army were to fight with the strength of ten, it was
to be the American Expeditionary Force.

Repression was only part of the commissions' approach. They also
sought to meet the soldier's needs for "wholesome" recreation. This took
numerous forms. Each base had a "Liberty Theatre" where the latest
movies, carefully censored, were screened. Many had "Hostess Houses"
where the men who had visitors could entertain. Singing and band music
were encouraged, and so were athletic events of all kinds. All of this,
even the baseball games, were seen by the commissions as contributing
to ultimate victory. The official history rhapsodized:

> . . . picture the activities of these men as fighters. What bomb-
> throwers those pitchers will make! How resourceful those
> first basemen will be in battle: How keen the catchers! Here
> is aid to discipline, self-discipline at that.[40]

Social experts not only cooperated in this campaign against the sins of
the flesh, they also came themselves to define social problems in terms of
drunkenness and promiscuity. This was an enormous step backward and
one taken as early as June 1917 when the National Conference of Social
Work's session on living and labor standards turned into a prohibition
rally. Prohibition was unanimously approved, "and the discussion seemed

to show," Arthur P. Kellogg reported, "that this was for a permanent policy and not just for war prohibition." Experts had for years struggled against the view that the living standard of the poor could be drastically improved if only they would not waste their substance on drink, but 1917 saw them reviving ideas their own research had discredited. In similar fashion public health took on a narrower meaning. Gertrude Seymour, who, as a collaborator of Dr. Alice Hamilton, was one of the most respected writers on the subject, hailed the war because it had "suddenly defined America's public health problem." Furthermore "the aroused public conscience has promptly enacted measures which, a few months ago, would have been tabled by leisurely officials and classed as visionary schemes. Into a year there has been packed the progress of a decade." The progress came from the "teamwork of many groups united in the determination to provide for a clean and normal social living, . . . in the campaign against venereal diseases."[41] The campaign, as we have seen, was one of repression, not prophylaxis.

Settlement houses also marched in the patriotic parade. Typified by Greenwich House, in New York City, they often acted as liaisons between the Federal War Risk Insurance Bureau and the families of servicemen. Greenwich House also converted "the entire neighborhood . . . into a knitting and serving auxiliary of the Red Cross." It ran Red Cross and Liberty Loan drives, registered alien women, showed war films, and sponsored war rallies. Not only did they heartily participate in the various forms of war service, settlement leaders also fully shared the grand illusion of social experts generally, namely, that the great hustle and bustle on the Home Front represented a triumph for their principles of scientifically directed social control. So Graham Taylor and Robert A. Woods, after acclaiming "the adaptability and readiness which the settlements have shown in meeting many emergency demands exacted by the war," asserted:

> Settlement principles and practices, long locally exemplified, have been embodied in measures taken by the government departments and the National and State Councils of Defense. Thus the Selective Service law has been democratically and successfully operated by utilizing the local resources of the neighborhood and its precinct. The community service being rendered in localities adjacent to war camps emphasizes and

> extends the fellowship in work and play and in the coopera-
> tion between the voluntary and official agencies which settle-
> ments all along have initiated, exemplified and promoted.
>
> Their line of attack against drink and vice in combining
> counter attractions with the enactment and enforcement
> of law has been carried out with such effectiveness by the
> War and Navy Departments and the Councils of Defense as
> to demonstrate these methods to be the best permanent
> public policies.[42]

This proclivity for discerning in the draft and the coercive campaigns
for virtue and patriotism the lineaments of a reformed postwar America,
for making the wish father to the thought, was shared by the academicians
in the social sciences. Reporting their Christmas conventions, Neva R.
Deardorff, assistant director of the Philadelphia Bureau of Municipal
Research, announced that "the theme that ran strongly through all the
annual meetings of the learned societies of the social sciences" was:
"Laissez-Faire is dead! Long live social control!" In the future, "education in idealistic concepts of service, toleration, justice are . . . to underlie
this social control and to make possible an enduring world democracy."
The actual future of higher education, as a recent authoritative study
makes plain, was quite different. The fall semester of 1918 witnessed the
appearance on hundreds of campuses of the Students' Army Training
Corps. "If the face of higher education had been altered previously by
cooperation with the cause," Carol S. Gruber writes, "it was now transformed totally, as the colleges and universities relinquished their function
as centers for the higher learning and dedicated themselves to serving the
needs of the War Department."[43] Academician and expert alike shared
an ideal of service and a vision of a reformed America that would be
guided by the scientific counsel they felt so well equipped to provide.
They also shared the belief that wartime social controls embodied their
favorite principles even when the reality of mobilization entailed the
actual elimination of their favorite programs.

For them the war became an exercise in wish fulfillment. Although
keynote speakers hailed the unparalleled extension of social service, the
reality behind the rhetoric was a diversion of effort from the ongoing
programs of the social agencies to vast campaigns for morale and morality.
The reality of wartime social control, and the role of the expert in it, can

be glimpsed in the campaign for fuel conservation. A statement from the
U.S. Fuel Administration told the social worker that "she" had "a new
opportunity and a new problem." She was to "spiritualize" the rationing
of coal. "In the homes of the poor she can be an interpreter of the sacri-
fices the war has made necessary." Of course, the task itself was trivial.
"The largest percentage of savings will not come from the poor, for
poverty is not wasteful on a large scale." On the other hand, "the social
worker has an opportunity to teach thrift in the stirring name and cause
of patriotism." The tone of this campaign was condescending, almost
contemptuous, toward "the poor." They were to "understand that they
are children of the United States and that our government asks for their
economies just as a father asks for assistance from his boys and girls."[44]
Social control was a family morality play in which the social worker, un-
failingly identified as a "she," was the mother figure charged with carrying out instructions from the Great Father in Washington.

Allen F. Davis has argued that the confidence experts had in wartime
social control was not entirely displaced, that it was reasonable for them
to regard mobilization measures as extensions of their crusades for social
justice. In part his case depends on citing gains made by groups like labor
unions, whose right to collective bargaining was recognized by the National
War Labor Policies Board, the U.S. Employment Service, and other wartime agencies. And the fact is that some mobilization measures did institute
some degree of planning of the sort experts had long been calling for.
What became of these measures we shall see later. For the rest, Davis's
case rests on his willingness to find a silver lining for every cloud. Thus
he writes: "The story of the treatment of the immigrant and alien during
the war was also not entirely bleak. . . . at the time the patriotic enthusiasm seemed in some cases to accelerate the process of Americanization."
Yet even Davis concedes that the experts "deluded themselves. They were
the victims of their own confidence and enthusiasm, for the social reforms of the war years were caused more by the emergency situation
than by a reform consensus."[45]

Davis's view, it seems to me, exaggerates the reformlike appearance
of mobilization and underestimates the experts' fatal infatuation with
social control. Experts started out in 1917 with high hopes of making
mobilization a means of reform. But they had also, under the leadership
of Devine, conceded the complete priority of military considerations and
had accepted the leadership of the Wilson administration and the eastern

philanthropic establishment. By 1918 they were captivated both by their own busyness in the war effort and the nobility of Wilson's internationalism, with the result that experts could hail the actual program of mobilization as a potential reform. Regarding their subordinate position on the Home Front as an aberration due to military necessity and sure to change as the value of scientific social control proved itself, experts bolstered their own morale with the notion that their work was contributing to the great victory. The war's end found them convinced, as they had been in April 1917, that the hour of scientific reform was about to strike. Devine congratulated his fellow engineers that "the war and all its limitations are behind us." What lay ahead of them was "the pursuit, not of peace—a negative and empty thing in itself—but of happiness, a social order in which all shall have income enough to live on, education enough to know how to live, and health enough to enjoy life."[46]

The vast extension of governmental activity the war brought had somehow not produced the unique opportunities Devine had forecast. Instead, war work had constrained the development of social expertise. Even so, experts were not discouraged. Most had been deeply involved in the war effort, and they shared in the general exultation victory produced. In addition, patriotic activity had proved a powerful deterrent to analysis. The full realization of what wartime social control had meant would await their bitter encounter with postwar realities.

The dream that a scientific reconstruction would follow the Armistice rested in part upon the mistaken belief that wartime volunteer activity could be converted into postwar reform campaigns. Lillian Wald, Mary E. Richmond, and Florence Kelley, for example, believed that their Council of Organizations for War Service in New York City "not only stimulates and directs the enthusiasm to work for the common good while the war lasts, but also prepares and helps to maintain a body of well-informed and socially minded citizens who will be needed for equally necessary national service during the sober period of reconstruction." Their council had functioned as a "clearing house" to direct "the large numbers of women willing to serve but ignorant of the most pressing needs, and to standardize the conditions and the quality of volunteer work. . . ."[47]

Another prop of this belief was a highly selective view of patriotism. In 1916 John Dewey had offered a hopeful distinction between "real Americanism," a "unity of feeling and aim, a freedom of intercourse," on the one hand, and "a sense of unity within a charmed area . . . accompanied by dislike, by hostility, to all without," on the other. Dewey thought it possible for Americans to have the first without the second. Edward T. Devine, as we have seen, was not so sanguine; but he too accentuated the positive, unifying, side of nationalism while downplaying its negative, repressive, side. The campaign of 1916 with its virulent anti-hyphenate rhetoric, the prosecutions under the Sedition Act, the strident advertisements of the Creel Committee, the Post Office's attacks upon the Socialist party, all demonstrated the utopian nature of Dewey's distinction and gave the lie to Devine's confidence that wartime sentiments could be channeled into reform. For, as George Creel described it, the goal of the Wilson administration was "no mere surface unity, but a passionate belief of the United States into one white-hot mass instinct with fraternity, devotion, courage, and deathless determination." And, as even Creel was willing to admit, the Wilson administration, with his help, had succeeded only too well. Creel condemned "the mad rumors that swept the country," the "persecution" of the Nonpartisan League in North Dakota, the actions of some State Councils of Defense "that would have been lawless in any other than a 'patriotic' body," and the "professional" Americanizers.[48] Those who play with "white-hot" masses are going to get burned.

Nonetheless, it was possible for wishful thinkers, even in 1918 or 1919, to seek to harness patriotism to the reform cause. For its full meaning had been appreciated only by its victims. Felix Adler, of the Ethical Culture Society, could wish "to perpetuate, to a degree, at least, the high tide of feeling, the moral exaltation of the war," because to him, patriotism was "the chevalier, romantic, idealistic spirit." Such a view was not baseless. The war had produced a good deal of selfless dedication. The experts' wishfulness arose from their belief that it was possible to have the "idealistic spirit" without the "mad rumors" or "persecutions." Experts shared, that is, Dewey's distinction. The experience of Charles F. Weller, associate secretary of the Playground and Recreation Association of America, helps to explain why this was so. Before the war Weller found the average American community characterized by "such extreme localism, such blind indifference to the needs and achievements of other cities, such smug complacency, that I declared: 'There *is* no America in the sense of a common consciousness, a national spirit.' " Meanwhile his association skimped along on an annual budget, for 1917, of $150,000. A year later, a member of the War Camp Community Service, which operated on a budget of $15 million, Weller found that "America was roused by war with its international ideals—that new America of the spirit which, except in great crises, has been potential only." Weller found too that "timidity and weakness in community undertakings have been superseded by a new great sense of power."[49]

Desiring to preserve this "new great sense of power," social experts chose to ignore the repressive aspects of the "chevalier" spirit. This was actually put to a vote at a *Survey*-sponsored Conference on Demobilization held for approximately 100 executives of social agencies held over Thanksgiving weekend in 1918. According to the *Survey*'s own account, Norman Thomas, of the National Civil Liberties Bureau, gave a "moving description of the abuse of conscientious objectors in federal prisons." This led to a "sterile discussion" of a resolution in favor of freedom of speech, press, and assembly. Its sponsor, Mary K. Simkhovitch, argued that "without freedom to meet, to speak and to print, social reform may as well shut up shop." The opposition urged that they did "not wish to criticize the government for any war action" and "assumed that all civil rights would be recovered as soon as, in the opinion of a wise administration, such action could be taken." In "a very small vote," at the end of a "prolonged session," the resolution was tabled by a majority of one vote.[50]

Attorney General A. Mitchell Palmer would soon demonstrate what plans the "wise administration" had for civil liberties. In the meantime, social experts busied themselves with plans for a new America. The most important of these had to do with economic arrangements, particularly with the questions of collective bargaining and full employment. Edward T. Devine's complacent optimism was widespread. "Hereafter," he announced, "all differences will be understood to have a public interest." This public interest, he was confident, would not only permit trade unions to organize and bargain, but would encourage and, in some cases, insist upon them. Collective bargaining, supplemented by compulsory arbitration, would replace the old era's labor wars, and labor would finally receive its just reward. "Trade unions will have pretty much their own way hereafter about hours of labor and standards of work."[51]

Felix Frankfurter, the chairman of the U.S. Labor Policies Board, had a more immediate knowledge of labor-management relations and took a more cautious position. While he acknowledged that "the standard of collective dealing received a great forward momentum during the war," the future Supreme Court justice pointed out that with war's end "these standards which the government has adopted and enforced . . . will lose the impetus which the government can give them." So although American business needed "a substitution of law and order for the present status between anarchy and violence by which it is governed," the American tradition of laissez faire was "tremendous" and "the direct participation of the government is likely to be a meager one in the next few years." Frankfurter placed his hopes not upon the government but upon "the consensus of public opinion." Frank P. Walsh, joint chairman [with former president Taft] of the National War Labor Board, was even more pessimistic. He told the Conference on Demobilization that, on the key issues of the right of workers to deal collectively with their employers through unions and of the right to a living wage, the five employers on the board all voted in the negative. These rights were approved only because he and Taft joined the five union members in voting for them. He warned the conference that "anyone who hopes to lay down a 'constructive' program that both sides to the labor situation will accept, is chasing rainbows."[52]

Despite this warning from one of their own, expert optimism remained unshaken. John A. Fitch, reporting on this session of the conference, wrote of "a better day for labor and a better day for mankind, a world in which democracy shall take on a new and deeper meaning—this was the vision of the future beheld by every speaker at the *Survey* dinner on November 30, and which they made visible also to the mind of every diner." This is an impression that reading the published minutes of the session does not corroborate. They do contain an abundance of optimistic forecasting; but they also contain, in addition to Walsh's forebodings, a warning from Alexander M. Bing, a mediator with the Industrial Service Section of the Ordnance Bureau, that "most manufacturers of ordnance are bitterly opposed to unionism," and one from W. H. Hamilton, of the War Labor Policies Board, that the too-rapid demobilization of the army would lead to falling wages and a possible depression.[53]

Less than two weeks later the Academy of Political Science held a conference on "Labor Reconstruction," capped by a banquet in the grand ballroom of the Hotel Astor to celebrate America's "industrial victory" in the war. Although "the number of men in overalls in the Astor ballroom was almost negligible," Frank A. Vanderlip, of the National City Bank, Charles M. Schwab, of Bethlehem Steel, and Samuel Gompers, of the American Federation of Labor, were there to toast each other as a "great captain of finance," the "greatest captain of industry in the United States," and the "greatest labor leader in the world" respectively. Beneath this veneer of good fellowship left over from wartime coopera-tion, however, were clear indications that 1919 would be a year of serious labor troubles. Vanderlip set the tone by calling for a "return to the old order [,] the sooner the restrictions are removed, the sooner we will be prepared to start on what will be a long, hard race." Schwab made the same point. Predicting, perhaps for the sake of form, that capital and labor would reach a "better economic understanding," and affirming that "one of the things we have learned from this war is that this is the age of democracy," his main point was that "we must have individual ownership and operation" of industry. Foreshadowing the stand his industry would take against the AFL's efforts to organize steel in the great strike of 1919, Schwab praised Gompers for his "stand against Socialism and Bolshevism." Gompers was not sure he deserved credit "because I am not a Bolshevik." And while he too paid homage to the language of industrial peace" and "cooperation," his message was plain. ". . . labor must not be asked to give up what it has won" during the war. "We shall never go back to the old conditions."[54]

Those who believed in omens might have pondered the meaning of the fact that the "Labor Reconstruction" banquet was held in the midst of a waiters' strike. In fact, it did prove a portent of things to come. The year 1919 saw an extraordinary number of bitterly contested strikes. Even without the omen, the stances taken by Vanderlip, Schwab, and Gompers should have been enough to chasten all but the most willful optimists. Neither capital nor labor had shown any interest in the ra-tional arbitration of disputes. Instead both sides were girding themselves for the coming test of strength. Nonetheless, Fitch told *Survey* readers that the conference was "as a whole forward-looking and constructive."[55]

Experts had no more success in persuading the government that it should regulate the labor market in the interests of full employment than they had in convincing labor and management of the merits of arbitration. A straw in the wind was Graham Taylor's proposal to use the selective service system to rationalize the impact of demobilization. He suggested that the local boards, "one of the greatest war achievements of modern democracy," could function as employment centers. To get the service-man to report to his local board, Taylor proposed that the military require that his last pay voucher be signed by a board member. This plan was no sooner offered than ignored. Within two weeks of first broaching it, Taylor had to report that "the general staff of the army has rendered its military decision upon the procedure in demobilizing soldiers with no perceptible regard for the very serious problem of reemployment." Worse still, Secretary of War Baker, who, as president of the National Consumer's League, was regarded by the experts as their special friend in Washington, had endorsed this "military" policy.[56]

Following hard upon the rejection of Taylor's idea came the collapse of the Federal Employment Service. The service had been the government's employment agency, and its demise occurred despite virtual unanimity among experts that it should have been continued. The platform adopted by the Conference on American Reconstruction Problems, called by the National Municipal League, for example, listed the Employment Service first among those "temporary [that is, wartime] powers" the American people should not let "slip through their fingers in the next few months." They urged that the service "be encouraged to extend its sphere to include the education of employers in modern principles of employment." The *Survey*'s own Conference on Demobilization called for it to be "perpetuated, extended and improved." Moreover, for a brief period, prospects for its continuation appeared to be good. Its assistant-director-general, Nathan S. Smith, told the Academy of Political Science's "Labor Reconstruction" Conference that "the Employment Service is now so thoroughly organized and has the backing of the government to such an extent" that he felt "very optimistic about the future." Robert W. Bruère, director of the service for the state of New York, shared Smith's rosy view of the future. He believed that the war had engendered in both employers and employees "the new habit . . . of working together for a common end." Because of this he expected "a considerable measure of progress towards peace in industry." He informed the Conference on Demobilization that "all efforts in that direction encouraged by the employment service were meeting with satisfactory response."[57]

There were portions of Bruère's report, however, that gainsaid his confident tone. He had to note that war industries in New York were demobilizing "practically without any concerted action between government and industry, but guided almost entirely by the exigencies of the actual economic situation." Furthermore, he "had to admit" that the Employment Service "only played a small part in the process" of demobilization. Finally, he and other state directors of the service had found themselves "without definite directions from Washington" and what cooperative action between the national government and the local offices did exist rested "almost entirely upon local initiative and capacity."[58]

Experts like Bruère did not realize that these early signs of federal neglect foreshadowed the policy of the Wilson administration to meet the labor problems of the postwar era with the repressive tactics of the Red Scare rather than with the rational techniques of social engineering. This did not become clear to them, despite the signs we have been cataloging, until a March 1919 White House conference of governors and mayors to discuss "the proper method of restoring all the labor conditions of the country to a normal basis as soon as possible." Secretary of Labor Wilson's opening address removed all doubts. He spoke of the dangers of radical propaganda and charged that the strikes at Seattle, Butte, Paterson, and Lawrence "were not industrial in their origin but political, having as their objective the establishment of a soviet form of government in America." A "depressed" Fitch reported the "conference apparently had two emotions, fear and a sort of aimless patriotism." Its social vision "reached no further than a patchwork of emergency employment"— measures motivated solely by "the fear of what may happen if men are hungry." For the rest "there was bitter denunciation, accompanied by flag waving, of theories that the conference disagreed with or could not understand."[59]

The awakening was as rude as the dream had been pleasant. Experts had hoped, in Felix Adler's words, "that we should have a new purchase in all the work we are doing . . . for the uplift of labor and all kinds of social work" because "the national consciousness has been developed during these few years and [the] people feel they want to do something for the nation." Experts sadly discovered that saying "for the sake of the *nation* we want this better condition of labor" could not compete with more virulent expressions of nationalism. The ax fell on the Employment Service the week after the conference. A Republican filibuster in the Senate had killed a deficiency bill to supply it with funds, and President Wilson decided against using his special fund to maintain it.[60]

The experts' other plans for rationalizing and regulating the labor market met the same fate. The most elaborate came from three experts of the War Labor Policies Board. They called for a "well-thought-out and consistent policy" and, having worked out an elaborate flow chart of the rate of demobilization and its likely effects, proposed a five-point program. It included extensive surveying of the employment market, continuation of the Capital Issues Committee and the War Finance Corporation, "proper distribution of government orders . . . to concentrate demand at strategic points where business is slack," a demobilization policy regulated by labor demand, and a system of "buffer employment" of public works projects to maintain full employment. The War Committee of the Union League Club of Chicago reprinted this proposal from the *Survey* and sent out 100,000 copies to members of Congress, governors, and other state officials, chambers of commerce and labor federations in cities, and all county commissioners. None of this lobbying, however, had any effect on the Wilson administration.[61]

Despite the Council of National Defense's grandiose claim that "the gigantic forces, such as the War Board and other newly created war agencies . . . are now demonstrating their far-reaching power and efficiency in the paths of Peace—in binding up the Nation's wounds by wisely considered plans of reconstruction and readjustment," the terrible fact, experts gradually discovered, was that the Wilson administration had no plans other than a rapid return to the status quo ante bellum. President Wilson informed Congress as early as December 1918 that "from no quarter have I seen any general scheme of 'reconstruction' emerge which I thought it likely we could force our spirited businessmen and self-reliant laborers to accept with due pliancy and obedience."[62] And, given their head, the spirited businessmen and self-reliant laborers spent the immediate postwar period locked in a struggle almost to the death.

While there was no lack of rhetorical commitment from administration officials to a new American democracy "purged of all class distinctions, of every vestige of privilege, of every hoary-bearded tradition that fetters justice," they saw the "acute problem of reestablishing ourselves upon a normal post-war basis," as Secretary of Labor Wilson put it, in terms of avoiding "any long sustained period of industrial unrest" that "might lead . . . to a recurrence of such horrors as those of the French revolution or to the spread of the menace of Russian Bolshevism." The solution the secretary saw was to get "business going and keep it going."[63] Given such an orientation, could the Red Scare be far behind?

If there was little in Secretary Wilson's views to distinguish them from those of the U.S. Chamber of Commerce or the National Civic Federation, they do possess the merit of being representative of administration thinking. Secretary of Interior Lane, for example, also had no use for "plans for making over our industrial or financial or economic lives." He cautioned against those who "in a tangle or a haze" cry out, "Let us refer the whole business to a body of experts." Some expertise, he admitted, was necessary in government, "yet experts . . . have the same capacity for imperialism, for cowardice, and for subserviency as all other men." When given authority, they "have a tendency to exercise it ruthlessly. . . ." Completing this catalog of experts' flaws, Lane noted, "they are also as weak-kneed as men in general before the hasty judgments and clamor of the multitude or the will of those who are politically powerful."[64]

With the Wilson administration joining the business community and labor in turning a deaf ear to expert schemes for a rationally reconstructed America, the social engineers could only deplore "the rapidity with which the interdepartmental organizations are breaking up in Washington" and lament that "in the general process of dismantling 'war services,' some uncommonly useful pieces of social work are in danger of going by the board." One example was the federal housing projects, "an unusually strong combination of public spirit and professional ability that might have been available at any time, had the nation cared to make use of it." There was the question of the hour for the experts: Did the nation care to use their services? As one member of the *Survey* staff put it, "only a strong and immediate expression of public opinion can rescue from an untimely end the new agencies and methods established during the war which would be valuable in preacetime."[65]

This hope was not as naïve as it may seem. If the experts sometimes spoke as though some great disinterested and intelligent public were waiting only to be aroused by the truth before demanding one or another reform, they also counted on the great "quasi-official" agencies like the Red Cross or the War Camp Community Service, which did enjoy wide popular support, to support their programs. The distinction here is analogous to the one Richard Hofstadter drew between the "hard" and "soft" sides of American agrarianism. In his "hard" role the American farmer was an aggressive speculator in real estate and commodities. When prices fell, however, he reverted to his "soft" role of stalwart yeoman, the moral guardian of the nation, and the innocent victim of financial intrigue.[66] The "hard" form of the experts' belief in public opinion rested upon the prestige and influence of the Red Cross and other "moral agencies."

Both the Red Cross and the War Camp Community Service (WCCS) had grown to enormous size by the end of the war. The WCCS employed 426 social workers and operated in some 600 communities. The Red Cross was larger still. Its Home Service section alone operated in some 10,000 communities. The full-time staff of 600 oversaw the activities of thousands of volunteers. About 1,000 of these had been graduated from the Home Service institutes, and another 5,000 to 7,000 had attended some sort of training program. In addition to their numerical strength the quasi-official agencies were financially sound. The United War Work Campaign, which funded the WCCS, had raised $170.5 million, a sum large enough to support its member agencies through September 1919. The Red Cross meanwhile launched, in late 1918, a campaign for $60 million.[67]

There were, then, some grounds for the expert hope that a "community service through which the morale and efficiency of industrial workers shall be developed as the War Camp Community Service has strengthened these same men while dressed in Khaki" and for the belief that the Red Cross's "Home Service sections will probably go on." These expectations were related to another. The connection was, as Devine expressed it, that many a businessman "has found his real vocation in some form of war-relief work." Because "the established varieties of social work" could match the interest of war relief, "social agencies in which volunteers are needed should reap the after-war harvest of the seed they have sown broadcast."[68]

However erroneous it proved to be, this belief recognized an important reality; the experts did not control the agencies they wished to use in reconstructing America. Businessmen did. This was true on the national level, where politicians, financiers, and industrialists monopolized the boards of trustees. It was true on the local level as well where merchants and bankers held sway. The WCCS, for example, had deliberately organized the "best" citizens in every community. As Charles Weller pointed out, the war had given the community organizer entree to the social elite. This stood in marked contrast to the prewar days when for "many toilsome years" community service had been "the work mainly of the less important men and women." These middle-class experts had "lingered humbly around the tables of the great to catch their falling crumbs" forced to offer "pathetic gratitude 'for small favors thankfully received.' " While, to judge from Weller's tone, the memory of those days still rankled, it also added a special savor to the glories of the war years. Once the war came, the "best" people were so frightened by the specters of venereal disease and sexual promiscuity haunting their communities that "now an ordinary social worker camouflaged as a representative of the United States government visits a city, summons several of the great ones to meet him and finally nominates 15 or 20 of the foremost men and women to Joseph Lee, who sends them letters of appointment from Washington."[69] The question, soon to be answered in the negative, was whether local elites would continue to defer to ordinary social workers *without* their camouflage as government representatives.

In similar fashion, W. Frank Persons had discovered that businessmen had shown "a remarkable interest" in Home Service during the war. The reason, he felt, was that they regarded the work "as a community responsibility which they, as leaders, must see through. . . ." Experts like Weller, glorying in their new sense of self-esteem, exulted that Americans "have learned that class distinctions are unimportant, that fellowship with different kinds of people is essential to democracy." Actually, as Persons— and Weller's own account for that matter—made clear, community organization work had recognized, built upon, and reinforced class distinctions. The prosaic truth is that there was little of democracy in the work of persuading the "best people" to clamp down on saloons and brothels or to sponsor "wholesome" substitutes. Jessica Peixotto, chairperson of the Council of National Defense's Department of Child Welfare, told the simple truth: ". . . that work has been for people, and not by people."[70]

Weller's scheme of developing "in each community a leader or organizer who will enable the local people to find satisfactory activities and relationships for their leisure hours" did not outlive the war. The cause of its demise, however, did not lay, as Weller feared, in "excessive individualism and provincialism" so much as in the fact that businessmen had their own ideas of community service expressed in organizations such as the Rotary. With the war over and the training camps dismantled, local elites could dispense with the services of the social worker, who became, once more, a humble petitioner. They could suppress the drinking of the lower orders with prohibition, segregate the red-light district, and display their patriotic fervor in the American Protective League.[71]

The Red Cross, with similar leadership, followed a path similar to that of the WCCS. Willoughby Walling, a Chicago businessman, replaced

Persons as director-general of the Department of Civilian Relief and oversaw the liquidation of Home Service.[72]

Reconstruction was a mirage. And once experts realized this, they
found themselves in that special desert of reformers, the 1920s. Allen
Davis has perceptively noted that "it was not the war itself which killed
reform, but rather the rejection afterward of the wartime measures which
seemed at the time to constitute the climax to the crusade for social
justice."[73] Surely it was not the experts' fault that they were unable to
persuade the relevant sectors of the American power structure to promote
their programs. On the other hand, they cannot escape responsibility for
their own disillusionment. For the wartime measures only *seemed* to
climax the crusade for social justice and then only in the limited sense
that they seemed to embody the *principles,* but not the substance, of
expert proposals. A man like Devine knew this very well. And for him,
as for the other experts, something more than social justice had been
at stake. Professional opportunity had been Devine's lodestone. And that
opportunity had proved to be a mirage as well.

James Weinstein has written that "the wartime experience . . . laid
bare, for those few who dared look, the essential powerlessness of the
reformers, social workers, and social engineers who joined the crusade to
save democracy." And, he added, "if they allowed themselves unwittingly
to be used, it was because they had the conceit to consider their intelligence and social values equal to the influence of the industrial and financial institutions that were the heart and muscle of American power."[74]
This is a harsh verdict. Experts did, however, badly miscalculate their
prospects of exercising real power. This was not because they fancied
they could outmuscle the financial and industrial giants[75] so much as it
was that they believed that expertise would make such tests of strength
obsolete. Arbitration and other forms of professional mediation, for
example, would—in their judgment—obviate the need for strikes or lock-
outs. So too scientific assimilation was to eliminate ethnicity as a divisive
issue. Experts, that is, failed to see that wartime cooperation between
capital and labor, or between native Americans and immigrants, was
possible only because of the larger international conflict. And so they
failed to understand how temporary that cooperation would prove.

Experts, as we have seen, had from the 1890s on defined themselves
as intermediaries and interpreters. Their own class position dictated as
much. And so they built their careers on the premise that conflict was

merely a byproduct of misunderstanding. They systematically under-
estimated the importance of divergent interests and disregarded the
possibility that social issues really could be settled by force.[76] The experts' besetting illusion in this regard was twofold. On the one hand,
despite the omnipresent example of the war, they assumed all problems
could be settled peacefully and, on the other, they fancied that they
could scientifically determine the content of those solutions. One can
label this latter "conceit," if one wishes; however, we should recognize
that it derived less from personal vanity than from professional aspirations.

NOTES

1. See H. C. Peterson and Gilbert C. Fite, *Opponents of War, 1917-
1918* (Seattle, Wash.: University of Washington Press, 1957), pp. 6, 27-28,
123, 216; and Charles Chatfield, *For Peace and Justice: Pacifism in
America, 1914-1941* (Boston: Beacon Press, 1973), who notes that the
"typical leader" of the pacifist organizations "was a social worker, clergy-
man, educator, or publicist" (p. 30). Allen F. Davis, "Welfare, Reform
and World War I," *American Quarterly* 19 (Fall 1967), states of the experts: ". . . when the United States declared war most of them went along
with the decision, with fear and trembling but with loyalty" (p. 518).

2. Statement by P. U. Kellogg, May 25, 1917. Survey Associates
Papers, Folder: 5. Clarke Chambers has written a comprehensive and
sympathetic account of *Paul U. Kellogg and the Survey: Voices for
Social Welfare and Social Change* (Minneapolis, Minn.: University of
Minnesota Press, 1971). He does not, however, examine the controversy
with the *Survey*'s editorial board over the issue of American entry into
the war.

3. Paul U. Kellogg, "The Fighting Issues: A Statement by the Editor
of the Survey," *Survey* 37 (February 17, 1917): 573.

4. Edward T. Devine, "Ourselves and Europe: I," *Survey* 37 (November 4, 1916): 100.

5. C. Wright Mills, "The Professional Ideology of Social Pathologists,"
American Journal of Sociology 49 (1943), reprinted in Irving Louis
Horowitz, ed., *Power, Politics & People: Collected Essays of C. Wright
Mills* (New York: Ballantine Books, 1963), pp. 525-52.

6. Edward T. Devine, "Ourselves and Europe: II Enduring Peace,"
Survey 37 (November 18, 1916): 158.

7. Kellogg, "The Fighting Issues," p. 574.

8. Devine, "Ourselves and Europe: II Enduring Peace," p. 158; Allen
F. Davis, *Spearheads for Reform: The Social Settlements and the Progres-*

sive Movement, 1890-1914 (New York: Oxford University Press, 1967), chap. 10, "The Progressive Crusade."

9. Kellogg, "The Fighting Issues," p. 575; Devine, "Ourselves and Europe: I," p. 100.

10. Paul U. Kellogg to Arthur P. Kellogg, October 10, 1917, Survey Associates Papers (SAP), File: 654; Edward T. Devine, "Social Forces in War Time," *Survey* 38 (June 30, 1917): 290-91, 297; Paul U. Kellogg, draft of a Report: To Survey Associates and All Survey Readers, 1917, SAP, File: 654, 5. Kellogg originally intended to include the statement, quoted in the text, concerning the three-month moratorium on discussion of the war, "but Mr. Devine, while he said it was entirely all right thought it would merely and unnecessary [*sic*] stir up things," Paul U. Kellogg to Arthur P. Kellogg, October 10, 1917. The Survey Associates Papers contain no record of the board meeting that, presumably, decided the matter.

11. Draft of a Report, 1-2.

12. Paul U. Kellogg, draft of a reply to Flora Davidson's scathing attack on the *Survey,* "Social Workers Present Arms," *Social Work Today,* October 1934, in SAP, File: 661, 2.

13. This was Kellogg's title for that section of his editor's report deleted on Devine's advice. Paul U. Kellogg to Arthur P. Kellogg, October 10, 1917.

14. Draft of a reply to "Social Workers Present Arms," p. 3; Open letter from Mary K. Simkhovitch, reprinted in the *Survey* 38 (April 7, 1917): 30. Simkhovitch's husband was a Russian émigré.

15. "In Support of the President," *Survey* 37 (March 10, 1917): 659; "Communications," *Survey* 37 (March 24, 1917): 729-30.

16. Trustee *Minutes,* pp. 393-95 (March 26, 1917); 402 (April 30, 1917). See Trustee *Minutes,* pp. 408-10 (October 29, 1917), for a list of eleven RSF staff members working more or less full time on the war effort.

17. "Mobilized on Moving Day: Red Cross Work in the Midst of Difficulties," *Survey* 37 (March 17, 1917): 687. For the full war program adopted by the Commission on the Church and Social Service of the Federal Council of Churches of Christ in America, see "What The Church Offers the Nation," *Survey* 38 (April 21, 1917): 70-71.

18. "Plans for the Care of Soldier's Families," *Survey* 38 (April 7, 1917): 20; "In the Rookies Playtime: Plans for the Recreation of Soldiers in Training," *Survey* 38 (May 12, 1917): 137; "War Resolutions," *Survey* 38 (June 23, 1917): 276-77.

19. Arthur P. Kellogg, "The National Conference of Social Work," *Survey* 38 (June 16, 1917): 253; Robert A. Woods, "Looking Forward:

A New Name and a New Era in the National Conference," *Survey* 38 (June 16, 1917): 269. The old name was the National Conference of Charities and Corrections.

20. Edward T. Devine, "Social Forces in War Time," *Survey* 38 (July 7, 1917): 314. This was one of a series of articles by Devine under this title. See "Organized Social Work and the War," *Survey* 38 (May 19, 1917): 71. Many academicians shared this view. See "What May Sociologists Do Toward Solving the Problems of the Present War Situation," *American Journal of Sociology* 23, no. 1 (July, 1917): 1-66, for forty-one replies, especially J. L. Gillin, "The Sociologist as Social Prophet," pp. 13-14.

21. Alice Hamilton, M.D., and Gertrude Seymour, "The New Public Health: III," *Survey* 38 (April 21, 1917): 59; "Social Forces in War Time," *Survey* 38 (July 14, 1917): 337; John A. Fitch, "A Reveille to American Industry: Some Social Consequences of the Stock-taking of Men and Machines," *Survey* 38 (March 17, 1917): 693; Henry P. Fairchild, "Land Distribution and Birth Control," in "What May Sociologists Do Toward Solving the Problems of the Present War Situation," p. 26.

22. See "Industrial Safeguards in War-Time," *Survey* 38 (March 31, 1917): 761; Petersen and Fite, *Opponents of War,* pp. 53-56; "Social Forces in War Time" (July 21, 1917), p. 353; John A. Fitch, "Sabotage and Disloyalty," *Survey* 39 (October 13, 1917): 36; "Social Forces in War Time (July 7, 1917)" p. 317; Kellogg memorandum to *Survey* staff, n.d. (April-May 1917), SAP, File: 654.

23. "Social Forces in War Time," p. 317.

24. "The Red Cross Civilian Relief Plan: Organization of the Chapters and a Great Campaign for Money," *Survey* 38 (May 19, 1917): 162-64; *Dictionary of American Biography,* 21: 446; *National Cyclopedia of Biography,* 6: 489; 18: 215; 20: 88.

25. "The Red Cross Civilian Relief Plan," p. 162.

·26. "Social Forces in War Time" (August 11, 1917), p. 424.

27. The *Survey* published these appointments as they were made, and the figure in the text is based upon this source. It should be noted that the *Survey*'s listings may not have been complete. For Deacon's appointment, see "Jottings," *Survey* 39 (February 23, 1918): 560.

28. Paul U. Kellogg, "Four Months in France: An Interpretation of the American Red Cross, I: Here to Work," *Survey* 39 (November 24, 1917): 182. Shortly after this article had been published, Kellogg was appointed to the Red Cross Emergency Relief Commission to Italy. See "Seven Weeks in Italy: The Response of the American Red Cross to the Emergency–I," *Survey* 39 (February 2, 1918): 486.

29. W. Frank Persons, "Home Service: The Work of the American Red Cross in the United States," *Survey* 39 (January 5, 1918): 397.

30. "Plans for the Care of Soldiers' Families," p. 20; "Training Civilian War Workers," *Survey* 39 (December 22, 1917): 351: "Home Service by the Red Cross," *Survey* 38 (September 1, 1917): 486.

31. Robert A. Woods, "The Trend of Social Service," *Survey* 39 (December 22, 1917): 339. This is a report on state social work conferences in Indiana, Minnesota, Wisconsin, Iowa, Missouri, and Massachusetts; and so Woods's opinion can be seen as reflecting a wide sample of social experts.

32. "Home Service at the Front," *Survey* 40 (June 15, 1918): 321; Edith Shatto King, "Wanted–Social Workers," *Survey* 40 (May 4, 1918): 126.

33. Edward T. Devine, "Social Forces in War Time," *Survey* 38 (July 28, 1917): 374; "Jottings," *Survey* 39 (October 6, 1917); "War-Time Training and Programs," *Survey* 38 (May 12, 1917): 146.

34. Edward T. Devine, "Social Forces in War Time," *Survey* 38 (July 14, 1917): 336; *Survey* 38 (August 18, 1917): 438; *Survey* 38 (September 22, 1917): 546.

35. Edward T. Devine, "Social Forces in War Time," *Survey* 38 (July 7, 1917): 314; *Survey* 38 (August 18, 1917): 438.

36. "After a Year of Home Service," *Survey* 40 (July 27, 1918): 482.

37. Bruno Lasker, "In the Rookies' Playtime," pp. 137-38; Woodrow Wilson, "Special Statement," in Edward Frank Allen, *Keeping Our Fighters Fit: For War and After* (New York, 1918). This was written "with the cooperation of Raymond B. Fosdick." Fosdick's name appears on the cover as the author. Wilson's statement is not paginated.

38. "Making Cities Safe for Soldiers," *Survey* 38 (July 28, 1917): 376; Allen, *Keeping Our Fighters Fit,* p. 15.

39. Winthrop D. Lane, "Girls and Khaki: Some Practical Measures of Protection for Young Women in Time of War," *Survey* 39 (December 1, 1917): 236; "Protective Officers for Girls Wanted," *Survey* 40 (January 26, 1918): 465.

40. Allen, *Keeping Our Fighters Fit;* the quotation appears on p. 51.

41. A. P. Kellogg, "The National Conference of Social Work," p. 255; Gertrude Seymour, "The Health of Soldier and Civilian: Some Aspects of the American Health Movement in War-Time," *Survey* 40 (April 27, 1918): 89, 92-93.

42. Anne O'Hagan, "A Settlement War Service Bureau," *Survey* 40 (August 24, 1918): 580-81; Graham Taylor and Robert A. Woods, "The War-Time Outlook of Social Settlements," *Survey* 40 (August 31, 1918): 616.

43. Neva R. Deardorff, "The Demise of a Highly Respected Doctrine," *Survey* 39 (January 12, 1918): 416; Carol S. Gruber, *Mars and Minerva:*

World War I and the Uses of the Higher Learning in America (Baton Rouge, La.: Louisiana State University Press, 1975). The quotation appears on pp. 213-14.

44. "Coal and the Social Worker: Prepared for *The Survey* by the United States Fuel Administration," *Survey* 40 (September 14, 1918): 659, 660.

45. Davis, "Welfare, Reform and World War I," pp. 521, 527, 532.

46. A measure of the priority given military priorities is the scant attention given in the *Survey* to the conviction of Eugene V. Debs on three counts of violating the Espionage Act. The *Survey* limited itself to commenting that this "constitutes perhaps the highest point reached by the government in its efforts to punish violators of that act." "The Trial Of Eugene V. Debs," *Survey* 40 (September 21, 1918): 695. For the experts' endorsement of Wilsonian idealism, see Paul U. Kellogg, "The 'Wilson Policies,' " *Survey* 41 (October 19, 1918): 59-61. For the atmosphere of postwar optimism, see Edward T. Devine [with the cooperation of the *Survey* staff] "Between War and Peace," *Survey* 41 (November 16, 1918): 180.

47. "A Clearing House for War Volunteers," *Survey* 40 (August 17, 1918): 565.

48. John Dewey, "Nationalizing Education," *National Education Association Addresses and Proceedings* (1916), pp. 183, 184; Petersen and Fite, *Opponents of War,* chap. 19, "The Sedition Act"; James Weinstein, *The Decline of Socialism in America* (New York: Monthly Review Press, 1967); George Creel, *How We Advertised America* (New York, 1920), pp. 5, 170, 180, 184.

49. Felix Adler, "A New Purpose," *Survey* 41 (December 7, 1918): 288. Adler made these remarks at a *Survey*-sponsored Conference on Demobilization of which he was chairman. Weller's remarks were made at the same conference. See Charles F. Weller, "Permanent Values in War Camp Community Service," *Survey* 41 (December 7, 1918): 297.

50. See "The Conference on Demobilization," *Survey* 41 (December 7, 1918): 287; and A. P. K. [Arthur P. Kellogg], "Shall Social Agencies Unite for Reconstruction," *Survey* 41 (December 7, 1918): 317. The record of social workers on civil liberties issues, although hardly commendable, was by no means worse than that of other groups. Paul L. Murphy's authoritative *The Meaning of Freedom of Speech: First Amendment Freedoms from Wilson to FDR* (Westport, Conn.: Greenwood Press, 1972) makes it plain that these years were the "nadir" of civil liberties in America.

51. Devine, "Between War and Peace," p. 184.

52. Felix Frankfurter, "The Conservation of the New Federal Standards," *Survey* 41 (December 7, 1918): 292. This was originally a paper presented to the Conference on Demobilization, as was Frank P. Walsh, "The War Labor Board and the Living Wage," *Survey* 41 (December 7, 1918): 301, 302, 303.

53. J. A. F. [John A. Fitch], "Gains to Be Consolidated in War-Time Industrial Relations," *Survey* 41 (December 7, 1918): 314, 315.

54. John A. Fitch, "Labor Reconstruction: The Conference of the Academy of Political Science," *Survey* 41 (December 14, 1918): 335, 336.

55. Ibid., 338.

56. Graham Taylor, "Selective Service Aid for Reconstruction," *Survey* 41 (November 30, 1918): 256-57; Taylor, "Demobilization and Reemployment," *Survey* 41 (December 14, 1918): 342; "Mr. Baker Still a Social Worker," *Survey* 41 (November 30, 1918): 264.

57. "Reconstruction Study Groups," *Survey* 41 (November 2, 1918): 133; "We Must Hold the Ground," reprinted in *Survey* 41 (November 30, 1918): 266; "Resolutions," reprinted in *Survey* 41 (December 7, 1918): 316; Fitch, "Labor Reconstruction," p. 336; B. L. [Bruno Lasker], "The Carrying Forward of War-Time Industrial Standards," *Survey* 41 (December 7, 1918): 309.

58. B. L., "The Carrying Forward of War-Time Industrial Standards," p. 309.

59. John A. Fitch, "Unrest as the Governors See It," *Survey* 41 (March 15, 1919): 858, 860. The first quotation is from Woodrow Wilson's welcoming address.

60. Adler, "A New Purpose," p. 260. Italics in original. "Employment Work Curtailed," *Survey* 41 (March 22, 1919): 894.

61. Walton H. Hamilton, "When Labor Comes to Market," *Survey* 41 (January 4, 1919): 425-28; "Buffer Employment," *Survey* 41 (February 22, 1919): 730. For more detail on this plan, see Harold G. Moulton, "Demobilization and Unemployment," in Frederick A. Cleveland and Joseph Schaefer, eds., *Democracy in Reconstruction* (New York, 1919), pp. 293-304. The third expert, in addition to Hamilton and Moulton, was G. S. Arnold.

62. "The Government's Reconstruction Plans Under the Council of National Defense," in Edwin Wildman, ed., *Reconstructing America: Our Next Big Job* (Boston, 1919), p. 418; "No Official Plan of Reconstruction," *Survey* 41 (December 7, 1918): 329.

63. Hon. Josephus Daniels, "Labor's Golden Age Here," in Wildman *Reconstructing America,* p. 230; Hon. William Wilson, "An Autocracy

of Anarchy Impending," in Wildman, *Reconstructing America,* pp. 234, 235.

64. Franklin K. Lane, "The Purpose of Reconstruction," *Survey* 41 (November 2, 1918): 120.

65. K. de S. [Karl DeSchweinitz], "Adaptation of Recreation and Community Service to Conditions of Peace," *Survey* 41 (December 7, 1918): 314, quoting John Collier, president of the National Community Council Association, to the Conference on Demobilization; "Salvage from Federal Housing," *Survey* 42 (January 4, 1919): 469; B. L., "The Carrying Forward of War-Time Industrial Standards," p. 308.

66. Richard Hofstadter, *The Age of Reform: From Bryan to F.D.R.* (New York: Vintage Books, 1955), chap. 1, "The Agrarian Myth and Commercial Realities." For a sharp critique, see Norman Pollack, *The Populist Response to Industrial America* (Cambridge, Mass.: Harvard University Press, 1962), which is dedicated to "The memory of my father . . . who worked himself to death in a vain search for the American Dream."

67. Weller, "Permanent Values in War Camp Community Service," pp. 296-97; W. Frank Persons, "The Contribution of the Red Cross Home Service to Organized Social Effort; Its Future," *Survey* 41 (December 7, 1918): 294; "Red Cross Asks All to Join," *Survey* 41 (December 14, 1918): 348.

68. Weller, "Permanent Values in War Camp Community Service," p. 298; R., "Home Service After Eighteen Months," *Survey* 41 (January 4, 1919): 453; Devine, "Between War and Peace," p. 184.

69. Weller, "Permanent Values in War Camp Community Service," pp. 295, 296-97, 297.

70. "The Contribution of the Red Cross Home Service to Organized Social Effort," p. 294; Weller, "Permanent Values in War Camp Community Service," 296; Jessica Peixotto, "Community Councils as a Basis for an Effective Recreation Program," *Survey,* 41 (December 7, 1918): 300. This was a paper presented at the Conference on Demobilization. She found this same "defect" in all seven wartime community service agencies.

71. Charles Frederick Weller, "Efficient Communities," *Survey* 41 (November 23, 1918): 218, 219. Membership in the league in 1918 was around 250,000. Members were "the leading men in their communities. They were bankers, they were railroad men, they were hotel men, they were the choice of the citizens in their particular locality." And they were sticklers for social and cultural conformity particularly concerned with purging dissident ministers, teachers and labor organizers (Petersen and Fite, *Opponents of War,* p. 19).

72. "Red Cross Swaps Horses," *Survey* 41 (January 4, 1919): 468.

73. Davis, "Welfare, Reform and World War I," p. 533.

74. James Weinstein, *The Corporate Ideal in the Liberal State: 1900-1918* (Boston: Beacon Press, 1968), pp. 214, 216.

75. Experts, as we have seen, rarely forgot who ran the institutions they depended on.

76. Lewis A. Coser published, in 1956, the first systematic analysis of the positive uses of conflict by an American social scientist. Not coincidentally, Coser is himself an immigrant whose theoretical orientation has been largely influenced by European thinkers, especially Georg Simmel. See Coser, *Functions of Social Conflict* (Glencoe, Ill.: Free Press, 1956).

chapter 7

The Price of Failure: The Red Scare in New York State

Experts, as we have seen, lacked the means to implement their programs, a fact that helps to explain their willingness to see the war as offering them a unique chance to display their skills. The kind of opportunity the war provided, however, was determined by the governing bodies of the Red Cross, the War Camp Community Services (WCCS), and the Council of Defense. One expert, Edward T. Devine, had a voice in these bodies; he used it only to mouth patriotic slogans and utopian hopes.[1] Nonetheless, he and other experts convinced themselves that their active roles in the wartime campaigns for morale and morality were laying the foundation for postwar programs of social control.

In an ironic sense, they were correct. It took only a few months, of course, for experts to realize that certain wartime agencies like the WCCS and the Red Cross's Department of Home Service would be quickly dismantled. Others, though, such as the defense societies and security leagues, would continue. A vast campaign of social control, known as the Red Scare, was about to commence. Perhaps the most flamboyant and illuminating instance of the politics of patriotism took place in New York State.[2] It provided a fitting denouement to the experts' attempts to determine social policy. If, as elsewhere, the main targets of the radical hunt in New York were the left-wing political parties, the new immigrants, and the more militant unions, the experts also came under fire. Their patriotism was questioned, and their programs came under legislative and judicial attack.

There was a certain poetic justice in this. In 1917, experts had vigorously supported John P. Mitchell's bid for reelection as mayor of New York City in a campaign featuring the same tactics that would be used against them in 1919. Mitchell had won their support by appointing many of them to high city positions. The *Survey* responded by calling the Mitchell years "the best example of the efficient, business-like type of government ever given us on this continent."[3] Whether that was the case or not, Mitchell lost the Republican primary in 1917 and ran on a "Fusion" ticket. As the election approached, Mitchell's "ardent patriotism,"[4] perhaps tinctured by his campaign manager's belief "that during the last three or four weeks of the canvassing an emotional issue was needed,"[5] led to a dress rehearsal of the Red Scare.

Typical of Mitchell's campaign was a "Political Primer" that, with appropriate drawings, taught such cautionary lessons as:

> This is a Soap Box Ag-i-tat-or. Does He Want To See the
> May-or De-feated? He Does. Why? Be-cause The May-or
> Pre-vent-ed Him From Talk-ing Se-di-tion and Stir-ring
> Up The En-e-mies At Home to Aid and Com-fort the
> En-e-mies That Our Sol-diers Are Fight-ing A-broad.[6]

Somehow escaping the charge of hyphenism himself, the mayor denounced his opponents, Democrat John F. Hylan, Socialist Morris Hillquit, and Republican William M. Bennett as "friends of the Kaiser."[7] Meanwhile Fusion speakers flailed "Turk, Teuton and Tammany."[8]

It was not until after the votes were in, after Hylan had defeated Mitchell by more than two to one, and Hillquit had run within 10,000 votes of Mitchell, that the *Survey* voiced its first criticism of the campaign. The war, it said, "was a distracting issue for a municipal campaign."[9] As the magnitude of the defeat registered, one expert went so far as to say "the selection of the patriot issue was a mistake."[10]

At no point did experts criticize Mitchell's campaign charges on the grounds that they were untrue. Nor did they find in his attempt to play the demagogue a basis for questioning his qualifications for office.[11]

Instead the *Survey* regarded Mitchell's defeat as an unrelieved tragedy. Its cover on January 19, 1918, featured a cartoon of the Tammany tiger stalking into the Department of Charities while three frightened children helplessly watched from a window. The caption read "The Tiger's Prey."

"They Used To Be His Regular Diet—Shall He Have Them Again?" Inside, the issue told of experts being replaced in the departments of charities, corrections, police, in the tenement house commission, and the parks commission.[12]

While some individuals such as Roger Baldwin or Norman Thomas rallied to the cause of civil liberties, most social experts did not as long as the practitioners of the politics of patriotism were those like Roosevelt, Wilson, and Mitchell, whom they regarded as potential supporters of their mobilization, reconstruction, and Americanization programs. The first indication that the experts were to be victims rather than beneficiaries of the loyalty hunts did not come until January 1919.

In that month a witness, Archibald E. Stevenson, claiming to be from the Military Intelligence Service, gave the Senate Judiciary Committee (the Overman committee) a list of names of those who allegedly had actively spread German propaganda. On the list were clergymen, labor leaders, and social experts, among others. One of those named was Paul U. Kellogg, who wrote in protest to Secretary of War Newton D. Baker. Baker then publicly repudiated both Stevenson, who, he said, had never been "an officer or an employee of the Military Intelligence Division," and Stevenson's list, which contained, according to Baker, the "names of people of great distinction, exalted purity of purpose, and life-long devotion to the highest interests of America."[13]

Stevenson, it appeared to a relieved Kellogg, was a powerless crank, who, with some associates at the Union League Club in New York City, had volunteered information to the War Department on those who, they thought, had deviated from the path of true patriotism. Baker's letter appeared to put an end to their activities. Such, however, was not the case. Partially discredited before the Overman committee, Stevenson and his fellow Union Leaguers turned to the New York State legislature.[14] There they obtained a more favorable hearing. State legislators agreed "Sufficient facts were adduced by the subcommittee of the Senate of the United States investigating this subject [the Overman committee] . . . to indicate the necessity of further inquiry and action. . . ."[15]

The committee created by this resolution was chaired by a first-term Republican senator, Clayton Riley Lusk, of upstate Cortland. Counsel to the committee were the attorney general, Charles D. Newton, and two of his deputies, Samuel A. Berger and Frederick R. Rich. Associate counsel was Archibald E. Stevenson.[16]

Stevenson's key role in the committee, associate counsel and chief author of its report, spelled trouble for social experts. For one thing, he was already convinced that Kellogg, Jane Addams, and others had been doing the kaiser's bidding during the war. For another, he was, in the judgment of Albert de Silver, of the Civil Liberties Bureau, "mentally in-competent to understand the intellectual position of a well-informed and liberal-minded person." According to Stevenson, said de Silver:

> If one believes in international understanding one must in
> some sly way be trying to promote international revolution.
> If one opposed the American entry into the war one doubt-
> less had German gold jingling in one's pockets, if only it
> could be proved. If one is active in the defense of civil
> liberty, *ex necessitate* one must do it with the tongue in
> cheek and for the real purpose of promoting violent change
> in the social order.[17]

One does not have to read far in *Revolutionary Radicalism* before en-dorsing this description. The Civil Liberties Bureau, to locate the immediate source of de Silver's dismay, was charged with "working up sympathy for revolutionaries, influencing public opinion, and generally spreading sub-versive propaganda."[18] Stevenson labeled the Union Theological Seminary a dangerous center "of Revolutionary Socialist teaching."[19] He found the *Survey* to be "the type of publication . . . that on numerous occa-sions had adopted an apologetic attitude toward extreme radical activi-ties."[20] Indeed, Stevenson thought it "a commentary on the increasing prevalence of revolutionary Socialist ideas among university men, that in 1917 and 1918, there did not exist in the United States a single purely literary weekly review that was not of this character."[21] Although the committee was out for bigger fish, social experts were bound to be caught in a net cast as widely as this.

The *New Republic* called the report "a sort of combined Who's Who and Town Topics of—it is difficult to find a sufficiently inclusive term—whatever the Lusk committee does not like."[22] Included in that category were Jane Addams, Frederick Almy, Charles A. Beard, Robert W. Bruère, Herbert Croly, John Dewey, Richard T. Ely, Florence Kelley, Walter Rauschenbusch, Lillian Wald, and almost countless others.[23]

Granting that Stevenson's narrow-minded notion of patriotism virtually guaranteed that such people would be attacked, the committee's operating procedures posed, in addition, an indirect, but serious, threat to social experts, particularly those associated with the United Neighborhood Houses (UNH) of New York City. A number of UNH member institutions held regularly scheduled "forums" where controversial topics were publicly debated. The committee, for its part, committed itself from the outset to pure opportunism. In retrospect, it seems it was only a matter of time before the committee got around to using the forums as "evidence" that the settlement houses were centers of radical propaganda.

The committee, however, got off to a slow start, doing nothing whatever until several days after the bombing incidents of May Day, 1919. Then, as headline space became available, Senator Lusk informed the press that reports had reached his committee indicating there was "a Bolshevist plan" under way "to hold up New York City in some unexplained way for an hour, as a spectacular demonstration to the world that the 'Red' brotherhood had developed fighting strength. . . ."[24] On the basis of this charge, Lusk was also able to announce that "on recommendation from the Attorney General," he had decided to organize "a secret service force to gather information. . . ."[25] This "force" allowed the committee to function with a staff sometimes exceeding a thousand persons.[26]

For the next several weeks the committee again did nothing until another series of bombings in early June provided another opportunity for publicity. Then "Chairman Lusk," as the press had begun to refer to him, alleged that the Bolsheviks in New York City numbered in the "hundreds of thousands" and announced his committee would begin its hearings the following week.[27]

The hearings did finally begin on June 12. They consisted of AFL General Organizer Hugh Frayne reading from IWW and anarchist publications. The real action was elsewhere. At 3:00 A.M. the following morning state troopers invaded the offices of the Soviet mission in New York City and seized its files. The spectacular raid was shrouded in mystery. Lusk admitted that he issued the subpoenas under which the material was carted away, but referred reporters to Attorney General Newton for information about the raid. Newton, for his part, "disclaimed any responsibility for the raid" and said the search warrant had been procured by Archibald E. Stevenson, who, to make matters more muddled, had yet to be appointed officially associate counsel and was thus still a private citizen.[28] Several days later, it came to light that the deputy state attorney, Robert S. Conkling, had obtained the warrant.[29]

The events of June 12-14 set the pattern for the committee's subsequent career. It preferred to work in the shadows. An unidentified "member" or "a person identified with the work of the Lusk Committee" would express alarm at "the ascendency of the alien element in the membership . . . of radical organizations" or "would welcome" similar investigations in other states so that "interesting documents," which were allegedly "secretly removed" before the committee's own raids, might be found.[30]

On June 22, 1919, at 2:30 A.M. the secret service force turned up at the socialist-affiliated Rand School for Social Science, the headquarters of the "left-wing" Socialists, and the IWW.[31] Two days later they opened a safe in the Rand School.[32] The committee, in fact, conducted raids all over the state.[33] All in all, they led to seventy-nine arrests for criminal anarchy. Overwhelmingly, those arrested were of southern or eastern European extraction. In Cortland County, Lusk's home county, for example, thirteen out of fourteen were new immigrants.[34]

The first hints that the Lusk Committee might direct its fire against the settlement houses came in late June 1919. At that time, Charles A. Starr of the Evangelistic Committee, publicly requested Attorney General Newton to investigate the "propaganda" activities of the United Neighborhood Houses.[35] The UNH reacted immediately with a public statement that "the [Evangelistic] committee has succeeded in defaming settlement houses whose sole object lies in developing that patriotic spirit and whose well-earned reputation in that respect has thus far been without a blemish."[36] For a while this defense looked as though it would be sufficient. The secretary of the Evangelistic Committee, Rev. Arthur J. Smith, declared that his committee supported the work of the UNH and that "any remarks made by Mr. Starr" were "made on his own responsibility."[37]

The Lusk committee was, so far, uninvolved in this squabble; and, in early July, Lusk wrote to Harold Riegelman, attorney for the UNH, denying "that he had ever said or intended that the committee should include the settlement houses in its inquiry."[38] Nonetheless, within a week, Starr appeared before the Lusk committee to charge once again that the settlement's open forums were centers of radical propaganda. Mary K. Simkhovitch, head worker at Greenwich House, indignantly replied "these houses have been and are the strongholds of genuine Americanism in the foreign quarters of the city."[39]

The UNH found itself in a very difficult position. For one thing, as Lusk's letter to Riegelman demonstrated, his committee was quite as untrustworthy as it was unpredictable. For another, the Luskers were an investigatory committee in name only. Their real interest was in charges, not in evidence. So, for example, Stevenson read into the committee record the names on a mailing list seized in the raid on the Soviet mission in New York City. The 500 or so names were, said Stevenson, the "cream of Reds and apologists for radical propaganda. . . ." It included, needless to say, people like Paul Kellogg and Lillian Wald as well as Norman Thomas and Morris Hillquit.[40] The UNH, of course, had nothing to fear from a bona fide investigation but found itself hard pressed to fend off baseless and damaging charges.

Its response was threefold. One tactic was to issue vigorous defenses of its work with immigrants such as we have already seen. This seemed sufficient until the fall of 1919. Then Joseph Levenson, chairman of the Republican Club's State Committee, resumed the attack.[41] After this the Executive Committee of the UNH decided on two further steps. One was to issue "a letter signed by outside friends of the Settlements [to] be published in the papers as an answer to hostile attacks in the press."[42] The other was to attempt to beard the lion in his den by appearing before the committee.[43] Neither strategy was noticeably effective.

The denials, while necessary, were not so newsworthy as the charges. Kellogg's protest against Stevenson's use of the Soviet mission's mailing list as a "smear tactic," for example, was buried on page 17 of the *New York Times* although the charges had been featured on page 1.[44] Similarly, the letter from "outside friends," "An Appeal for Settlements,"[45] was of limited value. This testimonial, like the statements the UNH put out in its own name, refrained from directly challenging the Lusk committee. But until the committee was discredited, the charges would tend to stick.

Opposition to Lusk's witch-hunt was, until the spring of 1920, virtually nonexistent. Those criticizing him or his methods would only convict themselves of wittingly or unwittingly aiding the "Reds." As the *New York Times* editorialized: "If there were any irregularities [in the Lusk committee's] procedures, our courts are open, but resort to them will have its dangers. . . ."[46] Thus, Democratic politicians like Governor Smith and Mayor Hylan at first cooperated even though an important Republican politician was thereby being created. The committee held its hearings in City Hall.[47] New York City police participated in one of the committee's raids.[48]

Smith, for his part, took a hard antiradical stand in his public addresses. Scarcely one week after the first Lusk raid, he told a commencement audience at Cornell that "nothing would be left undone to prevent a spread of radical ideas."[49] Smith also authorized an extra term for the state supreme court, on Lusk's advice, to handle the "radical" cases.[50] Under these circumstances the UNH turned to its third option, persuading the Lusk committee that its member houses provided sound Americanization programs. A more bootless quest can scarcely be imagined.

The UNH representatives[51] described their meeting with the Lusk Committee as "heated."[52] To judge from the partial transcript in *Revolutionary Radicalism,* the heat was on the UNH side of the table. Chairman Lusk is better described as coolly contemptuous. Counsel Riegelman tried to explain the settlement's belief that their forums had to be open to be effective.[53] Lusk interrupted to note "that in some of the radical literature . . . prostitution is commended and the prostitute held up as the ideal of womanhood." Would Riegelman, Lusk asked, "bring an advocate of prostitution into a forum and let everybody consider the question [?] " Would he "give the impression to foreigners who might come to such a forum that the question was debatable [?] "[54]

The question was a loaded one. And although there was no way of answering it without appearing foolish, Riegelman did attempt a reply. He said "I certainly don't think that the subject should be emphasized." Digging a deeper hole for himself, he went on:

> In other words, I do believe that the question impartially
> requires at least a strong presentation of the other side.
> Logically, I should say that if such a man were permitted
> to come into the house that I was entrusted with the
> guardianship of, I should take mighty good care that
> on the same platform, at the same time, there was a man
> who would completely answer the propositions that were
> made by the advocate of prostitution.

Lusk was apparently content that he had gotten Riegelman to discredit himself. The committee report, at this juncture, displayed one of its few instances of restraint, limiting itself to adding an exclamation point to Riegelman's final attempt to escape the prostitution question. "Mr. Riegelman further stated that if such an advocate should 'transgress the laws of decency' he should get him to leave the platform!"[55]

The UNH representatives had hoped to beard the lion. Instead they were eaten alive. Lusk had made them appear as foolish do-gooders.

"... it is a matter of extreme regret that the Committee must criticize sharply much of the work which is carried on in some settlements of New York City. . . ." With what the UNH must have found to be an intolerable condescension, the final report took

> this occasion to express its [the committee's] conviction
> that a citizen may be of immense value in the fields of
> philanthropy and social service and at the same time con-
> stitute a serious menace when he attempts to enter the
> field of reconstructing the social order and the government
> under which we live.[56]

Even though this whole episode can be seen entirely in terms of civil liberties, we should be wary of a view that duplicates that of Senator Lusk. For he, in fact, charged the settlements with nothing worse than granting "a dangerous freedom of thought" and "possibly" encouraging it.[57] In view of Lusk's record for making false charges, this one also needs to be carefully evaluated.

The settlements did, of course, occupy from time to time the high grounds provided by the Bill of Rights. Simkhovitch, for example, told the committee that "as to the idea of presenting ideas which involve a gradual change in our institutions which can be accomplished by con- stitutional methods, we think such a thing is necessary, desirable and fundamentally American."[58] Similarly, Riegelman wrote to the Lusk committee prior to their meeting that "truth cannot suffer in the long run from contact with fallacy."[59]

Nonetheless, it would be a mistake to conclude that the UNH rested its case on principle. Riegelman's sentence, quoted previously, is from a section labeled by him "Pro-American propaganda," the main thrust of which is that the forums are effective as propaganda agencies only because they appear to be open to the immigrants who attend them. "The new- comer is quick to suspect," argued Riegelman, "and not without justifica- tion." "He comes into the Neighborhood House now because he relies on its disinterestedness." Presenting one side only would "drive him away altogether."[60] In this argument, in other words, freedom of expression was defended as a tactic rather than as a principle. "The interest of the community," concluded Riegelman, "lies in making it possible to present the American ideals in a manner as attractive and vigorous as that which characterizes pernicious and subversive propaganda."[61]

This was an argument the UNH could not win because freedom of speech is, in fact, of dubious value as a propaganda technique. In his testimony, Riegelman conceded as much. He lamented that "one of the difficulties of the settlements has been that we have not been able to get enough men to expound in clear, vigorous fashion pro-American propaganda in language which will meet the particular objections raised by the disloyalists, the Bolshevists, the seditionists, and whoever else is opposed to our form of government."[62] The admission was fatal. One of the possibilities inherent in a free and open discussion is that any or all sides may win adherents. Ironically, it was the Lusk committee that pointed this out. It condemned the practice of inviting "radical or revolutionary speakers . . . for the reason that the audience is in many cases already predisposed toward radical ideals and the effect of radical or revolutionary speeches can be none other than to crystalize or confirm the radical beliefs of the hearers."[63]

The committee went on to attack "the attitude of many of the social workers" as "apologetic" and claimed they lacked "any actual convictions with respect to the value of American ideals and institutions."[64] While it is clearly based upon Riegelman's admission, the charge, like so much else in *Revolutionary Radicalism,* is patently false. Indeed, what is most striking about this long and "heated" discussion is that the UNH and the Lusk committee did not disagree over what was pro-American or what was subversive. Their quarrel was over the much narrower issue of how to promote the former and eliminate the latter. At issue were two opposing views of the immigrant. For the committee the immigrant was a menacing figure whose "seditious activities" threatened first the state and then the nation.[65] The UNH, on the other hand, viewed the immigrant as a docile, pliant subject for their benevolent expertise. At this point, another piece of negative evidence becomes relevant. At no point did the UNH seek to deny the committee's central contention that the immigrant was a menace. Instead, it adopted the by now familiar tactic of claiming its programs offered a better means of contending with him.

The claim was fraudulent. Open forums might foster assimilation by making the immigrant more familiar with his new surroundings, but it was wishful thinking (to put the matter in its most charitable form) to contend that this was in any way equivalent to what the Lusk committee meant by fostering loyalty. Although no evidence has been found to support it,[66] it is possible to conjecture that the UNH was adopting the only strategy open to it. One might argue that an open defense of the

immigrant would have been foolhardy, that the UNH had little choice
but to try to ride out the storm by adopting the verbal formulas of the
committee. On the other hand, the UNH did challenge the Lusk committee quite directly. Its "defense" was that it was a more effective
Americanizing agency than the committee.

The committee dealt with this competition in summary fashion. It
recommended that "the state shall control and supervise the curricula
of all public and private educational enterprises in this state," exempting
only schools conducted "by recognized religious denominations or
sects."[67] As embodied in Senate Bill No. 1274, this required UNH settlements to seek a license from the Regents of the University of the State
of New York for each of their estimated 4,000 clubs or classes.[68] Each
application had to contain a statement of the purposes of the classes as
well as a description of the educational content. "No license shall be
granted . . . unless the regents . . . are satisfied that the instruction proposed to be given will not be detrimental to public interests."[69] What
the Lusk committee meant by the phrase "detrimental to public
interests" is quite clear from its final report. "No person who is not
eager to combat the theories of social change should be entrusted with
the task of fitting the young and old of this State for the responsibilities
of citizenship."[70]

The UNH response was predictable. Although claiming to be "in
sympathy with the organic purposes of the Lusk Committee," it opposed
the bill because "it wholly defeats that purpose, oppresses neighborhood
houses, obstructs the free operation of innumerable informal educational
activities, and is unalloyed censorship legislation which will inevitably
stimulate, multiply and encourage the very elements that it purports to
suppress."[71] In addition to this memorandum, the UNH called an
emergency meeting of its head workers to work out a campaign of opposition. They sent letters protesting the bill to each senator and assembly-
man; delegates from the UNH went to Albany to testify against it; and
"newspaper publicity was given on the cooperation of a number of influential civic organizations enlisted to urge strong opposition on [sic] its
passage."[72]

Vigorous though it was, this campaign fell short of success although a
license fee of $5 that would have cost the UNH $20,000 the first year
and $4,000 a year thereafter[73] was dropped from the final version. The
Lusk committee disposed of UNH opposition through a cheap, but
effective, logical trick. Its final report strung together a series of excerpts

from a Socialist newspaper, the New York *Call*, which reported the UNH opposition. Blandly contending that "the only educational work which these bills could hamper being that which would be 'detrimental to public interest,' " the report commented that "it will be observed that there are wide discrepancies in the attitude of settlement workers who first assure us of the unqualified loyalty and Americanism of their houses, and later admit 'there is a lot of work done by settlements which such legislation . . . would hamper. . . .' " "An unbiased jury," the report went on, seeking "to determine which of their two attitudes the United Neighborhood Houses would permanently endorse," would seize upon "that by which they convict themselves by implying an admission that they fall into that class of educational effort which is 'detrimental to public interests.' "[74]

Once the bill had passed both houses of the legislature, UNH attention turned to trying to persuade Governor Smith to veto it. Special railway cars were rented so that settlement workers could appear at a public hearing the governor called for May 14, 1920.[75] Legal counsel Riegelman also sent a protest against the measure to Smith.[76] Smith did, in fact, veto the bill along with three companion measures known collectively as the "Lusk laws." There is, on the other hand, little reason to regard UNH activities as influential in his decision.

As both a Democrat and a public figure identified with the first- and second-generation immigrants of New York City, Smith had sufficient reason to oppose both Lusk and his witch-hunt irrespective of any concern he might have had for the UNH.[77] Whatever other considerations may have been operative, Smith's political position is enough to account for his vetoes. He defended them with two arguments that were also the main themes of his 1920 annual message.

One, very likely the more important, was a spirited defense of immigrants. We must not, said Smith in his annual message, confuse "the anarchist, the violent revolutionist, the underminer of our institutions" with "the hundreds of thousands of our brothers of alien stock." They "have made America their home" and "have helped to build up our great nation by self-respecting labor and their citizenship." They had contributed their sons to the nation on the battlefields of the Great War. Without mentioning the Lusk committee by name, Smith called on New Yorkers to "resent as sinister and as a new expression of the old know-nothing spirit, the attaching to all citizens of foreign birth the stigma of radicalism."[78]

Insisting on "the fundamental wholesomeness of citizens of foreign

birth," Smith's other argument was that while the existence of a state of
war meant that "every sane American relinquished some of his freedom,"
peace meant that "we should return to a normal state of mind, and keep
our balance, and an even keel."[79] This plea for "normal" governmental
processes was extended into a full civil libertarian position in his statement on the expulsion of five Socialist members of the New York State
Assembly. Smith declared it "inconceivable that a minority party duly
constituted and legally organized should be deprived of its right to
expression so long as it has honestly, by lawful methods of education
and propaganda, succeeded in securing representation. . . ."[80]

So, by the time the Lusk bills arrived on his desk, the governor had
staked out two positions the UNH had been unwilling to assume. He had
argued that the overwhelming majority of "hyphenates" were loyal; and,
unlike the UNH, he had defended civil liberties not as tactics but as
principles. "Our faith in American democracy is confirmed not only by
its results, but by its methods and organs of free expression."[81] The veto
messages simply carried forward these views. Of the bill opposed by the
UNH, Smith wrote that "in fundamental principle the bill is vicious. . . .
it strikes at the very foundation of one of the most cardinal institutions
of our nation—the fundamental right of the people to enjoy full liberty
in the domain of idea and speech." Invoking "the profound sanity of
the American people," he argued the bill was unnecessary "to achieve a
continuance of the patriotism of our citizenship. . . ."[82]

Welcome as they were to the UNH, the vetoes did not end the matter.
Smith lost the election of 1920,[83] which was also a Republican year nationwide. Lusk, meanwhile, had established himself as one of the most
powerful Republican politicians in the state. In January 1921 he became
president of the New York State Senate, while still in his first term,[84]
and in April of that year he reintroduced his "loyalty" bills.[85] They
quickly passed the legislature and were signed by the new Republican
governor in May.[86]

The UNH protested, of course—to no avail.[87] Most of its time, however, was devoted to denying the charges contained in *Revolutionary
Radicalism,* which was published at this time, and to answering public
restatements of those charges by Stevenson.[88] For the rest, the UNH
decided to accept the situation. Whereas the Rand School of Social
Science determined to challenge the constitutionality of the licensing
law by opening without the permission of the Board of Regents,[89]

Riegelman advised the UNH members to "take steps to conform with the Lusk Act if they are conducting classes other than extension classes of the Board of Education."[90] This advice was taken.[91]

It is difficult to assess the impact of the law upon UNH activities. There is no record in their files indicating that any of their classes or clubs was ever refused a license or that any prospective club was shelved because of anticipated difficulties in obtaining one. It is extremely likely that had such harassment taken place, the Executive Committee minutes would have indicated it. So the chief burden of the law, in one sense, was the immense amount of busywork involved in applying for thousands of licenses. On the other hand, the threat to UNH independence was real. The law gave the Board of Regents virtually unlimited discretionary powers. While Lusk's political star continued to wax, the UNH could take little consolation from the fact that the current board was not utilizing them.

The Lusk law regulating the "loyalty" of public school teachers operated with more immediate severity; so it was around this measure that the campaign for repeal organized. This law was particularly objectionable, from a civil libertarian viewpoint, because it presumed guilt rather than innocence. In practice it required each public school principal to complete a standard form. This listed all of the teachers within his jurisdiction followed by three columns. Column 1 was for teachers "for whose morality and loyalty as a Citizen" the principals could personally vouch. Column 2 was for teachers whom the principals could not vouch for "from personal knowledge, but can do so on information that you consider thoroughly reliable." All others, that is, those the principals simply did not know enough about to guarantee and those about "whose morality, or loyalty . . . you have reasonable doubt," were relegated to column 3.[92] These reports, supposed to be secret, went to a special committee appointed by the commissioner of education. The committee then held hearings, after which it could revoke the licenses of suspect teachers. One of the members of the committee was Stevenson.[93]

Liberals and progressive educators denounced the Lusk laws in no uncertain terms.[94] When a campaign for repeal began, the UNH joined in, though in a minor capacity. Prospects for repeal, needless to say, depended upon dislodging Senator Lusk from his position of power in the state. This, however, depended less upon an effective coalition of liberals and educators than upon the political fortunes of the Democratic party, particularly its Tammany Hall branch. As we shall see, the same Hylan administration that social experts had opposed in 1917 was instrumental in rescuing the UNH from the oppression of the Lusk laws.

Senator Lusk, emboldened perhaps by his success, decided to use his investigating committee for overtly partisan purposes. In late January 1921, an election year in New York City, he announced that the committee might have to investigate alleged corruption in Mayor Hylan's administration.[95] In February he followed this up with a speech before the New York County Republican Committee assailing Tammany politicians.[96] Yet as the investigation started, Lusk himself was suddenly implicated in a scandal. He had managed a bill through the state legislature requested by the Detective Bureau of the New York City police force. When the measure passed, the grateful detectives gifted Mrs. Lusk with a silver chest from Tiffany valued at $1,100.[97]

This was just the opportunity his opponents had hoped for. The *Outlook* was typical of the liberal press in arguing that "the man who waves the flag with one hand while with the other he takes presents from legislative constituents . . . is not a good American."[98] Lusk's position was seriously shaken. Restive members of his own party sought to oust him from the investigating committee, though without success.[99]

Lusk survived that crisis, losing mainly his chance to investigate Tammany. Another scandal broke the following year. Like many other legislators, he had operated a private law practice. In that capacity he represented the brokerage firm of Hughes and Dier. The New York Stock Exchange had removed the house's ticker service on the grounds that it was conducting an illegal "bucket shop." In his official role as president of the Senate, Lusk had interceded with the exchange to have the ticker service restored.[100] Tammany legislators kept the pressure on, and in June the firm's cashier testified he paid $5,000 to Lusk to get the service back.[101]

It was in this context of political scandal that repeal efforts began. As the *New Republic* editorialized, "Mr. Lusk has been having his troubles in Albany but his soul goes crawling on in the public schools of the State of New York."[102] The first steps in the repeal campaign were taken with considerable caution.

In May 1922 a group of professors from Columbia, Union Theological Seminary, and City College of New York wrote to Frank P. Graves, state commissioner of education, who had a reputation of being something of a progressive, "to remove the uncertainty as to the fundamental rights of teachers" by eliminating or clarifying the clause in the Lusk law empowering his Advisory Committee to revoke the license of any teacher who "has advocated by word or [sic] mouth or in writing a form of government other than the Government of the United States."[103] This was followed, months later, by another letter, this time from the New York City Teachers' Union.[104] This appeal was sent on October 17, 1922. Two days later, Commissioner Graves told the New York *Evening Mail* that "loyalty certificates had been withheld from many teachers because it had not been possible to reach them on the list."[105] The union, in other words, was to accept that it was mere coincidence that its members were the ones not yet reached.

So matters stood until the gubernatorial election of 1922. Smith had pledged during the campaign to work for repeal of the Lusk laws; and when he was elected, liberals, progressive educators, and social experts quickly formed the appropriate committee, the Citizen's Committee of New York City for the Repeal of the Lusk School Laws, on November 28, 1922. It included a host of organizations headed by the Public School Association and the Teachers' Union. Among the members was the UNH.[106] The committee wrote the usual stirring letters. One, to Benjamin Atin, chairman of the Senate Committee on Education, may stand for the rest. It denounced "conditions of possible terrorism" arising out of the Lusk laws and urged "the repeal of these reactionary laws."[107]

The UNH role in this campaign was nominal. Riegelman kept the Executive Committee informed and, at one point, told them it was unnecessary for the UNH to send a delegate to Albany to testify in favor of repeal. The settlements had a representative at the hearings only because Simkhovitch offered "to act for the United Neighborhood Houses at the same time as she is representing the Women's City Club."[108] The UNH could afford this nonchalance, a stark contrast to its feverish activism of 1920 and 1921, because Smith's election had virtually guaranteed repeal. It may have been, too, that experts were less than eager to associate themselves with Tammany any more than necessary. The author of the repeal legislation was the Hall's own Senator James J. Walker.[109]

Walker's bill passed the Senate in late February. Lusk's last hope of saving his laws died a month later when the Republican caucus in the Assembly resolved for repeal. As the Downing bill, the entire Assembly voted for repeal in April; and Smith added his signature in May 1923.[110] Lusk's political career barely outlasted the laws bearing his name. In October 1923 he was implicated in still another scandal, this one involving the purchase of the Black Elk Bridge; and in July 1924 he announced he would not stand for reelection.[111] Thus ended the Red Scare in New York State.[112]

This whole episode calls into question the common treatment of the Red Scare as "a study of national hysteria."[113] The simple fact that extreme rhetoric and absurd accusation characterized American politics for a full decade surrounding 1919-20 suggests that it is misleading to deal with those two years in terms borrowed from abnormal psychology. It is not necessary to deny actual instances of hysteria, mob actions against the IWW, race riots, and the like, in order to see that the Red Scare was part of a well-established pattern of politics, called here "the politics of patriotism." The connection A. Mitchell Palmer or Clayton R. Lusk saw between vociferous antiradicalism and their political careers was a realistic, not a hysterical, perception.

The politics of patriotism seems to have appealed to individuals and groups who sought to bypass the usual routes to power. Theodore Roosevelt was the pioneering example. In 1912 he split the Republican party in the name of the "new nationalism." In 1916 he had to find some means of coercing party regulars into forgiving him for the Bull Moose campaign; that is, Roosevelt could not follow the normal procedures of gaining the nomination by cultivating the party faithful. A new variant on the nationalism theme resulted. Mayor Mitchell, denied his party's nomination in the 1917 primary, adopted the same strategy. Meanwhile, the Wilson administration's wartime policies gave to many groups an opportunity to exercise power by invoking the mystical majesty of the state.

Lusk's career, then, followed a clearly marked pattern. Utilizing his investigating committee's extraordinary powers, he grasped the Senate leadership, an unheard-of step for a freshman legislator. There can be no doubt that social experts, in general, sought to play the same game— though with far less success. They too hoped to ride grossly exaggerated statements about the national emergency, and their special fitness for meeting it, to positions of influence otherwise beyond reach. In this, they, like Roosevelt, were hoping to retrieve the losses of 1912.

None of this is intended to prove that social experts were personally

insincere. Rather, it appears that their sincere belief in the benevolence
of their own intentions and their confidence in the merits of their
proposals blinded them to the risks they ran. It is no small irony that
these qualities, well founded as they were, led them to embark on so
dubious a course.

An understanding of the Red Scare as a system of politics, rather than
an outbreak of pathological frenzy, makes clear Tammany Hall's somewhat unexpected role as defender of civil liberties. Tammany practiced
a politics resolutely opposed to the politics of patriotism. It abjured issues
in favor of services. Far from wishing to bypass the normal routes to
power, it was itself a well-established route. Another reason has to do
with Tammany's long connection with immigrants.[114] Unlike the social
experts who also dealt with immigrants, Tammany Hall treated them as
voters who *had* problems. The experts instead had always justified their
programs on the grounds that the immigrant *was* a problem. Their expertise was to protect the rest of society from the immigrant.

Thus there was for the experts a strong temptation to acquiesce in
popular versions of nativism in the hope of converting them into support
for their programs. For Tammy the problem was the opposite. It wished
to return to normal politics. In New York, in the early 1920s, that included a return to civil liberties.

NOTES

1. On the other hand, Devine may have been chosen by the Council
of Defense to head its Committee on Publicity because of his well-known
view that the military effort had absolute priority. See Chapter 6.

2. Julian F. Jaffe, *Crusade Against Radicalism: New York During
the Red Scare, 1914-1924* (Port Washington, N.Y.: Kennikat Press,
1972), is the only monograph on the subject. He feels that his study
"substantiates the findings of Stanley Coben and other scholars" that
"the Red Scare [was] a movement of national regeneration dedicated to
the removal of the twin cancers of foreignism and radicalism from the
American body politic" p. 238. See also Stanley Coben, "A Study in
Nativism: The American Red Scare of 1919-20," *Political Science Quarterly* 79 (March 1964): 55-75.

3. *Survey* 39 (November 10, 1917): 144.

4. Ibid.

5. Karl DeSchweinitz, "Tammany by Default," *Survey* (November
17, 1917): 163.

6. Reprinted in ibid., p. 162.

7. *Survey,* p. 144.

8. DeSchweinitz, "Tammany by Default," p. 163.

9. *Survey,* p. 144.

10. DeSchweinitz, "Tammany by Default," p. 163.

11. Mitchell died the following year. An obituary by Charles A. Beard, then director of the Bureau of Municipal Research, sidestepped the issue: "It must be said, too, that he early saw the menace of German militarism in American life, warned his countrymen against it, sought to prepare for the coming storm, and then gave his all to the cause in which he believed." "John Purroy Mitchell," *Survey* 40 (July 13, 1918): 437. Several weeks later the *Survey* published a series of short commemorative articles by some of Mitchell's appointees: "John Purroy Mitchell: His Chief Contribution to City Government," *Survey* 40 (August 3, 1918): 505 ff.

12. "Only Democrats Need Apply," *Survey* 39 (January 19, 1918): 451-53. See also "Winding Up the Fusion Administration," *Survey* 39 (March 2, 1918): 604-5.

13. P.U.K. [Paul U. Kellogg], "The Taboo," *Survey* 41 (February 1, 1919): 648, 649.

14. *New York Times,* October 11, 1919, p. 24. See also Jaffe, *Crusade Against Radicalism,* p. 120.

15. Concurrent Resolution Authorizing the Investigation of Seditious Activities, reprinted in New York (State) Legislature, Joint Committee Investigating Seditious Activities, *Revolutionary Radicalism: Its History, Purpose, and Tactics with an Exposition of the Steps Being Taken and Required to Curb It,* filed April 24, 1920 (Albany, N.Y., 1920), 4 vols., 1: 1. (Hereinafter cited as *Revolutionary Radicalism.*) The chief author of the report was Archibald E. Stevenson. Collaborating were Arthur L. Frothingham, Samuel A. Berger, and Eleanor A. Barnes.

16. Ibid., title page.

17. Albert de Silver, "The Lusk-Stevenson Report: A State Document," *Nation* 113 (July 13, 1921): 39.

18. *Revolutionary Radicalism,* 1: 1095.

19. Ibid., 1: 1115.

20. Ibid., 2: 1409.

21. Ibid., 1: 1113. As "purely literary weekly review" is not the clearest of phrases, examples may help. Stevenson had in mind publications like the *New Republic,* the *Nation,* and the *Dial.*

22. "By Stevenson Out of Lusk," *New Republic* 27 (June 15, 1921): 64.

23. Drawn from the index of *Revolutionary Radicalism,* vol. 4.

24. *New York Times,* May 7, 1919, p. 7.

25. Ibid.

26. The estimate is Lawrence H. Chamberlain's; see *Loyalty and Legislative Action: A Survey of Activity by the New York State Legislature, 1919-1949* (Ithaca, N.Y.: Cornell University Press, 1951), p. 13. Chamberlain comments that "the financial record [of the committee] is hopelessly confused." It announced on January 29, 1920, that it had spent $80,000. Of this, $30,000 came as an initial appropriation to the committee. Chamberlain found the other $50,000 "had been advanced to the Committee, $10,000 at a time, by State Comptroller Travis as a private loan from an Albany bank." This last information seems not to be exact. The *New York Times,* June 5, 1919, reported that Attorney General Newton claimed approximately $50,000 was available to the committee under "the Peace and Safety Act of 1917." The money was "on deposit in a bank where it can be drawn on checks signed jointly by the Governor and the Attorney General" (p. 2). As will appear, Smith did cooperate with the committee in other ways for much of its career.

27. *New York Times,* June 4, 1919, p. 3.

28. *New York Times,* June 13, 1919, p. 1.

29. *New York Times,* June 15, 1919, p. 18.

30. *New York Times,* June 29, 1919, p. 9; July 15, 1919, p. 16.

31. *New York Times,* June 22, 1919, p. 1.

32. *New York Times,* June 24, 1919, p. 1.

33. See *Revolutionary Radicalism,* 1: 20-24, for an account of all of them by the committee.

34. Ibid., 1: 24-26. Nationality is not given as such. The compilation is based upon an analysis of last names.

35. *New York Times,* June 25, 1919, p. 12.

36. *New York Times,* June 26, 1919, p. 4.

37. Ibid.

38. *New York Times,* July 11, 1919, p. 24.

39. *New York Times,* July 20, 1919, p. 7.

40. *New York Times,* June 20, 1919, p. 1. The headline read: "Find Soviet Envoy Dealt in the Main with Radicals / Mailing List Included Anarchists, Socialists, I.W.W., and Fomenters of Discord."

41. "Uplifters as Aids to Socialist Propaganda/Republican Clubs Committee Reports That Settlements, Church Agencies, and Public Officials Share Blame for Growth of the Party in This City," *New York Times,* October 19, 1919, sect. 8, p. 1.

42. UNH, Legal Folder: 7, Scrapbook: 1-6A, Executive Committee *Minutes,* November 24, 1919.

43. Ibid.

44. *New York Times,* June 22, 1919, p. 17.

45. UNH, Folder: 461. Signed by Charles Evans Hughes and others.

46. *New York Times*, July 8, 1919, "More Than Politics Involved," p. 10. The *New York Times* consistently favored the committee, much to the disgust of the *New Republic*. "For shameless partisan misrepresentation of fact and motives on an important public issue, nothing has happened in American journalism worse than the manner in which the New York *Times* has misrepresented the contents of the Lusk educational bills, and the motives of those who opposed them." "The Times and the Lusk Bills," *New Republic* 26 (May 25, 1921): 369.

47. *New York Times*, June 13, 1919, p. 1.

48. *New York Times*, August 16, 1919, p. 18. This was a raid on the Russian People's House.

49. *New York Times*, June 21, 1919, p. 15.

50. *New York Times*, July 10, 1919, p. 1.

51. A five-member committee, chaired by Harold Riegelman, included UNH president Harriet Righter and past president Mary K. Simkhovitch. UNH, Legal Folder: 7, Scrapbook: 1-7, Executive Committee Meeting *Minutes*, December 2, 1919.

52. UNH, Legal Folder: 7, Scrapbook: 1-8, Executive Committee Meeting *Minutes*, January 5, 1920, p. 2.

53. *Revolutionary Radicalism*, 3: 2313, credits the UNH with "the statement that the Neighborhood Houses would lose much of their value if they tried to present a program of Americanism from one standpoint. They believe both sides should be given a hearing."

54. Ibid., pp. 2314-15.

55. Ibid., p. 2315.

56. Ibid., p. 2312.

57. Quoting superintendent of schools, of New York City, Ettinger, ibid., p. 2282. See also, ibid., pp. 2315-16. Ettinger led the attack on "radical" teachers in city schools; see Chapter 5. See, also Jaffe, *Crusade Against Radicalism*, chap. 4, "The Red Scare and the Schools."

58. *Revolutionary Radicalism*, 3: 2957.

59. Harold Riegelman to Joint Legislative Investigating Committee, Attention of Archibald E. Stevenson, December 30, 1919, UNH, Legal Folder: 13, Scrapbook: 3-3. Reprinted in *Revolutionary Radicalism*, 3: 2950-54. The quotation appears on p. 2954. The letter was later published by the UNH as "The Americanization Program of the United Neighborhood Houses of New York." See Chapter 5.

60. *Revolutionary Radicalism*, 3: 2953-54.

61. Ibid., p. 2954.

62. Ibid., p. 2315.

63. Ibid., p. 2317.

64. Ibid.

65. Ibid., p. 2306. This is simply one instance of upstate, or anti-New York City, bias on the part of the committee. The "seditious activities" are described as invariably "arising in New York City."

66. Because the position outlined here is one I at first inclined to, I ransacked the UNH files in an effort to find supporting data—with no success.

67. *Revolutionary Radicalism,* 3: 2333-34.

68. The estimate is Harold Riegelman's, in *Memorandum in Behalf of the United Neighborhood Houses of New York* [*City*], 1920, submitted in the Senate of the state of New York; UNH, Legal Folder: 13, Scrapbook: 3-6, p. 8.

69. Quoted in ibid., p. 1.

70. *Revolutionary Radicalism,* 3: 2343.

71. Riegelman, *Memorandum,* pp. 4-5.

72. UNH, Legal Folder: 8, Scrapbook: 1-11A, Executive Committee Meeting *Minutes,* April 5, 1920.

73. UNH, Legal Folder: 8, Scrapbook: 1-13, UNH Annual Meeting, May 11, 1920.

74. *Revolutionary Radicalism,* 3: 3001.

75. UNH, Legal Folder: 12, Scrapbook: 2-6. UNH Announcement, May 11, 1920.

76. UNH, Legal Folder: 8, Scrapbook: 1-12, Executive Committee Meeting *Minutes,* April 18, 1920.

77. I have not examined the Smith papers. I would like to thank two scholars familiar with the papers for their advice on what follows: Paula Eldot and Donn Neal.

78. Reprinted in *Progressive Democracy: Addresses and State Papers of Alfred E. Smith* (New York, 1928), p. 271. This collection was a campaign document. It is a measure of the significance Smith attached to them that it included this message, all four veto messages, and a 1923 call for the repeal of the Lusk laws.

79. Ibid., pp. 272, 271.

80. Reprinted in ibid., p. 273.

81. Ibid.

82. Reprinted in ibid., pp. 277, 278-79.

83. His stand on the Lusk laws seems to have been only one of a number of important issues in the campaign according to Eldot and Neal.

84. *New York Times,* January 5, 1921.

85. *New York Times,* April 7, 1921.

86. *New York Times,* April 15, 17; May 10, 1921.

87. UNH, Legal Folder: 9, Scrapbook: 1-24. Executive Committee Meeting *Minutes,* April 27, 1921.

88. UNH, Legal Folder: 9, Scrapbook: 1-25, Annual Meeting *Minutes,* May 10, 1921; and Legal Folder: 9, Scrapbook: 1-25A, Executive Committee Meeting *Minutes,* May 25, 1921. ". . . it was resolved that the thanks of the Committee be extended to Mr. Riegelman for his able handling of the delicate situation growing out of the Lusk Report."

89. See *New York Times,* September 25, 1921. The Rand School was a major target of the "Luskers."

90. UNH, Legal Folder: 9, Scrapbook: 1-26, Executive Committee Meeting *Minutes,* September 28, 1921.

91. UNH, Legal Folder: 12, Scrapbook: 2-20, U.N.H. Announcements, October 15, 1921, No. 1–Licenses for Settlements Conducting Classes Under the Lusk Act. "Mr. Riegelman believes that as long as the statute is on the books, settlements should conform with the law. He anticipates no difficulty in receiving such operating licenses."

92. Order from the Division of Examination and Inspection of the New York State Department of Education, reprinted in "The Degradation of Teaching," *Nation* 113 (December 7, 1921): 639. The order was publicized by the Teachers' Union of New York City, which opposed the law.

93. "Demoralized Schools," *New Republic* 31 (May 31, 1922): 8.

94. In addition to "The Degradation of Teaching" and "Demoralized Schools," see "The Subversion of Public Education," *New Republic* 29 (February 1, 1922): 259-62; "The Lusk Bills," *Outlook* 133 (March 21, 1923): 523-24; and "Educators Demand Repeal of Lusk 'Loyalty' Law for New York Teachers," *School and Society* 15 (June 3, 1922): 605-6.

95. *New York Times,* January 25, 1921.

96. *New York Times,* February 18, 1921.

97. *New York Times,* July 19, 20, 23, 24, 25, 1921.

98. "Small and Lusk," *Outlook* 128 (August 17, 1921): 597.

99. See *New York Times,* July 26, 27, 28, 1921. *Outlook* supported this with the comment: "On the grounds of political consistency, to say nothing of moral grounds, we think he should be deposed for while the Republican party is now on a gold basis, he is apparently an advocate of free silver" ("Small and Lusk," p. 597).

100. *New York Times,* January 7, 8, 1922.

101. *New York Times,* June 3, 1922; April 12, 18; May 27, 1922.

102. "The Subversion of Public Education," p. 260.

103. Reprinted in "Educators Demand Repeal of Lusk 'Loyalty' Law for New York Teachers," p. 605. Signers of the letter included John

Dewey, Franklin H. Giddings, Carlton J. H. Hayes, Samuel McClune Lindsey, C. Van Doren, and E. L. Thorndike.

104. Reprinted in "The Lusk Laws and New York City Teachers," *School and Society* 16 (October 28, 1922): 494. The letter was sent by union president Henry R. Linville.

105. Ibid., p. 495.

106. Permanent chairman was Howard W. Nadd, of the Public School Association. Henry Linville, of the Teachers' Union, called the conference. Member organizations included the ACLU, the Central Trades and Labor Council, the Men's and Women's City Clubs, the League for Industrial Democracy, the State League of Women's Voters, the National Consumers' League, the State Federation of Labor, the New York School of Social Work, the New School of Social Research, the PTA, the Rand School, and the YMCA and YWCA. See "Campaign to Repeal Loyal Laws in New York," *School and Society* 16 (December 9, 1922): 658-59.

107. Reprinted in "The Lusk School Laws," *School and Society* 17 (February 10, 1923): 154. The letter was signed by faculty members from Columbia, C.C.N.Y., Hunter, and N.Y.U. 108. UNH, Legal Folder: 10, Scrapbook: 1-47, Executive Committee Meeting *Minutes,* January 30, 1923. See also Legal Folder: 10, Scrapbook: 1-44, Executive Committee Meeting *Minutes,* November 28, 1922.

109. *New York Times,* December 17, 1922.

110. *New York Times,* February 28, March 28, April 25, and May 27, 1923.

111. *New York Times,* October 24, 25, 1923; July 15, 1924.

112. Its only legislative remains was a law censoring motion pictures.

113. Robert K. Murray, *Red Scare: A Study of National Hysteria, 1919-1920* (New York: McGraw-Hill, 1964). See also Jaffe *Crusade Against Radicalism* and Coben, "A Study in Nativism."

114. For the origins of this connection, see Seymour Mandelbaum, *Boss Tweed's New York* (New York: Wiley, 1965), especially pp. 67-70.

Conclusion

The campaign to repeal the Lusk laws prefigured a new political alliance between social workers, progressive educators, and other experts on the one hand, and machine politicians on the other. The alliance, first formed around the figure of Alfred E. Smith, marks a major turning point in the history of this portion of the "new" middle class even though it would not be until the New Deal that the alliance would be able to leave its mark on national policy. Its formation then marks the end of the first stage in the history of social engineering as well as the end of this book.

What can we say of this first stage? Clearly a group of allied social professions had succeeded in establishing themselves. These new experts had developed techniques, such as the survey and case work, which they claimed were necessary to rationalize the process of modernization. And they had developed an institutional base for themselves in the settlements, the charity societies, and the growing number of regulatory agencies and commissions. Moreover, the process of professionalization had been very rapid. As Vida Scudder put it, the "often futile, bewildered, but loving efforts of more or less amateurs" fast became "the well-organized activities of a set of experts."[1] By the turn of the century, graduate programs in "philanthropy" began to appear; settlements started to offer "fellowships" to college graduates eager to study the social problem, as it was still called; and scholarly journals, professional associations, in fact all of the paraphernalia of professionalism, had come to set the new experts off from their "Lady Bountiful" predecessors.

This first generation of social engineers had been drawn from the old Protestant middle class. More precisely, they consisted, if men, of those seeking a secular alternative to the ministry, and, if women, of those seeking a meaningful role for themselves outside of the genteel family. Both men and women, as a result, brought to their new careers a strong sense of mission that they defined largely in cultural terms. This often led them to speak as though they intended dramatic reforms, but this was rarely the case. A John Lovejoy Elliott, long the guiding spirit of the Hudson Guild, might proclaim that "The settlements are the bearers of a great hope, 'Hear O peoples of the earth, thy life is one life.' Settlement people must prove that message" or profess that "settlement workers have a power of determining the kind of civilization we want."[2] The reality behind the rhetoric, however, was that experts brought to their tasks an abiding faith in middle-class WASP culture that made any program more radical than a mild socialism unthinkable.

Thorstin Veblen noted this "quasi-religious or pseudo-religious character" of the new experts at the time; and while settlement and charity workers deserve a less acidic portrait than Veblen provided, his essential point still remains. The positive side of the experts' "social ministry," as Edward T. Devine phrased it, was their genuine desire to "serve" their fellowmen. Cut off from its traditional religious moorings, however, the social ministry contributed little more than a vague sense of *esprit* to their undertakings. The content of the new expertise derived from other aspects of the experts' middle-class experience. They would lift their immigrant clients up to genteel standards, an enterprise Veblen ridiculed as "the inculcation, by precept and example, of certain punctilios of upper-class propriety."[3] And they would derive their chief model of reform from the practices of scientific management, as Paul Kellogg's description of the Pittsburgh Survey as "social accounting" makes clear.

The sense of mission tended to disappear with the first generation of experts. By the 1920s laments for its passing were beginning to be heard. Walter Leo Solomon, head worker at the University Settlement in New York City, for example, wrote that the "founders" of the settlement movement had "vision." They had "something that fired them and was so big that its reflection illuminated all their contacts. They preached and fought and pled for a great idea, greater than themselves, a 'mythus,' that had power to animate and to inspire." Solomon thought that "most of us today [1927] have no such dream" and instead were "muddled and groping in our thought." Charles Cooper, of Kingsley House, Pittsburgh, sought to rekindle the sense of religious dedication in 1926 when, as president of the National Federation of Settlements, he brought the settlement pioneers together at the annual meeting. Kellogg found the 1926 convention "one of the most refreshing I have been to for years" because Cooper had given "the living species of experience and aspiration a chance." There was, Kellogg reminisced to Julia Lathrop, "a dynamic in their approach of twenty and thirty years ago which is invaluable in this decade, where there is so much sophistication and disillusionment and sag."[4]

What remained after the vision had fled was professionalism. This, as we have seen, had several defining characteristics. One was the connection experts forged between managing social change and furthering their own careers. They wished to be the scientific administrators of reform and, therefore, tended to define social issues in ways that magnified the need for their services. Often this involved crusading for the creation of the agencies of the welfare state. Thus instead of the opposition that Allen Davis posits between "professionalism" and "social action" we should recognize a more complex relationship. The very creation of these new professions was inextricably tied to reform. But this link did not necessarily persist once the regulatory agencies and the investigatory commissions had been established. At that point, most experts would follow whatever administrative routines had been established; and these, like routines in general, would tend to reinforce the status quo.

Another characteristic of the new professions was a product of the available range of institutional support. Experts again and again had to turn to the same philanthropic establishment composed of the industrial and financial elite. These aristocrats controlled the charity societies, the foundations, the Red Cross, the National Housing Association, and the National Americanization Committee. Over and over again, in other words, the social engineers had to convince members of the "old" upper class that expert proposals would implement *their* notions of social reform.

Whatever the case may be today, Talcott Parsons's equation of "superior competence" and "positions of power" as functional equivalents did not hold for the first generation of experts. The social engineers were dependent upon institutions they did not control. The results of this political situation were not uniformly negative for the experts. On some occasions—the Pittsburgh Survey is a leading example—experts succeeded in

obtaining generous support for their proposals. Yet the fact remains that
the philanthropic elite had its own ideas about social issues and was not
at all behindhand about implementing them. Forest Hills Gardens still
stands as a monument to this willingness to disregard expert advice.

The war seemed to offer experts the chance to break their chains of
dependence on private foundations. But, in fact, the same elite that controlled the peacetime charity societies also directed the War Camp Community Service, the Council of National Defense, the Red Cross, and the
other wartime relief agencies. Dependence remained. One response to this
situation was the strategy of accommodation. Experts presented their
programs as "scientific" solutions to problems of Americanization,
mobilization, reconstruction, and radicalism. The strategy did not work
over the long run; and, as in New York during the Red Scare, it sometimes actually backfired.

So it is quite clear that several of Robert Wiebe's generalizations do
not hold for this segment of the "new" middle class. None of the experts
discussed here, including Frances Kellor and Edward T. Devine, could be
called "indispensable." And certainly their version of "bureaucratic ra-
tionalism" did not revolutionize the politics of the issues they dealt with.
The opposite seems to have been more nearly the case. Kellor, Devine,
and many of their colleagues all too faithfully mirrored both the concerns and the tactics of the politicians. This was true even in cases where
accommodation to the prevailing political pressures eviscerated expert
programs. The acceptance of continence as the solution to the army's
venereal disease problem is a striking example. So is the incorporation of
"100 percent Americanism" into the experts' assimilation programs.

It is easy, in retrospect, to fault the experts for their accommodation-
ism. It is not so easy to suggest an alternative strategy that would have
worked more effectively. The engineers did not occupy the "positions of
power." Those who did had very definite ideas of their own about how to
proceed. Experts might challenge those ideas, as Veiller did when he tried
to persuade the Sage trustees not to build Forest Hills Gardens. But there
are no grounds for believing such challenges would have succeeded. In
addition, the intellectual characteristics of the new expertise, especially
its Baconian empiricism, its preoccupation with technique, and its uncritical acceptance of middle-class culture, reinforced the political pressures
for accommodation.

Social engineers gloried in "facts." Their first recommendation, no matter what the issue, was invariably the collection of information. A number of these surveys have proved to be of lasting value to later scholars, and they had a certain muckraking value at the time. Experts frequently publicized the existence of substandard living and/or working conditions and, in so doing, helped mobilize the social conscience of the nation. Still, as C. Wright Mills pointed out, these "masses of detail" were never systematically related to a theoretical view of the structure of society. The facts were somehow supposed to speak for themselves. Facts without theory led, argued Mills, to "a tendency to be apolitical." Experts studied large numbers of social "problems," but rarely attempted to relate them to one another. This produced a "liberal, 'multiple-factor' " understanding of causation. As Mills put it:

> If one fragmentalizes society into "factors," into elemental bits, naturally one will then need quite a few of them to account for something, and one can never be sure they are all in. A formal emphasis upon "the whole" plus a lack of total structural considerations plus a focus upon scattered situations does not make it easy to reform the status quo.[5]

Mills based his critique on a review of the textbook literature dealing with "social pathology." Yet his strictures apply with equal force to work in the "field." The Pittsburgh Survey, for example, did not include an analysis of the distribution of wealth or power in the steel district. So it could not connect living or working conditions to those key structural considerations. The Survey investigated work accidents, but not corporate power. In similar fashion, expert schemes to uplift immigrants were not based upon a theoretical understanding of assimilation. Lacking a social theory, experts fell back on techniques. How should Pittsburgh deal with the problems disclosed by the Survey? Kellogg called for "social accounting." Every city department should issue an annual report; Pittsburgh should "count" the social "cost" of the twelve-hour day.

All of this seemed very scientific, but it was also inadequate. The annual reports might measure efficiency, but they could not measure desirability. Once one knew the cost of the twelve-hour day, who was to say whether it was too high? Experts tended to answer such questions in terms of their commitment to middle-class "norms." As Mills observed, these norms functioned in place of theory. "Pathological" conditions were "not discerned in a *structural sense* (i.e., as deviations from central tendencies). This is evidenced by the regular assertion that pathological conditions *abound* in the city." The "norms," Mills decided, were those of "independent middle-class persons verbally living out Protestant ideals in the small towns of America."[6] What was wrong with the twelve-hour day, in other words, was its incompatibility with middle-class family life.

Neither facts nor technique provided a basis for resisting the political pressures experts found themselves facing. Neither addressed questions of what *should* be done about any particular social situation. Experts confronted those questions, not with theory, but with "norms," and with a missionary zeal to help those less fortunate than themselves.

Because this zeal was in the service of the dominant cultural values of the day, experts sought to moderate rather than resist the policies and goals of the politically powerful. Thus while the new professionals necessarily supported certain reforms, and brought a genuine concern for the downtrodden to their work, their emergence did not posit any long-run challenge to the status quo. This essential conservatism would become more apparent once the second generation of experts, without the "vision" or "mythus" of the first, appeared on the scene.[7]

NOTES

1. See Chapter 2, note 73.

2. *Minutes,* of Meeting of the UNH, December 13, 1921, Legal Folder: 9, Scrapbook: 1-30. This was the feature address, "Inspiration in the Technique and Spirit of Settlement Work."

3. Thorstin Veblin, *The Theory of the Leisure Class* (New York, 1934), pp. 344-45.

4. Walter Leo Solomon to Mrs. Emily Bernheim, December 14, 1927, in UNH Papers, Folder: 168. Paul Kellogg to Julia Lathrop, June 10, 1926, SAP, Folder: 690.

5. "The Professional Ideology of Social Pathologists," *American Journal of Sociology* 49 (September 1943), reprinted in Irving Louis Horowitz, ed., *Power Politics and People: The Collected Essays of C. Wright Mills* (New York: Ballantine Books, 1963), p. 531.

6. Ibid., pp. 541, 552. Italics in the original.

7. See Frances Fox Piven and Richard A. Cloward, *Regulating the Poor: The Functions of Public Welfare* (New York: Random House, 1971). Fittingly, this book won the C. Wright Mills Award.

Bibliographical Essay

Because they provide a guide for others, bibliographical essays may be the most effective way of trying to repay intellectual debts. Even so, this essay is not intended to be a comprehensive survey of the available material. That would take another book. Instead, it is a description of the sources I found most useful in writing this one.

ARCHIVAL COLLECTIONS

The place to begin any study of social engineering is at the Social Welfare History Archives at the University of Minnesota, Twin Cities. Clarke E. Chambers, founder and director of the archives, has compiled a rich array of valuable collections. One of the richest is the National Federation of Settlements (NFS) Papers. Included are numerous annual reports and other publications of member houses, correspondence between settlement leaders on a variety of topics, and diverse publications by and about settlement residents. A second collection of settlement house materials is the United Neighborhood Houses (UNH) Papers. The UNH was composed of New York City houses; and, like the NFS Papers, the papers contain extensive records dealing with the settlements' day-to-day operations. Of particular use were the Legal Scrapbooks detailing the UNH's response to the Red Scare in New York.

Perhaps the most useful collection among the center's holdings is the Survey Associates Papers (SAP). The Survey Associates were formed to

oversee the publishing of the *Survey* magazine and also published the
final volumes of *The Pittsburgh Survey*. The *Survey* was the semiofficial
organ of the social engineers. The papers contain editorial records concerning the policies of the *Survey* and an extensive correspondence with
Survey contributors. The contributors were a "Who's Who" of social
engineering, and expert opinion on a wide range of subjects can be
followed in this correspondence. I made extensive use of the records
touching upon the *Survey*'s editorial position on World War I, a topic
largely undescribed in Clarke Chamber's otherwise definitive *Paul U.
Kellogg and the Survey: Voices for Social Welfare and Social Change*
(Minneapolis: University of Minnesota Press, 1971).

The Russell Sage Foundation generously granted me permission to
use their Trustee *Minutes*. The *Minutes* do not disclose everything one
might wish to know about the inner workings of the foundation because many important early decisions were taken by an executive
committee whose records have not been preserved. Even so, the Trustee
Minutes are very useful, particularly in following the financial aspects
of the foundation's history. Several foundation employees, including its
long-time director, John M. Glenn, have written a two-volume official
history. See John M. Glenn, Lillian Brandt, and F. Emerson Andrews,
Russell Sage Foundation, 1907-1946 (New York, 1946), an accurate but
uncritical account.

The Immigration History Research Center, directed by Rudolph
Vecoli, holds several collections that are indispensable to anyone interested in the Americanization movement and the experts' role in it. Like
the Social Welfare History Archives, the center is housed at the University
of Minnesota, Twin Cities. For my purposes the center's key holding was
the American Council of Nationality Services (ACNS) Papers. The ACNS
Papers include the records of the Foreign Language Information Service
(FLIS), an agency that provided materials to both the foreign-language
and English-language presses. Daniel E. Weinberg, "The Foreign Language
Information Service and the Foreign Born, 1918-1933: A Case Study of
Cultural Assimilation Viewed as a Problem in Social Technology" (Ph.D.
dissertation, University of Minnesota, 1973), is a useful history of its
career although it is mistakenly preoccupied with exonerating FLIS from
the charge of nativism. My reading of the evidence is that the charge
should stick. The ACNS Papers include press releases, pamphlets, and a
variety of other materials including correspondence. The center has in-

creased their usefulness by obtaining Xerox copies of American Red Cross Papers covering the year or so FLIS was part of that agency. The center has also obtained microfilm copies of portions of the Committee on Public Information (CPI) Papers (FLIS began as the committee's Division of Work with the Foreign Born) and the Josephine Roche Papers (Roche was FLIS's first director).

My interest in Americanization led me to two other useful collections. One is the Americanization and War Work records in the Bureau of Education Papers, Record Group 12 in the National Archives, and the other is the General Records of the Department of Labor, Record Group 174, also in the National Archives. The Bureau of Education Papers are difficult to use because they were compiled in no discernible order and then shipped to the archives. Although there are extensive gaps, they nonetheless contain extremely valuable information about the federal government's role in the movement. So, to a lesser degree, do the Department of Labor Papers. For a somewhat detailed sketch of the federal role, see John McClymer, "The Federal Government and the Americanization Movement, 1915-1924," *Prologue: The Journal of the National Archives* 10 (Spring 1978): 22-41.

PRINTED SOURCES

Social engineers were, as a group, prolific writers. Until its demise in the 1940s, the *Survey* was their favorite outlet. It was originally published by the Publication Committee of the New York Charity Organization Society under the name of *Charities and The Commons* and then, after the Pittsburgh Survey, as the *Survey* by Survey Associates, Inc. In addition to articles on literally every phase of social engineering, the editorials and letters to the editor are useful sources of expert opinion. The *Survey* also published a "Personals" column that listed appointments and promotions, so that individual careers can also be traced in its pages.

Experts also often wrote for general-circulation magazines such as the *New Republic, Forum, Outlook, Nation,* and *Century* as well as for journals with small circulations but elite readerships like the *North American Review* or the *Yale Review.* Other important sources for expert ideas and proposals are the annual *Proceedings* of the National Conference of Charities and Corrections (later the National Conference of Social Work) and the *Annals* of the American Academy of Political and Social Science.

Experts also wrote for a wide range of scholarly journals. The *American Journal of Sociology* is perhaps the most useful of these, but one can also find material in the *Quarterly Journal of Economics,* the *Journal of Political Economics,* the *American Political Science Review,* the *Eugenics Review,* and the *Journal of Heredity.*

Educational questions, particularly as they bear upon Americanization, are covered in the annual *National Education Association Addresses and Proceedings* and in several specialized periodicals: *School and Society, Education,* and *Educational Review.* For this writing there was no attempt made to survey newspapers. The *Literary Digest*'s samplings of press coverage were supplemented with a reading of the *New York Times.*

The richest contemporary statement of the vision of scientifically managed change at the heart of social engineering is Walter Lippman's early masterpiece, *Drift and Mastery: An Attempt to Diagnose the Current Unrest* (1914 rpt., Englewood Cliffs, N.J.: Prentice-Hall Inc.). And *The Pittsburgh Survey,* findings in six volumes, edited by Paul U. Kellogg (New York, 1909-14), is undoubtedly the fullest prewar application of the new techniques it inspired. John Dewey was the most eminent and most consistent defender of "mastery." Many of his most important essays are collected in Joseph Ratner, ed., *Characters and Events,* 2 vols. (New York, 1929). The most acute critic, then and now, of "applied" pragmatism is Randolph Bourne, whose most important writings were edited by Carl Resek, in *War and the Intellectuals, Collected Essays, 1915-1919* (New York: Harper & Row, 1964). Frederick Howe's autobiography, *Confessions of a Reformer* (New York, 1925), echoes some of Bourne's criticisms, as does Lincoln Steffens's even more famous *Autobiography,* 2 vols. (New York, 1931).

Historians have vigorously debated the role of social engineering in the progressive movement. The strongest, and perhaps most influential, statement is Robert Wiebe's, in his *The Search for Order, 1877-1920* (New York: Hill and Wang, 1967), that "the heart of progressivism was the ambition of the new middle class to fulfill its destiny through bureaucratic means" (p. 166). Richard Hofstadter, in his classic *The Age of Reform: From Bryan to F.D.R.* (New York: Vintage Press, 1955), argued that, on the contrary, expertise did not really come into its own until the New Deal. Wiebe's thesis has received some, largely unintended, support from the left as revisionist scholars like Gabriel Kolko and James Weinstein have emphasized planning as a key to the period. See Gabriel Kolko, *The Triumph of Conservatism: A Reinterpretation of American History,*

1900-1916 (New York: Free Press, 1967), and James Weinstein, *The Corporate Ideal in the Liberal State, 1900-1918* (Boston: Beacon Press, 1968). Both were following Wiebe's lead because his *Businessmen and Reform: A Study of the Progressive Movement* (Chicago: Quadrangle Books, 1968) documented the business support for governmental regulation. Perhaps the earliest statements of this "new organizational synthesis" can be found in the works of Samuel P. Hays, particularly *The Response to Industrialism, 1877-1920* (Chicago: University of Chicago Press, 1957) and "The Politics of Reform in Municipal Government," *Pacific Northwest Quarterly* 55 (October 1964): 157-69. More recent versions of it are collected in David M. Kennedy, ed., *Progressivism: The Critical Years* (Boston: Little, Brown & Co., 1971). An important dissenter to the Wiebe thesis is David P. Thelen, who argues in *The New Citizenship: Origins of Progressivism in Wisconsin, 1885-1900* (Columbia, Mo.: University of Missouri Press, 1972) and *Robert M. LaFollette and the Insurgent Spirit* (Boston: Little, Brown & Co., 1976) that the depression of the 1890s created a new Progressive constituency organized around consumer issues. William E. O'Neill has tried to combine elements of Wiebe's and Thelen's views in his *The Progressive Years: America Comes of Age* (New York: Dodd, Mead, 1975). One reason why the debate over social engineering has remained unresolved is that few case studies have yet been done. Fortunately, this is beginning to change. Two recent, and outstanding, examples are Carol S. Gruber, *Mars and Minerva: World War I and the Uses of the Higher Learning in America* (Baton Rouge, La.: Louisiana University Press, 1975), and Ellen Ryerson, *The Best-Laid Plans: America's Juvenile Court Experiment* (New York: Hill and Wang, 1978).

The best introduction to the origins of social engineering is via the settlement house movement, and the best introduction to the movement is Jane Addams's masterpiece, *Twenty Years At Hull House* (New York, 1910). Also useful are Paul U. Kellogg, "Social Settlements," *Encyclopedia of the Social Sciences,* vol. 14; and Arthur C. Holden, *The Settlement Idea: A Vision of Social Justice* (New York, 1922). Robert A. Woods and Arthur J. Kennedy, eds., *Handbook of Settlements* (New York, 1911), is a convenient reference that lists, for each house, its founders, officers, trustees, facilities, programs, and religious affiliation (if any). One of the earliest fruits of the settlements' concern with the systematic study of their neighbors was *Hull House Maps and Papers* (New York, 1895). Another early, and influential, outcome was Robert Hunter's study of *Poverty*

(New York, 1904). *Hull House Maps and Papers* and *Poverty* provide a quick introduction to what experts knew about social conditions prior to the Pittsburgh Survey. Their ultimate goal was to match the herculean effort of Charles Booth in *Life and Labour of the People in London* (London, 1889-1903), a work encompassing seventeen volumes of carefully arranged statistics.

There are a number of biographies of early settlement residents. Some are by relatives, like Eleanor Woods, *Robert Woods, Champion of Democracy* (Boston, 1929), whereas others are by professional historians like Louise C. Wade, *Graham Taylor: Pioneer for Social Justice, 1851-1938* (Chicago: University of Chicago Press, 1964). The most useful source for biographical information is Allen Davis's *Spearheads for Reform: The Social Settlements and the Progressive Movement, 1890-1914* (New York: Oxford University Press, 1967). This is also a good general survey of the settlements' early years. Clarke A. Chambers carries the story to the New Deal in *Seedtime of Reform: American Social Service and Social Action, 1918-1933* (Ann Arbor, Mich.: University of Michigan Press, 1967). There are now two able surveys of social welfare in the United States: Walter I. Trattner, *From Poor Law to Welfare State,* 2nd ed. (New York: Free Press, 1979); and James Leiby, *A History of Social Welfare and Social Work in the United States* (New York: Columbia University Press, 1978). Neither, however, supplants Robert Bremner's *From the Depths: The Discovery of Poverty in the United States* (New York: 1956), which recognizes the important role played by novelists, painters, and other artists in shaping popular attitudes toward the poor. An incisive recent study places the social engineers in the context of a century of American concern for social order. This is Paul Boyer's *Urban Masses and Moral Order in America, 1820-1920* (Cambridge, Mass.: Harvard University Press, 1978). Two works are especially helpful for appreciating the religious context in which social engineering arose: Henry May, *The Protestant Response to Industrial America* (New York: Octagon Press, 1963); and Robert Cross, ed., *The Church and the City* (Indianapolis: Bobbs-Merrill, 1967). Roy Lubove has written a basic work on the development of social work as a profession, *The Professional Altruist: The Emergence of Social Work as a Career, 1880-1930* (Cambridge, Mass.: Harvard University Press, 1965), and Nathan Irwin Huggins has treated the same process in microcosm in *Protestants Against Poverty: Boston's Charities, 1870-1900* (Westport, Conn.: Greenwood Press, 1971).

Studies of the "war years," 1914-1925, do not exist. There are, however,

primary materials in abundance. Most of my research was in the manuscript sources already mentioned or in the contemporary periodicals.
There are also some book-length materials of interest. Edward Frank Allen
("with the assistance of Raymond Fosdick") wrote a remarkably naïve
account of training camp activities, *Keeping Our Fighters Fit: For War
and After* (New York, 1918). George Creel, the director of the Committee
on Public Information, described his agency's activities in *How We Advertised America* (New York, 1920). And there are several collections of
essays detailing plans for the postwar reconstruction that never came.
One is Frederick A. Cleveland and Joseph Schaefer, eds., *Democracy in
Reconstruction* (New York, 1919); another is Edwin Wildman, ed., *Reconstructing America: Our Next Big Job* (Boston, 1919). The Red Scare
in New York left a four-volume monument of sorts behind in the form
of the New York (State) Legislature, Joint Committee Investigating Seditious Activity's *Revolutionary Radicalism: Its History, Purpose, and
Tactics with an Exposition of the Steps Being Taken and Required to
Curb It* (Albany, 1920).

Although no interpretation of the "war years" as a whole is available,
there are a host of useful studies on various topics related to them. What
scholarly attention has been paid to the impact of the war on social engineering has concentrated on the effect of the war upon different "reforms."
Arthur Link began this discussion with his "What Happened to the Progressive Movement in the 1920's?" *American Historical Review* 44 (July
1959): 833-51. And Allen F. Davis has continued it with his "Welfare,
Reform and World War I," *American Quarterly* 19 (Fall 1967): 516-33.

Much of the analysis of the domestic impact of the war focuses upon
civil liberties. The best survey is Paul L. Murphy, *The Meaning of Freedom
of Speech: First Amendment Freedoms from Wilson to FDR* (Westport,
Conn.: Greenwood Press, 1972). Also interesting is Howard K. Beale's
muckraking *Are American Teachers Free?* (New York, 1936). Two works
detail the fate of those opposed to the war: Charles Chatfield, *For Peace
and Justice: Pacifism in America, 1914-1941* (Boston: Beacon Press,
1973); and H. C. Petersen and Gilbert Fite, *Opponents of War, 1917-1918*
(Seattle: University of Washington Press, 1957). James R. Mock and
Cedric Lawson wrote an admiring history of the wartime Committee on
Public Information on the eve of World War II, *Words That Won the War:
The Story of the Committee on Public Information, 1917-1919* (Princeton, N.J., 1939).

The Red Scare has received a good deal of attention. Unfortunately, the two most influential studies treat it as an aberration rather than an integral part of American history. See Robert K. Murray, *Red Scare: A Study in National Hysteria, 1919-1920* (New York: McGraw-Hill 1964), and Stanley Coban, "A Study in Nativism: The American Red Scare of 1919-1920," *Political Science Quarterly* 79 (March 1964). The story of the Red Scare in New York can be followed in Lawrence Chamberlain, *Loyalty and Legislative Action: A Survey of Activity by the New York State Legislature, 1919-1949* (Ithaca, N.Y.: Cornell University Press, 1951), and Julian F. Jaffe, *Crusade Against Radicalism: New York During the Red Scare, 1914-1926* (Port Washington, N.Y.: Kennikat Press, 1972). Christopher Lasch has written a study of the liberal preoccupation with radicalism during this period, *The American Liberals and the Russian Revolution* (New York: McGraw-Hill, 1962). Finally, Burl Noggle has suggested some of the continuities between the immediate postwar days and the 1920s, *Into the Twenties: The United States from Armistice to Normalcy* (Urbana, Ill.: University of Illinois Press, 1974).

   Americanization has received more continuous attention than the domestic side of the war, but it too is a subject characterized by a relative paucity of studies. And it is also characterized by a wealth of manuscript materials. There is also a remarkably useful series of contemporary analyses sponsored by the Carnegie Corporation, *Americanization Studies,* in ten volumes (1918-21, rpt. Montclair, N.J.: Patterson, Smith, 1971). The series is unquestionably the place to begin a study of both the movement and the role of experts in it. In fact, the Carnegie studies are a leading instance of expert attempts to direct the movement. Edward Hartmann's *The Movement to Americanize the Immigrant* (New York, 1948) was the first historical study of the movement. It reprints or quotes a great deal of useful material, but John Higham's sketch of the movement in his masterful *Strangers in the Land: Patterns of American Nativism, 1860-1925* (New Brunswick, N.J.: Rutgers University Press, 1955) is far more persuasive. *Strangers in the Land* is, in fact, the indispensable guide to nativist thought. Another key overview is Oscar Handlin's *Race and Nationality in American Life* (Boston: Little, Brown & Co., 1957), a book that is required reading for anyone intending to do research in the forty-two volume *Reports of the Immigration Commission* (Washington, D.C., 1911). For those who blanch at the thought of plowing through the *Reports,* two economists associated with its preparation wrote a single-volume précis of its "findings." See Jeremiah W. Jenks and W. Jett Lauck, *The*

Immigration Problem: A Study of American Immigration Conditions and Needs (New York, 1917), 4th ed., revised and enlarged. Isaac A. Hourwich wrote a rebuttal, *Immigration and Labor: The Economic Aspect of European Immigration to the United States* (New York, 1922). Hourwich's study is far more convincing today than it proved to his contemporaries. A representative statement of the dominant view is John R. Commons, *Races and Immigrants in America* (1920, rpt. New York: A. M. Kelley, 1967). In addition to the works of Handlin and Higham, Thomas Gossett's *Race: The History of an Idea in America* (Dallas: Southern Methodist University Press, 1963) is useful for putting the issues in perspective. So is Milton M. Gordon, *Assimilation in American Life: The Role of Race, Religion and National Origin* (New York: Oxford University Press, 1964), and David A. Hollinger, "Ethnic Diversity, Cosmopolitanism and the Emergence of the American Liberal Intelligensia," *American Quarterly* 27 (May 1975): 133-51, although both considerably overestimate the importance of cultural pluralism at the time.

STRATIFICATION THEORIES

As indicated in the text, historians have preferred description to definition when it comes to discussing the role of class in American society. Robert Wiebe argues that "the new middle class was a class only by courtesy of the historian's afterthought" (*The Search for Order,* p. 112). And he contents himself with listing the occupational categories that make it up. Richard Hofstadter also constructed a list and went on to comment that the "enthusiasm of middle-class people for social and economic reform" was "a rather widespread and remarkably good-natured effort of the greater part of society to achieve some not very clearly specified self-reformation" (*The Age of Reform,* p. 5). This usage makes class a matter of attitudes more or less generally held in society, a usage in which class is synonymous with culture. Samuel P. Hays, in his *Conservation and the Gospel of Efficiency* (Cambridge, Mass.: Harvard University Press, 1959), labels professional conservationists "a special group" (p. 4), and Christopher Lasch calls his radical intellectuals a "social type" in *The New Radicalism in America, 1889-1963: The Intellectual as a Social Type* (New York: Knopf, 1965). Lasch then refers to this "social type" as an intellectual "class" to which he adds the parenthetical qualifier "(or, more accurately, a 'status group')" and then cites Max Weber "for the distinction between classes and status groups (subcultures?)" (p. x). Lasch is not only more

open than most historians in detailing his doubts about the meaning of
these terms, he is also more successful than most in overcoming these
confusions. But his success in providing a host of incisive ideas about
some intellectuals is idiosyncratic and so partial. Does, for example, his
analysis of the middle-class family life of radical intellectuals hold for
proponents of the "gospel of efficiency"?

In part this lack of consensus among American historians over concepts
like "class," "status group" and "subculture" reflects the absence of any
continuous concern with the problems of social stratification. In Britain,
on the contrary, there is a tradition stretching from Engels through the
Webbs and the Hammonds to present-day scholars like E. P. Thompson,
Eric Hobsbaum, and George Rudé. Here, as John P. Diggins notes in his
The American Left in the Twentieth Century (New York: Harcourt,
Brace and Javanovich, 1973), the "left" has been reinvented every generation and the debate over stratification rekindled. The result is that each
new study grapples with the same old questions.

In addition, American sociologists have produced a bewildering variety
of stratification theories, and this has inevitably made for confusion.
Indeed, confusion over the meaning of class is as old as American sociology
itself as Charles H. Page's study of its "fathers" indicates. See his *Class
and American Sociology* (New York, 1940). A study of more recent
theorists, Milton M. Gordon's *Social Class in American Sociology* (Durham,
N.C.: Duke University Press, 1958), found "no general agreement . . . as
to what factor or combination of factors delineates a 'social class' " (p.
13). Gordon did find, however, a growing inclination to adopt "multi-
dimensional" approaches to the problem; and this trend has continued.
Typically, these studies seek to integrate the various factors that operate
to stratify American society. As Leonard Reissman phrases it, the goal is
to assess an individual's "total standing" in the "hierarchies of several
institutions" (*Class in American Society* [Glencoe, Ill.: Free Press, 1959],
pp. 203-5).

Additive models of class presuppose that one's "standings" (as measured
by, say, wealth, occupational prestige, education, ethnicity, and religion)
really do add up. And, for elites, they do. For the remaining 95 plus percent of the population, however, they tend to cancel each other out.
Hence these models produce a picture of American society with a sharply
defined top and bottom but a vast and amorphous middle. The models
have little, if any, predictive value. This recognition that "observations

of congruent objective data about and of societal regularities related to social class . . . when forced into a theoretical scheme, are invariably plagued with inconsistencies, aberrations, and imperfections" has led some, like Thomas E. Laswell, to define class in terms of "the cognitive schema of individual human beings" who, alas, often do not mean quite the same thing by it. See Thomas E. Lasswell, *Class and Stratum: An Introduction to Concepts and Research* (Boston: Houghton, Mifflin, 1965), pp. 469-70. This may explain the "inconsistencies, aberrations, and imperfections." It does not explain what class itself is.

The dominant school of American sociology since World War II has been functionalism. And it has spawned two major explanations of class. One, sponsored by Kingsley Davis and Wilbert Moore, held that the differential allocation of status, income, and other social rewards corresponds to the functional value of various social roles. This argument set off several decades of tendentious controversy, much of it reprinted in Melvin Tumin, ed., *Readings on Social Stratification* (Englewood Cliffs, N.J.: Prentice-Hall, 1970). Now that the smoke has largely cleared, two critical problems with the Davis-Moore thesis stand forth. One is that any social arrangement of roles that does not lead to chaos is "functional." The theory, in other words, provides no way of distinguishing the functional value of different roles. The second problem is that rewards that may have been functionally distributed in the first instance come to be inherited, for one key reward is the power to hand over to one's children the fruits of one's success. Hence, in any real social system, the theory recognizes there will be a wide gulf between social strata and the functional value of their members.

Talcott Parsons, the leading figure in functionalism, also provides an explanation of "class," albeit one so hedged about by qualifying phrases that it defies simple paraphrase. His theory holds that although "in a rather loose and insecure way" the "business managerial elite" is "the unequivocal top class in an occupation sense," it is but part of "the family-occupation-income complex" which "by and large" is "the core of the [class status] complex." Making matters more muddled still, Parsons further postulated that the business managerial elite is challenged for supremacy by professional elite groups "greatly reinforced by the increasing importance of scientifically based technology." Between these "elite groups" and "a broad band of what is usually called the 'upper middle class,' " there "is no clear break." The "upper" and "lower" middle classes also shade into each other, and lines between "white collar" and "labor" groups are fast fading. All of this is from his "A Revised Analytical Approach to the Theory of Social Stratification," in Reinhard Bendix and Seymour Martin Lipset, eds., *Class, Status, and Power: A Reader in Social Stratification* (Glencoe, Ill.: Free Press, 1953), pp. 120-24.

The Parsonian theory of stratification thus yields a social spectrum in which positions fade into one another with "no clear break." Parsons attributed this to "a highly diversified occupational structure that no longer displays a clear division between the 'controllers' and the subordinate class." And the occupational structure, in turn, reflected "the prevalence of large-scale organization" and "the greatly increased role of many kinds of competence." Both factors make "for inequalities in power and authority" while inviting "the possibility of differentiating over a far wider range than, in general, was possible under simpler conditions." The increase in inequality went along with a decrease in the ascription of status and power. The result is "the achievement complex," discussed in the text. (See "Equality and Inequality in Modern Society, or Social Stratification Revisited," in Edward O. Laumann, ed., *Social Stratification: Research and Theory for the 1970's* (Indianapolis: Bobbs-Merrill, 1970), p. 18.

What is most remarkable about Parsons's view is that it most resembles the "open" classes postulated by Charles Horton Cooley or the "sociocracy" of Lester Frank Ward. Parsons, that is, continues the long tradition in American sociology that the United States is a classless society.

The sum and substance of the matter is that while Parsons conceded the existence of "higher ranges" of "institutionalized power," his theory offers no way of focusing upon them as coherent groups. Similarly, although the "achievement complex" explicitly recognizes the birth of a new middle class, it does not clearly state where it belongs in the social structure. This is because Parsons held that authority was diffused throughout the whole society. The question "Who is in charge here?" had no answer. However, as Ralf Dahrendorf pointed out in *Class and Class Conflict in Industrial Society* (Stanford, Calif.: Stanford University Press, 1959), in any "specific association" there is always a "dichotomy of positions" with respect to authority (p. 171). In the large-scale organizations that Parsons saw as characteristic of modern society, some positions carry with them decision-making powers, and others do not.

Hence the question of the new middle class can be stated in political terms: What kinds of decision-making power do its members enjoy?

There are two main schools of thought on this matter. C. Wright Mills, in his classic *White Collar: The American Middle Classes* (New York: Oxford University Press, 1951), argued that these salaried employees are "becoming more and more similar" to "wage workers" (p. 297). Reinhard Bendix, in *Work and Authority in Industry: Ideologies of Management in the Course of Industrialization* (New York: Wiley, 1956), took the contrary position, that the new middle class was an extension of the old bourgeoisie (Chapter 4).

I lack the temerity to advance any grand theories of my own concerning the meaning of class. Nor do I feel competent to choose among the many theories already discussed. I do wish to reiterate the point made in the text. There are enough areas of agreement about the dynamics of stratification to frame meaningful historical questions about the new middle class. All of these studies assume the development of various kinds of technologies and of complex organizations to institutionalize them. This is the framework in which authority is exercised according to Dahrendorf. It is the setting for Parsons's "achievement complex." The key question is how positions of authority are allocated in complex organizations. The question can be raised in terms of each of the theoretical models; it can only be answered historically.

Index